'Gareth Williams, Emeritus Professor at t
has devoted his academic life to studying
higher education policy. This *Festschrift* pi
deserved appreciation in honour of his w(
scholars who use the opportunity to con   _ ...ai кеis,
managerialism, and the uses of higher education – all themes that Gareth
Williams himself pursued with passion, rigour and acumen.'

**Michael A. Peters, Professor of Education, Waikato University,
New Zealand**

'Gareth Williams helped to create higher education as a distinctive field for
study. He never staked out disciplinary or sectoral boundaries; although
his starting point was an economic view he was never constrained by it.
Perfectly titled, *Valuing Higher Education* is a fitting tribute to his work,
organized by contemporary themes – marketing, the academic life, and
the uses of higher education – which reflect Williams' constant concern
to make research and teaching influential and relevant for policy. The
contributions from many leading academics recapitulate theory and
policy development in ways that provide a valuable overview for students,
policymakers and researchers alike, and remind us how Gareth Williams
has played his part in shaping the whole field of research into HE.'

**Rob Cuthbert, Emeritus Professor of Higher Education Management,
University of the West of England**

'A *Festschrift* in the truest sense of its German origin, to honour an
eminent and highly renowned scholar by contributions from his equally
renowned peers. Interesting and readable, the contributions provide a
state-of-the-art overview of a wide range of topics central to the field of
higher education studies and research.'

**Barbara M. Kehm, Professor of Leadership and International Strategic
Development in Higher Education, University of Glasgow**

Valuing Higher Education

Valuing Higher Education

An appreciation of the work of
Gareth Williams

Edited by Ronald Barnett,
Paul Temple, and Peter Scott

IOE Press

First published in 2016 by the UCL Institute of Education Press, University College London, 20 Bedford Way, London WC1H 0AL

www.ucl-ioe-press.com

British Library Cataloguing in Publication Data:
A catalogue record for this publication is available from the British Library

ISBNs
978-1-78277-174-6 (paperback)
978-1-78277-175-3 (PDF eBook)
978-1-78277-176-0 (ePub eBook)
978-1-78277-177-7 (Kindle eBook)

Typeset by Quadrant Infotech (India) Pvt Ltd
Printed by CPI Group (UK) Ltd, Croydon, CR0 4YY

Cover image © amadeustx/Shutterstock.com

Contents

Notes on contributors

Alberto Amaral is a Professor at the University of Porto, Portugal, and a member of the Centre for Research in Higher Education Policies (CIPES). He is also president of the Portuguese national quality assurance agency for higher education. His main research interests are in the fields of higher education quality, governance, and European higher education policies.

Ronald Barnett is Emeritus Professor of Higher Education at the UCL Institute of Education, London. For 35 years, he has been developing a social philosophy of higher education, his most recent book being *Understanding the University: Institution, idea, possibilities* (2016).

Tessa Blackstone is a Labour peer and former UK government minister. She has been Master of Birkbeck College, University of London, and Vice-Chancellor of the University of Greenwich, UK. She was Professor of Educational Administration at the Institute of Education, University of London, and worked with Gareth Williams as Deputy Director of the Leverhulme inquiry into higher education (1981–3).

David D. Dill is Professor Emeritus of Public Policy at the University of North Carolina at Chapel Hill, USA. His research interests include public policy analysis, research policy, and the regulation of academic quality.

Jill Johnes is Professor of Production Economics at the University of Huddersfield, UK, and has published widely on education economics. She is co-author of *Performance Indicators in Higher Education* (1990) and co-editor of the *International Handbook of the Economics of Education* (2004).

D. Bruce Johnstone is Distinguished Service Professor of Higher and Comparative Education Emeritus at the State University of New York at Buffalo, and Chancellor Emeritus of the State University of New York system. His principal scholarship is in higher education finance, governance, and policy formation.

Louise Morley is Professor of Education and Director of the Centre for Higher Education and Equity Research (CHEER) at the University of Sussex, UK. She has an international profile in the field of the sociology of higher education.

Rajani Naidoo is Professor of Higher Education and Director of the International Centre for Higher Education Management at the University of Bath, UK. Her research analyses the links between shifts in global political economy and the changing roles of universities, with a particular focus on new forms of imperialism and global well-being.

James Pringle is Assistant Professor in the School of Health Services Management at Ryerson University, Toronto, Canada. His research is grounded in exploring the impact and influence of private sector forces on public sector spaces including universities and hospitals.

Peter Scott is Professor of Higher Education Studies at the UCL Institute of Education, London. He was Vice-Chancellor of Kingston University, UK, from 1998 until 2010; Professor of Education at the University of Leeds, UK, from 1992 until 1998; and Editor of *The Times Higher Education Supplement* from 1976 until 1992.

Michael Shattock was Registrar of the University of Warwick, UK, until 1999 when he became a Visiting Professor at the Institute of Education, University of London, where, with Gareth Williams, he established the MBA programme in Higher Education Management. He has published widely on higher education topics, including recently *Making Policy in British Higher Education 1945–2011* (2012).

Ulrich Teichler was from 1978 until 2013 a Professor at the University of Kassel, Germany, and for many years Director of its International Centre for Higher Education Research (INCHER-Kassel). His 1,300 publications concentrate on graduate employment and work, higher education systems, internationalization, and the academic profession.

Pedro Teixeira is Associate Professor of Economics and Vice-Rector for Academic Affairs at the University of Porto, Portugal, and Director of the Centre for Research in Higher Education Policies (CIPES). His main research interests are in the economics of education and the history of economics.

Paul Temple is Emeritus Reader in Higher Education Studies at the UCL Institute of Education, London. He was until 2013 Co-Director of its Centre for Higher Education Studies (CHES). His research interests include the study of the physical form of the university. His most recent book is *The Hallmark University: Distinctiveness in higher education management* (2014).

Gareth Williams, whose home discipline is economics, is Emeritus Professor at the UCL Institute of Education, London, where he established its Centre for Higher Education Studies (CHES) in 1986. Previously he worked at Oxford University (as an agricultural economist), the OECD, LSE, and Lancaster University. Most of his academic work has been concerned with various dimensions of the economic underpinnings of higher education policy.

Maureen Woodhall is Emeritus Reader in Education Finance at the UCL Institute of Education, London. She worked with Gareth Williams at the Institute of Education Centre for Higher Education Studies (CHES) from 1984 until 1996; was a consultant for many international agencies, including the OECD, UNESCO, and The World Bank; and has published extensively on the economics of education, particularly the finance of higher education.

Foreword

Tessa Blackstone

I am delighted that a group of distinguished academic experts on higher education have come together to celebrate the work of Gareth Williams. For more than 50 years Gareth has been a leading thinker on the development of contemporary higher education. Drawing on his expertise as an applied economist, he has analysed the dramatic changes that have taken place in higher education systems across the developed world since the 1960s.

He started his academic career not long after the Robbins Report was published in 1963. When the Robbins Committee started its work, 5 per cent of young people went to university and 8 per cent into higher education, which included the Teacher Training Colleges. Most of these students were school-leavers: there were very few mature students; 75 per cent of them were male; tuition was free, and there were relatively generous grants for maintenance. There were only a few overseas students, mainly from the USA and the Commonwealth. Postgraduate study was focused on research, and seen mainly, although not exclusively, as training and preparation for an academic career. Universities were small institutions: few of them had more than ten thousand students and many had far fewer.

The transition from these early 1960s universities to today's very different system began with the expansion of student numbers recommended by Robbins. Gareth Williams has dedicated his career to analysing these changes and examining their impact on the labour market for high-level skills, on the academic profession, on the development of a global market for higher education, on new ways of financing it, and on the participation of students from different social origins.

I first met him at the Centre for the Study of Higher Education at the London School of Economics in the late 1960s. Not long after we worked together on a study of the academic labour market commissioned by the Prices and Incomes Board (PIB), which had been given the remit to make recommendations on the pay of university teachers. With David Metcalfe, a labour economist at LSE, we wrote a book which was published in 1974, based on our research for the PIB. In the early 1980s I worked with Gareth again, on the Leverhulme inquiry on higher education, which is described in this book. He masterminded this wide-ranging inquiry, bringing together many organizations and many individuals as contributors to the series of volumes that made up the report. He demonstrated his organizational skills, as well as his drive and tenacity in producing a large output of work in a short space of time. The research was published in a form that was accessible to a wider audience than academic experts in the field, and was designed to influence policymakers and practitioners.

Although my career changed direction, Gareth's fascination with research on higher education continued. As well as publishing widely on the subject, he has taught many generations of postgraduate students, not just from the UK but from around the world too. Some of his former students have become academics, but others have become policymakers. As a former minister with responsibility for all forms of post-school education, I know how valuable it was to be able to draw on the findings of well-conducted research and to rely on the advice of well-trained policy analysts. Gareth's contribution has stretched way beyond the narrow confines of the academic world.

British higher education continues to enjoy high prestige internationally. The justifiable high regard in which it is held needs to be cherished. To preserve it requires high levels of investment as well as securing the best possible value for money from this investment, whether in research or teaching.

Gareth Williams knows better than anyone just how challenging this is, especially in a context where the system of financing it is through loans to pay for tuition fees, many of which will not be repaid. As a consequence, there will eventually be a vast hole in the public finances as one of the chapters in this book indicates. Perhaps Gareth can address this problem and come up with a solution? His work is surely not yet finished!

Introduction
A will to connect: Perspectives, publics, and prospects
Ronald Barnett, Peter Scott, and Paul Temple

Gareth Williams: An academic life

A *Festschrift* can serve a number of purposes. It can seek to reflect the esteem in which an academic is held by his or her immediate friends and colleagues, it can seek to recognize a lifetime's intellectual achievements in a field, and it can honour an individual's broad contribution to the scholarly life. This Festschrift in honour of Gareth Williams does all of these things. The contributions here are testimony to the warmth many feel towards Gareth Williams, who has done so much as a scholar, teacher, researcher, and academic colleague for over four decades. Evident here, in the breadth of the chapters in this volume, are intimations of very broad concerns and interests on the part of Gareth Williams in his field; but evident, too, is the considerable regard that so many have for Gareth as someone who has made a large contribution as a player in the larger academic community, much of it in unheralded and quiet ways in supporting students and newer – and not so new – colleagues.

At the heart of the contributions here is, as stated, a recognition of the contribution that Gareth Williams has made to his field. But what *is* or has been Williams's field? It is not so easy to identify it succinctly. One may start by saying that the main focus of Williams's work has been that of the economics of higher education. Immediately, though, there are two difficulties with such a proposition. The first is that Williams has never taken a narrow approach to the economics of higher education; and the second – which is linked to the first – is that Williams has broad interests that go beyond economics as such.

One way of backing up these propositions is simply to note the range of topics prompted by Williams's work that appears in the chapters here. Those topics include: the economics of higher education; government policy on higher education; markets in higher education and market failures; human capital theory and manpower planning; institutional income generation and resource dependency; the widening of institutional boundaries and the emergence of private institutions; the labour market and 'employability'; public and private goods; the costs of higher education and its financing including student fees; the knowledge society and university research; institutional competition and stratification; mass higher education and equity matters; governance and leadership; league tables and institutional gaming; emerging forms of capitalism; and the effects of macro changes on academic identity and the academic profession more broadly.

Wide ranging as it is, such an enumeration of issues that come within or naturally lead on from Williams's oeuvre is inadequate in two ways. Firstly, there are some large matters hidden within such a list that are properly attracting contemporary attention, and which have their appearance here: for instance, those of institutional 'branding' (Pringle and Naidoo). But, and even more significantly, such a list cannot do justice to the interconnections between the aspects of higher education and – as several of the contributions here observe (Amaral and Teixeira, Dill, Teichler) – it has been a feature of Williams's work that key issues cannot be understood without a sensitivity to their interconnections. Economics of higher education has to be placed in the context of its relationship with sociological inquiry into equity and access; the funding of higher education should be put into contact with inquiries into the effects of different policy options on the balance between public and private goods that higher education can offer; and both manpower planning and markets should be brought into view alongside their implications for the potential of higher education to open life-chances.

Such an intellectual openness is no better demonstrated than by pointing to the Leverhulme Programme of Study into the Future of Higher Education, which ran in the early 1980s and was directed by Gareth Williams (with Tessa Blackstone as the Programme's Deputy Director). Out of the Programme's seminars – each of which had a lay chair – emerged no fewer than 11 volumes covering topics as wide as access, the labour market, institutional change, the arts, professionalism, accountability, resources, and structure and governance. Each volume contained research papers specially commissioned for the respective seminar. 'Perhaps more important than the detailed recommendations was the fact that the Programme opened up higher education policy issues for public discussion in a comprehensive way that had not been attempted since [the] Robbins [Report, some twenty years earlier]' (Shattock, 2015: 11).

Putting it simply, Gareth Williams has perhaps become mainly associated with his work in the economics of higher education, especially with matters of its funding. But, as implied, Williams's work has consistently underscored the need to take a broad and interconnected view of matters. So we see in Williams's corpus a continuing stream of shrewd observations about the limitations of any particular approach. Four examples drawn from across the decades of Williams's work may help to substantiate the point. The first is taken from a collection on *Perspectives on Higher Education* edited by the late Burton Clark:

> The main weakness of the market model results from its possible effects on the supply of educational services ... Unrestricted competition can lead to reductions in quality as institutions indulge in price competition and hard-selling tactics.
>
> (Williams, 1984: 97)

Although these remarks appeared three decades ago, they retain a freshness for higher education in the twenty-first century, in which much concerted attention is focusing on the benefits and possibly pernicious aspects of markets. And it is indicative of Gareth Williams's abiding preparedness to see matters in the round, always sensitive to interconnections between elements, including unintended and even unforeseen consequences of policy options. In many ways, this volume can be seen as a set of collective attempts to identify and to examine unintended consequences of national policies in relation to higher education.

Here is a second comparable quotation from Williams's work:

> ... the main danger of market financing is that it will become progressively more difficult for higher education institutions to teach broadly cultural subjects or to teach other subjects in a way that does not promise an immediate economic return.
>
> (Williams, 1989: 116)

This quotation is important, for it reveals Gareth Williams's interests in the wider roles that higher education can play in the formation of culture both in society and among individuals. Conventionally, in work in the sociology of higher education, the central term has come to be that of 'cultural capital'. This is not a term that Gareth Williams would turn to naturally, but the concept of cultural capital is clearly at work in this quotation. Again, we have here a hint about the limitations of a narrowly economic approach to understanding higher education, but we see, too, a critique of the dominant market-led policy environment that has developed across much – but by no means all – of the world over the past three decades.

A third quotation is the following:

> The relationship between higher education institutions and the society which surrounds them is a reciprocal one. It is a partnership. ... any government that attempts to use its control of the purse as a way of controlling academic life risks having a very mediocre intellectual elite and graduates who are unable to take initiatives.
>
> (Williams, 1992: 850)

Here, again, we see a sensitivity to the interconnectedness between multiple facets of the higher education world and to unintended consequences of national policy frameworks. But we also see, in this quotation, a concern for the academic life itself. That the academic life has its own internal vitality is a key matter for Williams, one that constitutes much of the substance of a higher education system in possession of its own integrity. This is not to suggest that Williams is an advocate of absolute autonomy for higher education. Definitely not. That quotation runs on:

> A university that divorces itself entirely from society rapidly becomes an irrelevant ivory tower; [but] equally, one that only responds to outside pressures cannot perform its proper function of disinterested scholarship, research and criticism ... [However], there is no single correct balance between the two extremes.
>
> (ibid)

Williams also adds there that 'It is (the) different solutions [to this tension] that makes the study of higher education ... intrinsically rewarding and practically useful' (ibid). And for a final quotation here, in a concluding chapter in a recent volume, Williams's sense of the interconnectedness of matters is vividly conveyed:

> It is, in fact, impossible to separate particular ideas of a good society from the idea of education, including higher education, as a public good ... My own starting point is Durkheim's proposition that educational systems reflect dominant ideologies ... Thus education cannot be theorised in isolation from theories of the wider society of which it is part, and higher education cannot be theorised except as a late stage of education generally.
>
> (Williams, 2015: 185–6)

Interconnectedness is here in several senses. There is a sense that higher education is part of a larger education system and so cannot be satisfactorily understood as a discrete entity. It is *not*, therefore, susceptible of analysis as if it is an independent institution entirely separate from the rest of education, only deserving of particular concepts, analytical frames, and theories. There is, too, a sense that ideas of higher education are intimately connected with larger social sentiments and values. As it might be said, imaginaries of higher education reflect social imaginaries (Taylor, 2007). And there is, further, a sense that an understanding of higher education must take its place in the wider context of an understanding of the nature of society in the twenty-first century.

This dual sense that we glean from all of these quotations – both of higher education as interconnected with the wider world and of the economics of higher education as needing to be connected with other disciplinary frames – has implications for the understanding of any topic in the field. We see all of this in an analysis that Gareth Williams offers on the matter of public and private goods provided by higher education.

In a characteristically balanced analysis, Williams shows that even if, analytically, public and private goods can be demarcated (and 'it is clear that higher education has the attributes of both public *and* private goods'), in practice, matters are more complex. For example, 'it is easy to make the case that all higher education should have ethical underpinnings and that this is a public service. But which public should decide?' (2015: 195). In other words, there are multiple publics at large. Even so, 'whether political choices made by persuading representatives of the majority are more legitimate than market choices resulting from the sum of individual choices is ultimately a question of value' (ibid: 201). Furthermore, 'the question arises of whether the public benefits, economic, social or cultural, are equivalent in all the activities that come under the heading "higher education"' (ibid: 200).

From this admittedly somewhat cursory overview of his oeuvre, it is clear that Gareth Williams has sensitively dissected many of the major contemporary issues concerning the funding, organization, and policy framing of higher education. In doing so, and in the way he has done so, Williams's work exhibits a number of achievements. It has implicitly chastised those who are wedded to work within discrete disciplinary frameworks (such as the economics, sociology, politics, and philosophy of higher education). It has pin-pricked the self-assuredness of those who want to insist on particular readings of higher education. It has demonstrated the complexity of the field, and reminded us of the unintended consequences of policies and actions. It has posed questions that do not yield anything approaching simple or consensual answers, and so in turn show that careful work by researchers and scholars is worthwhile. And it has indicated that ultimately many of the large issues pose profound value challenges. They cannot be solved with technical instruments and procedures, but call for value choices. A non-choice is a choice.

The lure of markets

In his chapter, Bruce Johnstone graphically observes that higher education poses to governments a particular set of challenges. On the one hand, the costs of higher education are set on an upward trajectory; on the other hand, governments are faced with increased demands for public expenditures on all manner of ends. Unsurprisingly, governments characteristically try to find ways of limiting public expenditure on higher education. This is far from being straightforward, not least because the rising costs of higher education accrue from a number of directions: expanding demand, with more would-be students seeking access, rising costs of salaries (higher education being staffing-intensive with relatively high-paid personnel), and expensive physical resources. In responding to these challenges, some countries have developed policies such that universities are encouraged – or obliged – to understand that they possess highly valuable resources, the value of which can be revealed in market situations.

This neoliberal turn has been especially marked in some countries. Temple observes that, on OECD international data, the UK is exceeded only by South Korea and Chile in the extent to which the state has limited its direct support of higher education. And since the latest OECD data were released, it is worthwhile noting that: first, England has introduced a student fee ceiling of £9,000 per year but has already – as Michael Shattock observes – opened the way to even higher fee levels (for institutions faring well in a forthcoming Teaching Excellence Framework); second, partly following a student radical movement, a left-oriented government has been returned in Chile with a mandate to find ways of *limiting* the private costs of higher education.

It follows that matters of the funding of higher education and the adoption of any balance between public and market-led expenditures are far from being a simply technical matter. It also follows, in turn, that there is no such thing as a proper relationship between the state and higher education. And it follows again that while economics can help in identifying some of the consequences of different policy options, it cannot be deployed to determine unequivocally any particular strategy in funding higher education.

Many of the chapters here indicate that just such a nuanced understanding of economics has characterized Gareth Williams's approach. Perhaps this is Gareth Williams's largest contribution, and it is in a way a double contribution, both to advocate economics as a valuable disciplinary perspective in understanding higher education and also to show its limitations. Universities may legitimately be understood as enterprises possessing and indeed producing numerous valuable resources, which are consequently in demand; and, under certain circumstances (such as a heightened use of market mechanisms), the strength of that demand or desire might be tested. And given the need to adjust to financially straightened circumstances, it is hardly surprising that some states at least have opened the way to universities to find ways of responding to economic incentives and that, in turn, universities – to different degrees – have accepted that challenge. Accordingly, a plausible story can be told of the response of universities to market mechanisms.

In their different ways, the three chapters of Amaral and Teixeira, of Temple, and of Shattock draw out this story. Amaral and Teixeira show that the economic perspective has been drawn upon to support quite different stances on the part of the state. When first taking a close interest in higher education, and sensing that it had a key part to play in economic development, states considered that they had a role to play: human capital theory justified a level of manpower planning. However, the very desire to expand higher education brought with it an increase in its total cost that not all states (including the UK) were prepared to meet. As a result, we witnessed not just an 'economisation of higher education', as Amaral and Teixeira put it, but also a marketization of higher education. This policy shift has had a differential impact on institutions. Some institutions are more 'resource dependent' than others and have needed to become imaginative in finding new ways of generating income streams.

Amaral and Teixeira go on to observe that this policy shift has not been unproblematic. There are 'issues of market failures': for example, of institutions withdrawing subjects that are valuable to the wider society; of imperfect information (just how is reliable information about university activities to be gleaned and to reach interested parties?); of the maintenance of standards (in which all universities vapidly proclaim their 'excellence' (Readings, 1997)); and of unequal power wielded by different universities. Consequently, the state has retained much influence and has sought to steer the developing market; hence the term 'quasi-market'. Internally, within universities, these changes have been accompanied by a heightened managerialism (the 'new public management'), resource allocation mechanisms, and close scrutiny of processes and academic staff.

Focusing especially on England, Temple charts the marketization of higher education and shows that it has proceeded through stages, amounting to different market models. Broadly, 'it has moved ... from concentrating on the needs of institutions to an almost exclusive focus on the needs of students'. In the first stage, Market 1, the government – through its agent – turns to 'buying outputs from competing (at least, theoretically) providers on behalf of the public', with the government 'paying money to institutions'. In the second stage, Market 2, an explicit focus on students emerged, so promoting 'students-as-customers', with a switching of much of the financing to purchases by the students themselves (supported by a government-backed loans scheme). This student market was accompanied by successively higher levels of fees and the abolition of the 'cap' on student numbers, so shifting power 'away from central bureaucracies ... towards the intended beneficiaries ... the students'. That this intensifying of markets in higher education has attracted critical comment from informed analysts has done nothing to impede its path. To the contrary: in a recent 'Green Paper', a further shift is being contemplated towards a 'Teaching Excellence Framework' that would both raise fee levels still further and intensify competition among universities.

In reflecting on these (and other accompanying) changes over the last half-century or more, Michael Shattock attributes much of the momentum to the UK's finance ministry, the Treasury. In all of the key policy moves, including the so-called abolition of the binary line which had divided universities and polytechnics, the main driver was that of reducing public expenditure and securing 'value for money'. An initial strategy lay in the imposition of 'cash limits' which, combined with an expansion of the system, inevitably led to a significant fall in the system in the resource per student (that is, in the 'unit of resource'). Subsequently, it was concluded that the only way to protect and even raise the unit of resource lay in recourse to the students sharing part of the cost of their education.

Shattock asks 'whether the Treasury itself had policies in relation to higher education' and concludes that 'it did not'. However, even if 'the Treasury's task ... was not to make policy ... that was a natural consequence of [its] negotiations [with the Ministry responsible for higher education]': 'issues affecting access ... entry standards ... postgraduate study, the viability of institutions and the shape of the sector [are being] determined on financial criteria'. We might add that the pedagogical relationship between students and lecturers (as students become 'customers'), standards (as evident in the proportions of students gaining 'good' degrees), and decisions about subjects taught, are also being influenced by the wider political and economic environment.

Shattock also observes that whereas 'the old system was aimed at the public good the new system is weighted much more heavily towards the private good. That was perhaps inevitable'. It is a further question whether such concomitant changes were intended as a matter of political policy, to reduce the power of the academic community and to open higher education to the influence of markets.

Several of the chapters in this volume touch on the matter of performance indicators. After all, it is understandable that the state, when intent on ensuring 'value for money' from its expenditures on higher education or in wanting to steer the system in certain directions (for example, more towards 'teaching excellence'), should want to use performance indicators to assist its developing policy framework. In turn, it is hardly surprising that either purchasers of university services or university managers should want to deploy performance indicators, in making informed choices and in 'performance management' respectively.

In her chapter, Jill Johnes tackles this matter of performance indicators directly. Perhaps the key message of the chapter is that there is always a trade-off, between simplicity and complexity, or between usefulness and validity. These are not matters susceptible of easy resolution. 'Higher education institutions are multi-product firms with complex production processes.' Accordingly, issues arise as to the products and processes felt to be significant; the dimensions by which those products and processes will be judged; the relative weights to be accorded to them, to their measurement, and to their possible uses. It follows that a 'simple approach can provide a misleading picture of performance with adverse consequences for institutional behaviour'.

It follows, in turn, that 'in trying to give a simple overview of performance, composite indicators [of the kind portrayed in national and global league tables] can be misleading'. Furthermore, 'rankings are open to manipulation and gaming ... a university has an incentive to change its behaviour in response to the rankings; but changed behaviour may not benefit performance'.

In analysing data derived from performance indicators, it may be seen that indicators do not cluster together: 'there is no reason to expect that a university that is good in one area will necessarily be good in another'. For example, in the UK, 'the student satisfaction indicator generally appears to provide a noticeably different picture compared to the other measures'. Analysis of the data reveals too that, while 'merger policy has ... been promoted in the UK in the belief that greater size leads to ... greater efficiency', 'typically economies of scale are exhausted and ... there are diseconomies of scope in English higher education ... [F]or the [university] of average size, there are no further opportunities for economies of scale from expansion in size'. Accordingly, 'the user of performance indicators and rankings should beware: university rankings come with a serious health warning and should be handled with care'.

A changing academic life

As intimated, it was unsurprising that within an environment being shaped significantly by external forces, the management of universities emerged as one of their key features. Currently, both in the USA and in the UK, academics account for a minority of the staff of universities. Many attribute this rise in the numbers of managers and administrators – and staff fulfilling an ever-widening array of functions in marketing, quality assurance, human resources, curriculum design, information supply, and so forth – to the emergence of markets. Ensuring that universities, as highly complex organizations, are fully effective in and take advantage of new opportunities that markets may present, calls for sophisticated management capabilities. And the increased presence of management, in guiding, steering, evaluating, and monitoring university activities, has in turn heightened universities as bureaucracies. Routines, procedures, controls, and audits become more present and more visible.

Against this background, many have become exercised by this turn, voicing concerns both with 'neoliberalism' and 'managerialism'. However, it is worth posing the question: are there perhaps different forces at work here? To put it simply: perhaps universities' bureaucracy presents more of a challenge to their fulfilling their potential than marketization?

Such a question is tacitly under the skin of David Dill's contribution here. Dill examines different models of university organization: the bureaucratic model (closely associated with New Public Management) is but one of four models that can be espied, the others being the Political Model (focused on power and hierarchy), the Organized Anarchy Model (which recognizes academic life as characterized by random intersections of happenings), and the Academic Collegial Model (especially associated with the development of research and doctoral schools). Dill goes on to glimpse and advocate a fifth model, the Commons Model, formed on the basis of 'universal design principles that permit individuals in self-governing organizations to address collective action dilemmas effectively'.

Such 'models' should surely be regarded as indicative of tendencies and – to use Dill's own term – as metaphors. Less ideal types, they are much more insights into a melange of aspects of the complex organizations that universities have become. Most universities are some kind of mix of a number of these models, albeit with each university evincing dominant tendencies in one or other direction. More than that, there are conflicts at work here. Democratic collegiality, entrepreneurial anarchy, rule-governed bureaucracy, and power-dominated decision making: these tendencies pull against each other. And in mass systems, with universities placed in different positions of the ecosystems that comprise higher education, it is likely that these tensions, both within and across institutions, will not just be evident but are likely to grow in the future.

Being positioned differently in the total higher education space, it is inevitable that universities will respond in different ways to the situations with which they are confronted. Two conditions especially mark out the contemporary setting across the world, those of massification and austerity, and it is these two conditions and their interplay that provide the focus of Bruce Johnstone's chapter. While both massification and austerity are part of the wider societal–political and economic environment, they play themselves out differently across universities. Some universities may respond 'by increasing class size and teaching loads and employing low-paid, part-time faculty', although '*cheaper instruction* is not necessarily more productive higher education'. [Johnstone's emphasis.] Others may be favourably placed to generate additional income, especially from research.

A crucial part of the story that Johnstone weaves is that of the changes taking place within universities as they attempt to accommodate both massification and austerity. Changes 'at the margin of institutional expansion' bring changes both in the composition of the student cohort and in the academic faculty. 'The concept of marginal … does not mean inferior, but merely statistically different from the typical past or current average.' Ultimately, however, the limits of the capabilities of existing institutions to changing circumstances may be reached and under those circumstances, new institutions are likely to emerge, 'more likely to feature less costly programmes, shorter cycle programmes', and more likely to be 'teaching-oriented'. Even well-established research universities are unlikely to be immune from internal changes: there, 'academic staff are being increasingly differentiated' and subject to 'varied payment contracts'. We are witnessing then 'fundamental changes in the academic profession' and they are 'here to stay'. The question is just how might they be 'further developed'?

Louise Morley examines one way in which changes afoot are working their way deeply into academic life, in particular into the research process itself. Under the new market conditions and amid a developing global knowledge economy, knowledge itself has become 'a significant form of capital'. Accordingly, knowledge has become caught up in a 'neoliberal research economy' and, in turn, 'research [is becoming] a vehicle for performance management'. Under such conditions, issues arise both about academic identity and about the nature of the research and scholarship that is now being favoured. Academics are increasingly subject to subtle and not-so subtle injunctions to steer not just their work but their academic personas in the direction of income-generation. Failure to generate research income can lead not just to institutional opprobrium but even institutional shame. (Morley cites the instance of an experienced professor at a leading UK research-based university committing suicide in the wake of admonition at a failure to win research grants.)

All this is backed by a heightened regime of 'performance management', itself resting on a greater use of performance indicators, where the favoured indicators link especially to income. This amounts to a 'financialization' of academic life, namely attempts 'to reduce all value that is exchanged either into a financial instrument or a derivative of a financial instrument'. Superficially, the 'impact' of research may be judged in a relatively open-ended way, but it is a 'tactic' intending to reassure external audiences that they are getting a return on their investment in research. Even global league tables have the latent function of being 'mechanisms by which neoliberal principles are inserted into organizations'.

Under these conditions, what it is to be an academic changes. Pressures mount not simply to publish, but to publish in selected journals and to gain research income on a continuing basis. Since these are highly competitive activities, and success cannot be assured, time is spent pursuing these goals. Anxiety levels rise, risk is lessened – such that counter views and critical scholarship are diminished – and academic identity comes to be structured within tightly drawn boundaries, marked out by numerical performance indicators. There is a need, therefore, 'to imagine and [to] research desired futures'.

Another way in which academic life is changing lies in a greater use of branding, through which universities project themselves in a competitive environment. This is the topic of the chapter by James Pringle and Rajani Naidoo, who present empirical evidence from a study of three rather different Canadian universities. Again, we see what, *prima facie*, may appear to be a relatively superficial phenomenon, having effects on the deep character of academic life. After all, 'brands ... become the sign of different types of social identity'. 'Employees' engagement with and enactment of the values and vision of the brand thus becomes a key element in [institutional] differentiation', staff being encouraged 'to live the brand'. Again, under such conditions, 'employees [may be] prevented from expressing critical thought'. Again, too, accompanying institutional branding and a wish to project one's university as distinctive, is to be found a heightened competitiveness between universities. However, and not atypically in market situations, there are tendencies towards 'more standardization', both in the curriculum and in organizational structure.

Here arise profound issues of authenticity: what is it to be a real university? Are universities as they appear? Is institutional deception a common feature of this marketization? The chapter cites the use of a photograph of three female students to promote engineering in a university being described as 'disingenuous' by some of its staff. Authenticity, accordingly, has to be achieved, and achieved not only with external audiences but with universities' internal audiences.

The uses of higher education

It is apparent that many of the chapters in this volume, at least implicitly, are raising matters to do with the uses of the university. Who is to benefit from the presence of universities in the world? They certainly bestow private benefits and large economic benefits on their regions and nations, but is there more to it than that? Does the idea of public benefit hold water, and if so, in what ways? Under market conditions, it is the private and economic benefits that are trumpeted aloud but perhaps there are public goods that may be attributed to the university. The sheer growth of professionals who have had the advantage of a university education might itself be counted as a public good (for the professional is supposedly characterized by a disinterested concern for the client). And perhaps it might be possible that *new* spaces are opening for the university to widen the public sphere – for example, through the growth of public understanding of issues – a possibility that the new digital technologies and open access systems are offering.

And so large issues arise here about the relationships between the university and the wider society, issues that have been long-standing but which resonate still. Ulrich Teichler puts a key question succinctly: 'Do we have too few or too many graduates?' This apparently simple question, however, generates complexities, for issues arise about the nature of the students – the would-be graduates – and about the ways in which such graduates assume their places in the wider society and through which graduates are valued.

For Teichler, four 'discourses' open here: the *economic* (with its largely quantitative analyses), the *sociological* (with its concerns for structure and agency), the *functional* (which attempts to discern the range of functions that higher education might play), and the *educational and process* (concerned to fillet out the different kinds of student qualities and the connected curricula and pedagogies that might be envisaged). Each of these four perspectives generates its own complexities *and* there are links to be observed between them; *and* views have varied over time in each domain.

Unpicking these complexities shows that large ideas – such as 'employability', 'skills', 'vocationalism', 'graduate work', and 'competence' – are themselves fraught with difficulty. Even the notions of 'profession' and 'professionalism' are continually on the move. As such, the design of curricula and the shaping of pedagogies have to remain open matters. They cannot fall into place through any simple reading of the relationships between higher education and the wider society. For example, what is to count as 'breadth' and its usefulness are in part matters of value, of the value attributed to the potential for universities to educate for a changing world and an unforeseeable future. After all, some students enrolling today (2016) will be alive in the twenty-second century, so readings of the contemporary world are bound to short-change the potential of higher education.

Peter Scott delves further into these matters, deploying in part a historical perspective. The opening paragraph of that chapter puts the matter directly. 'The consensus … is that higher education has never been more in thrall to the needs of the economy' but '[t]he links between higher education and the economy were almost certainly stronger in the 19th and early 20th centuries.' Scott's main target, though, is to account for the connections now being made between higher education and the economy and to reveal the complex set of structures in play that are encouraging this development. The growth of the 'knowledge society' and the emergence of the knowledge economy (in which knowledge has come to have an economic value), 'user-payments', in which university services are purchased by customers (who seek a return on their investment), and the rise of mass higher education (with higher education being promoted as a provider of economic life-chances) are just some of the macro factors at work.

The story, though, is complex, and Scott shows how different strands – and even apparently contradictory strands – interweave and, thereby, come to open spaces that are not understandable in simple categories. For example, the development of 'open research systems' certainly has economic and controlling aspects but it contains, too, possibilities for new relationships between higher education and society, not only through 'open-source and open-access publishing' but also through the efforts of (some) universities to open themselves up to engagement with the wider world over their research activities and outputs. 'These more open knowledge systems … combine both *dirigiste* and democratic elements.'

Large and even global movements are in train and so the relationships between universities, the economy, and society are liable to become ever more unstable, exhibiting contradictory forces at work. But that very instability and complexity could yet open new spaces for these profound relationships to be thought anew. Such a prospect is much to be desired, for 'perhaps only the university is still constituted to be able to increase human understanding of these truly epochal challenges'.

References

Readings, B. (1997) *The University in Ruins*. Cambridge, MA: Harvard University Press.

Shattock, M. (2015) *The Society for Research into Higher Education and the Changing World of British Higher Education: A study of SRHE over its first 25 years*. London: Society for Research into Higher Education.

Taylor, C. (2007) *Modern Social Imaginaries*. Durham, NC, and London: Duke University Press.

Williams, G. (1984) 'The economic approach'. In Clark, B. (ed.) *Perspectives on Higher Education: Eight disciplinary and comparative views*. Los Angeles, CA: University of California Press.

— (1989) 'Prospects for higher education finance'. In Ball, C. and Eggins, H. (eds) *Higher Education into the 1990s: New dimensions*. Stony Stratford: Open University Press/SRHE.

— (1992) 'Introduction'. In Williams, G. (ed.) *The Encyclopedia of Higher Education, Vol. 2: Analytical perspectives*. General editors Clark, B. and Neave, G. Oxford: Pergamon Press.

— (2015) 'Reflections on the debate'. In Filippakou, O. and Williams, G. (eds) *Higher Education As a Public Good: Critical perspectives on theory, policy and practice*. New York: Peter Lang.

Gareth Williams: An appreciation

Maureen Woodhall

'Education, education, education' – Tony Blair's mantra for the 1997 General Election – has also been the theme for Gareth Williams' long and distinguished career. He comes from a family of Welsh school teachers: both his parents, as well as his brother and sister, were teachers, and Gareth has been a dedicated and inspirational teacher of hundreds of undergraduate and postgraduate students at Lancaster and London universities, as well as making a huge contribution to educational research and policy analysis. Not long after being appointed Professor of Educational Planning at Lancaster University, aged only 37, Gareth was interviewed for the *Times Higher Education Supplement* by Tim Albert, and was remarkably practical and pragmatic:

> I must confess I don't have any high falutin' ideas on education. I take the view in general that most people view education as largely instrumental towards achieving something else … it's wrong for us in education to believe that everybody has the same interest in education with a capital 'E' – a sort of unfolding of the human spirit for its own sake.
>
> (Albert, 1975)

But he concluded the interview with the stirring declaration: 'I do believe, in spite of my cynicism, that education in the real sense is probably the one hope for mankind. I'm sure it is.'

In the 1975 interview, in which he presciently predicted the end of the binary line and the introduction of student loans, he said, 'It's a bit premature to say what should be on my monument, but I suppose the only thing I can expect to be remembered for at the moment is having some tiny involvement in the great expansion of higher education in the sixties'. Forty years later, Gareth will be remembered for far more than that. 'Tiny involvement' is the last phrase that comes to mind when considering his contribution to higher education policy in the UK and internationally. His contribution has been far-reaching and influential, not only through his research and publications on higher education finance, planning, and management, but also through his work as Chairman of the Society for

Research into Higher Education (SRHE) (1977–9 and 1986–8), Director of the SRHE-Leverhulme Programme of Study into the Future of Higher Education (1981–3), Planning Editor for the journal *Higher Education* (1973–93), General Editor of *Higher Education Quarterly* (1996–2001), and founding Director of the Centre for Higher Education Studies (1986) at the Institute of Education in London.

In 1977, Gareth wrote a report for UNESCO, *Towards Lifelong Education: A new role for higher education institutions*, and his own belief in the value of lifelong learning could be seen early, during National Service in Cyprus, when he chose to spend his spare time learning modern Greek. This stood him in good stead when he worked at the OECD in the 1960s on the Mediterranean Regional Project, an early experiment in educational planning, in which Gareth worked on the application of a statistical forecasting model in Greece and helped write the OECD report on *Econometric Models of Education* (1965). Before working for the OECD Gareth had been a Research Assistant at the Agricultural Economics Research Unit at Oxford, but it was the economics of education, rather than agricultural economics, that captured his interest, and indeed it was on the strength of a student paper on the economics of education, presented to the Political Economy Club at Cambridge, that he was hired by Colin Clark at Oxford. After six years at the OECD, Gareth returned to London in 1968 to become Joint Director of the Higher Education Research Unit, set up in 1964 at the London School of Economics by Sir Claus Moser, following his work for the Robbins Committee on Higher Education. This was where I first met Gareth, as I was working at that time with Mark Blaug at the Research Unit on the Economics of Education at the University of London Institute of Education, and our research units worked closely together. It was an auspicious meeting, and I enjoyed working with Gareth for over 30 years. I consider myself remarkably fortunate that during my own academic career at the Institute of Education I enjoyed the generous guidance of two such outstandingly stimulating scholars as Mark Blaug and Gareth Williams.

During his time at the LSE, Gareth contributed to several influential studies on higher education, including *Patterns and Policies in Higher Education* (Brosan *et al.*, 1971), in which he and Richard Layard argued for the abolition of the binary line, and he was a joint author, with Tessa Blackstone and David Metcalf, of the first serious study of the labour market for academics in the UK (Williams *et al.*, 1974).

After five years at the LSE Gareth found that the Higher Education Research Unit was focusing increasingly on economics and statistics, whereas he was fascinated by policy issues, so in 1973 he moved to Lancaster University, as Professor of Educational Planning and Director of the Institute for Research and Development in Post-Compulsory Education. It was significant that the title emphasized post-compulsory education, rather than higher education, as Gareth told his *THES* interviewer in 1975: 'I try to resist being stereotyped as a higher education person – particularly as opposed to a further education person.' Indeed, it was Gareth's interest in further education that led to our first joint publication, *Independent Further Education* (1979), which reported on a survey of independent vocational and other post-secondary colleges conducted by the Research Institute at Lancaster. We concluded that this 'forgotten sector' of education could offer some lessons to traditional higher education institutions, particularly with regard to flexibility, accessibility, and emphasis on the cost-effectiveness of short intensive courses and on consumer satisfaction. While he was at Lancaster, Gareth directed the SRHE-Leverhulme Study into the Future of Higher Education (1980–3), which produced a series of ten edited volumes on the future of higher education, culminating in a joint book with Tessa Blackstone, *Response to Adversity: Higher education in a harsh climate* (1983).

In 1980, the House of Commons Education, Science, and Arts Committee published a report on *The Funding and Organisation of Courses in Higher Education,* which stated: 'We believe that higher education is at a watershed in its development and that the time is right for a great national debate'. The SRHE-Leverhulme Study on higher education was seen as a significant contribution to this debate, and Gareth personally played an increasingly prominent part in the debate over the next decades. In 1984, he was invited to join the Institute of Education, University of London, as Professor of Educational Administration. His Inaugural Lecture in December 1986, on *New Ways of Paying the Piper,* argued that changing mechanisms for funding education could have just as much impact as cuts in the level of funding, and in the next few years Gareth directed an extensive research programme in the Centre for Higher Education Studies on 'Changing Patterns of Finance in Higher Education', in which I enjoyed taking part. His book (1992), analysing the changes in funding higher education in the 'turbulent decade' of the 1980s, began with the introduction of full-cost fees for overseas students in 1979, examined the effects of cuts in public funding for universities and polytechnics, the trend towards selective government funding of teaching and research, and the growth of entrepreneurship in higher education institutions, and ended with the establishment of the Higher Education Funding Council for England (HEFCE) in 1992. Gareth had no illusions that what he called this 'period of great turbulence, uncertainty and change' (Williams, 1992: 3) would be followed by a period of calm and stability for higher education, and he continued to offer penetrating analyses and wise counsel in his extensive publications on higher education, even after his retirement in 2001.

His influence was not confined to the published word. Always an imaginative and inspiring teacher, it spread to many countries through his PhD students and a period as a Visiting Professor in Australia, as well as consultancy work for UNESCO, OECD, and the World Bank in countries as diverse as Algeria, Belarus, China, Ghana, and Thailand. We worked together on a World Bank higher education project in China, which for operational reasons required us to visit China in July 1990. We were reluctant to go in July, as we both had teenage daughters who would be on their school holidays, but the World Bank was adamant about the timing, so Gareth took his daughter and I took two of my daughters on a fascinating visit that none of us will forget. We were also able to take with us one of Gareth's Chinese PhD students, who provided invaluable translation services, while also visiting his family in Beijing.

This vividly demonstrated the skill with which Gareth has always been able to combine his strong commitment to a happy marriage and family life with a commitment to the highest intellectual and professional standards. I was fortunate to be able to attend his eightieth birthday party in October 2015, and see for myself the love and pride with which his family joined friends and former colleagues in celebrating his birthday and his long and distinguished career. One of his sons had asked all his grandchildren to give a brief encapsulation of the qualities of their beloved grandfather, and the results were revealing, including not only his 'dry wit', 'wisdom', and 'big belief in learning and education', but also his love of 'quizzes, crossword solving and stupid bets', and the fact that the greatest compliment he can pay is 'that's not altogether a stupid idea'! Anyone who knows Gareth will recognize many of these characteristics. His interests have always been amazingly diverse and far from confined to intellectual pursuits. He discovered after a brief foray into boxing at school that 'brains rather than brawn' were more likely to bring him success, but as an undergraduate at Cambridge he loved rowing, and he was a member of the Board of Red Rose Radio, described as 'the jewel in the crown of independent local radio'[1] in Lancashire, from 1982 to 1992.

The quality and breadth of the chapters in this book are a testament to the importance and influence of his distinguished academic career. Another notable achievement is that he helped design and establish the MBA in Higher Education Management at the Institute of Education. Gareth and Michael Shattock, the first Joint Directors of the MBA programme, designed it as a predominantly distance learning course with several week-long intensive residential blocks each year. At the launch of the MBA in 2002, Gareth said: 'It's supposed to be for people who are perceived to be high flyers in the management of the universities' and expressed the hope that 'some recruits will go on to become heads of administration, heads of schools or university registrars', adding that he hoped one or two might become vice chancellors, while stressing that 'one of the things we're trying to do is establish a network of people who have a modern, holistic and realistic view about management of universities'.[2] The latest publicity for the MBA provides ample evidence that this hope has been fulfilled, with glowing comments from past students, including a Pro-Vice Chancellor who says: 'A day does not go by when I do not draw upon what I learned on the course.'[3] In 1975, Gareth thought that he might be remembered for 'having some tiny involvement in the great expansion of higher education in the sixties'. Forty years later he is remembered fondly by colleagues and former students from around the world for so much more, as this volume testifies.

Notes

[1] See the 'Red Rose Radio Memories site' at http://30111.tripod.com (accessed 4 November 2015).

[2] *The Guardian*, 1 November 2002. See www.theguardian.com/education/2002/nov/01/highereducation.uk7 (accessed 4 November 2015).

[3] UCL Institute of Education (2015) *Brochure for MBA Higher Education Management 2015–16*. See www.ioe.ac.uk/research/departments/lce/156.html (accessed 4 November 2015).

References

Albert, T. (1975) 'From promising young man to accomplished Eurocrat'. *Times Higher Education Supplement*, 4 July.

Brosan, G., Carter, C., Layard, R., Venables, P., and Williams, G. (1971) *Patterns and Policies in Higher Education*. Harmondsworth: Penguin.

House of Commons Education, Science, and Arts Committee (1980) *The Funding and Organisation of Courses in Higher Education*. Fifth report. London: Her Majesty's Stationery Office.

OECD (1965) *Econometric Models of Education: Some applications*. Paris: OECD.

Williams, G. (1977) *Towards Lifelong Education: A new role for higher education institutions*. Paris: UNESCO.

— (1987) *New Ways of Paying the Piper: An inaugural lecture*. London: Institute of Education, University of London.

— (1992) *Changing Patterns of Finance in Higher Education*. Buckingham: SRHE/Open University Press.

Williams, G. and Blackstone, T. (1983) *Response to Adversity: Higher education in a harsh climate*. Guildford: Society for Research into Higher Education.

Williams, G. and Woodhall, M. (1979) *Independent Further Education*. London: Policy Studies Institute.

Williams, G., Blackstone, T., and Metcalf, D. (1974) *The Academic Labour Market: Economic and social aspects of a profession*. Amsterdam: Elsevier.

Part One

The rise and rise of markets
in higher education

1

An economic view of higher education theory

Alberto Amaral and Pedro Teixeira

The university is one of the oldest institutions in the world. Throughout its long life it has been confronted with changes in its environment. However, changes occurring over the last decades seem to have had more drastic consequences than before, putting the fundamental values and mission of the institution in question. The ideas of markets, competition, or marketization, which today are a normal component of higher education theory, were totally alien to the university culture less than three decades ago.

In the UK these changes were profound and occurred earlier, which makes the analysis of UK higher education policies an interesting tool for understanding changes occurring later in other European countries.

Gareth Williams, an economist by background, has approached higher education theory with higher education examined as a set of linked economic activities and as such open to the analyses used for any other economic activity (2009, 2011). At the 2009 Society for Research into Higher Education (SRHE) Annual Conference, Gareth Williams presented a paper entitled 'An economic view of higher education theory', recognizing that his arguments could 'be seen by some as a neoliberal approach and therefore merely ideological. But any analysis must start from somewhere' (2009). He argued that universities were always economic enterprises, using resources to produce multiple products such as educational services and knowledge. However, there has been a change from a situation of generous public funding with few accountability demands to a situation of short cash, fierce competition, and detailed government control. Instead of 'being institutions dedicated to research and high-level learning and teaching many [universities] have become quasi-commercial enterprises selling services in the knowledge industry to a wide range of purchasers' (Williams, 2004: 251).

Under the pressure of drastic economic stringency, universities were forced to enter a market-type competition where some of the traditional academic values and principles had to be seen with more flexibility, to say the least. Universities expanded their organizational boundaries to include new activities that could provide additional resources to make up for the cuts in public funding.

In this chapter we closely follow Gareth Williams, as his economic analysis of higher education policy offers a convincing interpretation of the reactions of universities to market regulation and unravels the rationale for government intervention aiming at steering the system by offering economic incentives that institutions, hard on cash, could not easily refuse. But before doing so, we propose a short digression on a number of theoretical questions, including sociological institutionalism, resource dependence, and institutional boundaries, in order to understand Gareth Williams's research better.

The economization of higher education: Human capital theory and manpower planning

Gareth Williams initiated his professional career at a time when economics started to make inroads into the analysis of education. In the post-war decades, economists' interest in education increased significantly, leading to the development of multiple studies exploring the potential contribution of education to national and individual betterment (Rostow, 1990; Schultz, 1963). This gained particular significance with the development of the human capital theory (Teixeira, 2005) that stimulated significant theoretical and empirical controversies about the extent of education as an important factor in promoting economic growth and development (Bowman, 1966; Blaug, 1985). Subsequent to these debates, it became increasingly important to discuss how far government policies could (or could not) enhance that contribution, notably by promoting a faster expansion of access to education.

These debates about the economic role of education and about the role of governments in this regard were increasingly taken over by several of the international organizations that emerged in the post-war period. Organizations such as the International Monetary Fund (IMF), the International Bank for Reconstruction and Development (IBRD), and the Organisation for European Economic Co-operation (OEEC)/Organisation for Economic Co-operation and Development (OECD) became significant actors in intergovernmental and transnational economic relations (Pechman, 1989). The influence of these organizations grew in the definition of priorities for economic policymaking, and they increasingly engaged in debates about the economic role of education.

By the early 1960s, when the human capital research programme was taking off, there was increasing attention from the OECD to the economic role of education (Papadopoulos, 1994). This became more visible with the Washington Conference entitled 'Economic growth policies and educational investment' (16–20 October 1961), in which a definition of the objectives of educational expansion for OECD countries that met foreseeable demographic, social, and economic needs was attempted. This initiative indicated a clear confidence in the capacity of education to promote growth as part of a broader optimistic perspective on social change. This conference was followed by the creation of the Study Group in Economics of Education in 1960, which operated mainly between 1962 and 1965 and was responsible for organizing some relevant conferences in this field. The group started with Henning Friis, Friedrich Edding, Seymour Harris, Raymond Poignant, Ingvar Svennilson, and John Vaizey, and was later joined by Michel Debeauvais, Selma Mushkin, and Jan Tinbergen. Also among this group was a young British economist named Gareth Williams.

This group included several pioneers in the Economics of Education who had become interested in the topic either through the analysis of its costs and funding (Edding for Germany, Harris for the USA, Vaizey for the UK, and Poignant for French-speaking African countries), or via the analysis of economic growth (Svennilson and Friis). This group was largely pro-Keynesian, in favour of some degree of planning, and somewhat sceptical about the perfect working of the market. Most of its members believed that markets had far more failures than neoclassical models assumed, and education was clearly one of the issues in which markets underperformed. They saw the role of education in economic development as a matter of long-term planning that should not be left to the working of market forces as most of the human capital pioneers believed.

Although short-lived, the activities of this Study Group were important in shaping the initial views of the OECD about the economic role of education. Their work contributed to disseminate the idea of 'investment in education' and human capital/education became established as an engine of growth. However, the organization tended to assume that educational expansion was too important to be left to private decisions and embarked on a series of activities that promoted educational planning and manpower forecasting. Most of the members of the Study Group considered that the specificities of education and the imperfections of the labour market prevented a straightforward application of microeconomic neoclassical theory, rather choosing an approach that called governments to play a much more active role in the development of educational provision. These suspicions and the dominance of manpower planning in terms of the OECD's views on education lasted almost until the early 1980s and only by then would the OECD (with other international organizations) embrace a more market-friendly attitude towards higher education.[1]

Nonetheless, these early decades were important in starting to change societal and political views about higher education and about the role of economic motivations and rationality in underpinning higher education's regulatory framework. With the development of the human capital theory, and the subsequent increasing interest of many economists in education, perceptions about the nature and purpose of higher education would eventually change. By stressing the economic motivations of higher education's demand, educational economists have opened the door for reconceptualizing the role of educational institutions themselves. By viewing educational decisions as being largely motivated by economic factors and calculus, economics has contributed decisively to recognize educational institutions (also) as economic institutions. Moreover, by presenting them as a kind of economic unit, economists quickly moved to encompassing the educational system into the basic framework of a market system. Over the last decades, societies and governments have evolved in their views about the social role of higher education, with significant implications for the identity of higher education institutions (HEIs) and the organization of the higher education sector. In the latter part of the twentieth century those have come to be shaped by an increasing influence of economic rationality in education in general and in higher education in particular (Teixeira, 2009). Before analysing that process, we will briefly present the higher education reality that these ideas would change in recent decades, notably by reflecting on the institutional fabric of higher education.

Social institutionalism and resource dependence theories

The coming of the modern university occurred between the end of the eighteenth and the beginning of the nineteenth centuries, following the reforms of von Humboldt in Prussia and Napoleon in France (Neave and van Vught, 1994). The modern university was an instrument in the construction of the nation-state and provided qualified manpower to fulfil the recruitment needs of the apparatus of the state (ibid).

The legitimacy of the modern university resulted from the idea that knowledge was independent of both religion and the state, being inseparable from the ideas of education, reflection, creation, and critique (the university educates, it does not merely train).

Institutions are capable of influencing institutional actors' actions and vice versa, in a way that organizations cannot, which makes the university seem to be more important and efficient as an institution than as an organization (Meyer *et al.*, 2007: 199). Institutions not only affect the strategic calculations of individuals, but also their basic preferences and identity (Hall and Taylor, 1996: 948).

March and Olsen (2009), whose work had strong influence on sociological new institutionalism, argued that human behaviour is guided and shaped by a *logic of appropriateness*. Individuals not only react to their institutional environment but they also shape their interactions with institutions and with others through frames of reference, moral templates, and normative orientations (DiMaggio and Powell, 1991). Neo-institutionalism explains why well-established universities, with strong academic norms and values, are far more careful than newer universities in offering new activities and products, such as cross-border programmes or franchising.

In 1978, Pfeffer and Salancik published *The External Control of Organizations: A resource dependence theory perspective*, which is considered the starting point of Resource Dependence Theory. The theory's fundamental assumption is that 'because organizations are not self-contained or self-sufficient, the environment must be relied upon to provide support' (1978: 43).

Resource dependence explains, for instance, why some institutions (mainly polytechnics and private institutions) offer programmes scheduled after working hours, or why private institutions are traditionally careful in their choice of study programmes, avoiding those that demand large investments in facilities or running costs.

Institutional boundaries

The notion of boundaries assumes a preponderant role in organizational theory (Heracleous, 2004). As described by Santos and Eisenhardt (2005a), there are different definitions of organizational boundaries. Some authors see organizational boundaries as the limits of the social structure, which constitutes the organization with an identity whose logic determines how it operates (Dutton *et al.*, 1994; Kogut, 2000). Others see boundaries as the limit of the organizational resources, which shape growth strategies and trajectories (Helfat, 1997). Finally, some authors see boundaries as determining the sphere of organizational influence (D'Aveni, 2001; Santos and Eisenhardt, 2005b).

Santos and Eisenhardt (2005b) stress the importance of the notion of identity for the understanding of organizational boundaries. Identity translates the set of norms and values constituting an organization's distinctive character, allowing both for its self-assertion and its demarcation in relation to other organizations and the environment (ibid).

The recent decline in public funding has forced universities to look for alternative sources of funding, which have resulted in shifting their boundaries to include new activities, such as collaborations with non-academic organizations, provision of cross-border higher education, and participation in private companies or agencies. This expansion of activities beyond 'its core mission of scholarly teaching and research' just to get extra funds, raised questions about its appropriateness (Williams, 2004: 245).

From system to institutional marketization

Economists have conceptualized markets as a powerful mechanism of social choice that, through rational utility-maximizing behaviour of individuals as if by an invisible hand (as metaphorically proposed by Adam Smith in the late eighteenth century), will distribute goods in such a way that no one could be better off without making anyone else worse off (Wolf, 1993; Teixeira and Dill, 2011). However, economists have also warned that markets do not always produce the optimal outcome from a society's point of view. Some markets can persistently produce too many or too few goods and services, challenging the self-regulating capacity that economists usually associate with a market mechanism, i.e. the capacity to adjust to situations of excessive or insufficient supply (or demand). This is a case of *market failures*.

The development of public economics has focused attention on the issue of market failures, namely in the case of public goods, the existence of externalities (spillovers), information asymmetry, and monopoly powers. With the exception of the public goods issue, all of the other examples of potential market failure are considered relevant for higher education (Johnes, 1993). First, self-interested individual decision making does not take into account that investment in higher education will affect the functioning and well-being of others in a positive way. The same holds for firms investing in research or Research and Development (R&D). Both examples may increase the risk, from the society's point of view, of an underinvestment in higher education and research. Second, there are important information-related problems in the higher education sector when it comes to assessing the outcome (including the quality) of the efforts of academics and students. Imperfect information also shows up in the student loans market, where information asymmetries exist between students taking up loans, on the one hand, and banks (or government agencies) that supply loans, on the other. Thirdly, while natural monopolies may not exist in the case of higher education, market power may be concentrated in a selected number of providers, causing them to behave like a cartel and to erect barriers to entry for potential new providers.

These examples of market failures have provided the traditional economic rationale for government intervention, which can take the shape of public production, the provision of government subsidies, the provision of information, and the issuing of laws and regulations. Government intervention may also work to introduce incentives to ensure that providers reveal the quality of their services and students express their demands and capacities, because sufficient information is a vital ingredient for any market. Government regulatory bodies are also charged with overseeing market concentration, preventing collusion practices or monopolies, and promoting a market structure without unjustified barriers for potential new providers entering the market. When it comes to the higher education market, one of the major goals of government intervention is also to provide equal opportunities to all qualified individuals who wish to participate in a higher education course.

Some have been arguing that the peculiar nature of higher education limits the relevance and applicability of economic assumptions about competitive markets. They suggest that because university prices do not reflect true costs (due to government subsidies, private endowments, or cross-subsidies), the traditional economic framework of 'market failures' may be inappropriate for assessing the performance of higher education. A related argument is that higher education differs from traditional markets in that they are publicly funded 'quasi-markets' introduced into existing state systems of higher education in order to increase efficiency and responsiveness (Le Grand and Bartlett, 1993).

Many also argue that the application of market forces to higher education is inappropriate because higher education is a 'public good'. These critics, however, use the term 'public good' as equivalent to public benefits, and seem to assume that such benefits must be publicly provided. This common usage of the term, however, often obscures the contribution that an economic perspective can make to higher education policy. Mainstream economists have instead defined a pure public good as a good or service that will not be provided by the market because of the inability of private providers to exclude those who do not pay for it (Barr, 2004). But academic degrees, research, and most of the other outputs of higher education are provided by the private sector. Therefore, public economists prefer calling higher education a merit good rather than a public one. By this they mean that governments should promote private consumption of this type of good because of its individual and social benefits, but this promotion does not require its public provision.

Despite significant social and political resistances, over the last decades higher education has been experiencing a growing influence of marketization forces (Teixeira *et al.*, 2004; Teixeira and Dill, 2011). For instance, they have seen the strengthening of competition (nationally and internationally) for students, financial resources, and academic staff. Privatization has been taking place not only through the development of private sectors, but also and quite significantly through the adoption of private-like rules and practices in public HEIs, aiming at attaining more flexibility, but also a better level of efficiency.

The growing influence of a perspective that views higher education as an industry and a part of the economic system (and an increasingly important part of it) has had important effects on the way HEIs are perceived. Increasingly, HEIs have come to be regarded as quasi-corporate units that produce a wide range of educational goods and services (including, but not only, educational ones) to an increasingly competitive and demanding external environment (Teixeira and Dill, 2011). Therefore, there is an increasing need for those institutions to adapt and respond to the changing requirements of multiple economic and societal actors. Thus, although governments have, in the context of mass higher education, awarded greater autonomy to HEIs, they have also steered them to face increasing and more diverse demands through marketization and to adopt a quasi-corporate approach to those demands.

The microeconomic theory of non-profit enterprises

This view of HEIs as quasi-corporations was built upon the microeconomic theory of non-profit enterprises (Hopkins and Massy, 1981; James, 1986; Massy, 1996, 2003). This view proposes a model that distinguishes non-profit from for-profit organizations in the way they deal with surpluses. While for-profits will eventually distribute the surplus money among the shareholders, this is not allowed for non-profit organizations, which use surpluses to boost mission accomplishment by means of internal subsidization (Massy, 2004: 26). It is through this capacity for discretionary spending that universities can, for instance, finance specific research projects or valuable cultural activities, though they are not profit generators. If there is no discretionary spending capacity, as is the case for non-profits in a difficult economic situation, then they tend to behave as for-profits, thus threatening the accomplishment of the institutional mission.

Perceiving HEIs as quasi-economic organizations has tended to obscure their distinctive nature, even from a microeconomic perspective (Winston, 1999). Most of them are motivated by non-profit rather than commercial interests: they use a production process that is much dependent on the collaboration of the so-called customers, and they adopt a selective approach regarding those demanding their services, calculating the prestige to be derived from each association. Moreover, we can find a level of diversity of units and production processes in the higher education sector much beyond what is usual in other sectors.

Universities as economic enterprises

As a consequence HEIs are increasingly motivated to adopt an external orientation, often translated into a discourse calling for greater customer focus. This customer-orientation is often received with mistrust and perplexity. One of the main concerns has to do with its stimulation of student consumerism. The trend has steered the system from the notion of clients that rely on professional expertise, to customers (who are always supposed to be right) to be pleased. The emphasis on students' sovereignty has had important effects in matters such as curriculum, since student satisfaction has become an important institutional objective. Thus, academic staff perceive their influence over student learning as clearly weakened and have felt the pressure of a certain anti-intellectual drift. Moreover, institutions have become increasingly adverse to any behaviour that could have negative short-term impacts on student satisfaction.

Gareth Williams has approached the changes taking place in British universities from the late 1980s from an essentially economic point of view. British universities until then had a substantial level of autonomy, and the government funded them generously without too many demands on accountability. The budget was allocated through a buffer organization dominated by representatives of the academy, which softened eventual political pressures. In economic terms, British universities were independent, non-profit, multi-product enterprises, whose core business was the creation and dissemination of knowledge (Williams, 2004: 242). Their non-profit character was granted by their status as charitable foundations, which did not allow for profit distribution but granted full discretionary powers over any financial surpluses they achieved. Gareth Williams agrees with Bill Massy (2004), in considering that there is only one strategy for achieving academic freedom in a market economy: to ensure a surplus (Williams, 1998: 86), which will allow for cross-subsidized operations. Otherwise they will tend to behave like private for-profits. However, by the late 1980s, overall enrolments in British higher education lagged behind those of most European countries and universities were short of cash following almost a decade of financial stringency (Williams, 2004: 246).

After the first election, in 1979, of Margaret Thatcher as Prime Minister, the British government decided to lower the overall levels of public expenditure. In the case of higher education, a first measure consisted in removing any public subsidies for foreign students, followed one year later by a 15 per cent decrease in the funds for higher education. In the case of foreign students, universities soon realized that they could get significant income by increasing foreign student numbers, and started very aggressive recruitment policies. In the case of national students, universities reacted to the 15 per cent cuts by lowering student enrolments, claiming that they did so to maintain the quality of provision. On the contrary, polytechnics, which did not have the same level of autonomy as universities, did not initiate marketing strategies to recruit more foreign students, but realized that the only way they had to round up their resources depended on recruiting more national students, a policy that was vigorously pursued.

The re-election in 1983 of Margaret Thatcher's Conservative Government with an increased majority was a clear sign that 'the post-war age of unconditional government generosity to the universities was over and that new sources of finance had to be found' (Williams, 2004: 244). Universities started to expand their boundaries by pursuing diversified income-generating activities, including recruiting as many full-paying foreign students as possible, creating university companies and services to sell teaching, research, and consultancy services, creating science and business parks, and even renting its facilities when they were not being used by staff and students (Williams, 1992).

Gareth Williams (1997: 276) interpreted the reactions of both universities and polytechnics as typical market responses from 'economic enterprises' determined 'by the mechanisms by which universities and polytechnics received their funding and the regulations which govern them'. In other words, HEIs were seen to have the capacity to 'respond quickly to financial opportunities from outside their traditional sources of funds regardless of the conditions imposed' (Williams, 1997: 282), behaving 'like any other organisation to market and quasi-market incentives' (ibid). And he argued, 'the lessons were not lost on the government' (ibid). Faced simultaneously with the need to increase enrolments and to reduce public expenditure, the government was able to devise a system of incentives that has allowed for the implementation of a mass higher education system at reduced costs for the taxpayer.

What the government did was to introduce a form of privatization under the guise of quasi-markets to create competition among institutions. In a quasi-market a well-informed buyer (the government or a government agency) substitutes an immature, under-informed client (Dill, 1997: 181) making contracts with the institutions on behalf of the final consumers. Students may choose which programme and institution to attend, but 'the main element of market power is exercised by the state on their behalf' (Massy, 2004: 15).

The expansion of the British higher education system in the late 1980s was the result of a combination of budget emaciation with manipulation of the rules for allocation of public funds to institutions in order to force them to compete for additional students while accepting lower per capita funding. This change in the attitude of institutions was made easier by keeping them short of money. For Gareth Williams the achievement of mass higher education at relatively low cost to the taxpayer owed much to the almost accidental early lessons (Williams, 1997) collected from the elimination of subsidies for foreign students and early budget cuts. The reactions of institutions made clear that they were able to react swiftly to market pressures just like any commercial private company. The 1988 Education Reform Act, supported by the Dearing Report (National Committee of Inquiry into Higher Education, 1997) and the results of that earlier experiment, transformed universities from 'partners of the state in the provision of high-level reaching and research into audited vendors of academic services to the state' (Williams, 2004: 246). As argued by Gareth Williams, there is a very considerable difference between the Robbins Report (Committee on Higher Education, 1963), considering that 'Universities existed to preserve, extend and disseminate a [common] culture', and the Dearing Report, stating:

> ... the issue is one of customers and suppliers. It is considered appropriate for providers to be paid for the specific services they provide and for individual consumers to pay at least part of the cost of the services they receive.
>
> (Williams, 1998: 85–6)

The mechanism designed by the government consisted in allowing institutions to compensate for budget cuts by competing for additional students at marginal costs. To guarantee that the buffer councils would promote the policies set by the government, the former University Grants Committee was dismissed, being replaced by a new higher education funding council with its members being chosen from outside higher education (Williams, 2004). To create financial incentives for the implementation of a mass higher education system, the government used about 20 per cent from the traditional core funding of universities to subsidize the direct payment of fees by students to universities and polytechnics. This meant that institutions were allocated a reduced budget for a fixed number of full-cost students (as defined by the Funding Councils) and they could compensate for this loss of revenue by recruiting extra students paying fees that were about 30 per cent of the normal teaching full costs, 'which government statisticians guessed to be about the level of the real marginal costs of additional students in many institutions' (Williams, 1997: 284).

This exercise has forced institutions to recruit the maximum possible number of full-cost students and then to recruit as many students as they could at marginal costs. However, in the following year, 'the average allocation per student was reduced to the realized average after the bidding was completed, thus reducing standard income per student for all institutions whether or not they had participated in the bidding process. All had to join in or lose money' (Williams, 2004: 247).

The result of this policy was a 75 per cent increase in new first degree enrolments in a five-year period from 1988 to 1994, while the per capita public funding of students had a 25 per cent decrease (Williams, 2004: 247). This too-fast expansion raised two major concerns:

a) The constant increase in enrolments together with a decrease of per capita funding raised concerns about the quality of provision. This concern was met by creating a Quality Assurance Agency responsible for monitoring the quality of the education provided.

b) A 75 per cent increase in enrolments, even at decreasing per capita costs and with a partial replacement of maintenance grants with loans, resulted in the end in increased public expenditure.

In 1995, the government reversed the expansion policy by imposing a ceiling on student numbers. A new Labour Government, elected in 1997, ended this restrictive policy but further expansion was to rely mainly on the shorter two-year foundation degrees and on developing the skills of mature students already in the workforce (DfES, 2003: 60).

The introduction of quasi-markets has transformed non-profit institutions like universities into 'self-interested, market-oriented institutions seeking short-term profit maximisation [and as a result the] government [has] unsheathed its latent powers to regulate them' (Williams, 2004: 265). This has resulted in increasing complexity and detail of the financial control over universities, as the government provided 'financial incentives to encourage agents to behave in desired ways and market monitoring to ensure that they do so effectively' (Williams, 1997: 278).

The increasing government control over financial matters has resulted in changing from a lump sum core funding system without many accountability requirements into a much more detailed funding system where each individual activity is paid separately, thus making the generation of surpluses more difficult. With these control policies, the government went further in reducing the capacity of universities to have discretionary policies and made the behaviour of universities converge further with that of for-profits. This was reinforced by a technical clause in the 1988 Education Reform Act determining that 'any financial allocations to individual universities [...] be accompanied by Financial Memoranda that specified within fairly defined limits what was expected in return for these financial allocations' (Williams, 1997: 283). This amounts to the introduction of a contractual system, one of the instruments of New Public Management.

As recognized by Gareth Williams (2004), universities reacted to market competition like any other economic enterprise, trying to diversify their clientele to survive and extending their boundaries in three major directions:

a) Expansion of the number of higher education programmes.
b) Inclusion of new market niches, namely 'professional areas such as nursing and tourism and quasi-professional areas such as media studies' (Williams, 2004: 261).
c) Inclusion of new profitable activities beyond the traditional ones of teaching and research, to include a public service function, nowadays classified as 'the third mission'.

However, as universities had a non-profit status as charitable foundations, this expansion of institutional boundaries to include income-generation activities and the incursion into what were barefaced market activities raised a number of questions, which can be interpreted using the notion of identity for understanding organizational boundaries (Santos and Eisenhardt, 2005a). All those questions were related to ensuring the coherence between the identity of the university and its activities: how far was it appropriate for a university to expand its boundaries beyond its core mission of scholarly teaching and research just to make some money? How could these new profit-generating activities develop side by side with traditional academic activities without harming them? How could a charity become responsible for profit-generating activities without jeopardizing its favourable fiscal situation? And Gareth Williams adds:

One aspect of this debate that still generates tensions in the academic profession is the extent to which success in income-generating applied research and consultancy should supplement, or replace, traditional academic criteria in making staff appointments or promoting staff to senior positions.

(Williams, 2004: 245)

Analysis and conclusions

One characteristic of the recent changes in higher education is 'the active experimentation with market-oriented policies by states intent on maximising the social benefits of national higher education systems' (Dill *et al.*, 2004: 327). And, as argued by Gareth Williams, the important issue for public policy purposes is not the existence of a market but the extent and the way markets are regulated (Williams, 2004: 265). However, he agrees that ideology underpinned most changes taking place in the UK (ibid).

Gareth Williams further argued that scepticism about the efficiency of centralized public services and saturation with high levels of taxation favoured experimentation with economic market regulation, which was 'usually expressed through the resource dependency inspired concepts of new public management, [and] became an attractive way of providing a very wide range of services' (Williams, 2004: 265).

Such changes had profound influence on the universities, as education is no longer regarded as a social right but rather as a service, universities having become the providers of that service while students are seen as the clients.

One consequence of these changes was the diversification of funding sources, which extended the boundaries of universities by broadening the activities considered legitimate for them. And the importance of the identity concept in organizational boundaries was accommodated by institutional mission drift (Massy, 2004: 31), in order to preserve the coherence between the identity of the organization and its activities.

Bob Massy presents as an example of mission drift the proliferation of 'market-oriented programmes like executive education and technology transfer' (Zemsky and Massy, 1995, cited by Massy, 2004: 29). Another example is the expanding provision of cross-border higher education that several scandals associated with low quality of delivery have shown resulted from operations having been mainly aimed at profit generation without paying due attention to long-term institutional strategies or the traditional ideal of transferring knowledge. However, none of the universities that in general occupy the top positions of international rankings has participated in those activities, which is consistent with the 'logic of appropriateness' of new institutionalism or the influence of a strong organizational identity over its boundaries.

Another problem was the complexity of the details and procedures of the funding of teaching, research, and third leg activities, which made it difficult for a university to determine 'the appropriate strategy to maximise institutional income and [safeguard] it in the future' (Williams, 2004: 249). The diversification of external funding sources went together with increased responsibility of senior management teams and governing bodies, and made the proactive management of universities and polytechnics much more visible while financial management in particular was strengthened (Williams, 2004: 251). Gareth Williams recognizes that 'many British universities are now large commercial enterprises and need, at least in part, to be run as such. Business acumen is now at least as important as academic expertise for their top managers' (Williams, 2004: 263).

There were also additional internal consequences at the level of financial management, as most institutions have introduced Resource Allocation Models (RAMs), a planning and management tool for allocating resources to the diverse cost centres in a university. RAMs allow central management to steer the activities of the institution by using allocation criteria that will favour, for instance, the recruitment of foreign students, which brings additional income, or the attraction of well-funded grants or service contracts.

This new financial situation has also been reflected in the composition of the academic staff: as tenure has been eliminated, there has been an increasing recourse to part-time or non-permanent staff in both teaching and research, while many subsidiary activities have been outsourced.

As recognized by Gareth Williams, 'the emergence of formula funding of universities by government and of RAMs for resource allocation within them are clearly indications of a very market-oriented approach to the funding of universities' (Williams, 1997: 278). However, this does not mean that there is a real free market for higher education, as some of the conditions of a market are not present (Jongbloed, 2003) due to government regulation that strongly conditions its operation, both externally and internally. Good examples of restrictive conditions are the limits set to the number of enrolled students, or to the value of tuition fees (Williams, 1996).

To conclude, the reforms taking place in the UK have produced substantial change in the way universities are funded and managed. Resource dependence and scarcity of funding have forced institutions to extend their boundaries, including new for-profit activities even if their legal status as registered charities would limit the use of any profits to purposes compatible with their charitable status (Williams, 1997: 286), and raised questions about possible negative influences over the core mission activities of teaching and research.

The work of Gareth Williams has helped us to understand better the potential and limitations of using economic analysis and concepts in higher education, and its implications for a policy orientation that privileges economic rationales. He has taught us that HEIs cannot escape the fact that they need resources to develop their activities and that they are part of the economic system. However, they need to accommodate market signals and to respond to short-term economic and social demands with a longer-term commitment to their enduring institutional mission. This is something commendable, even from a management perspective, since it is doubtful that firms can endure if they limit themselves to responding to short-term incentives and pressures, losing sight of their long-term goals. The use of economic rationality in academic management is not a means to avoid problems and difficulties; rather it is another possible criterion to organize the decision-making process and legitimize institutional decisions.

Notes
[1] Gareth Williams would also evolve towards a more careful tone regarding the role of planning in higher education, considering that some planning was necessary, but that the specificities of higher education required a less heavy approach than the one adopted in the 1960s (Williams, 1972).

References
Barr, N. (2004) *Economics of the Welfare State*. Oxford: Oxford University Press.

Blaug, M. (1985) 'Where are we now in the economics of education?' *Economics of Education Review*, 4 (1), 17–28.

Bowman, M. (1966) 'The new economics of education'. *International Journal of Educational Sciences*, 1, 29–46.

Committee on Higher Education (1963) *Higher Education: Report of the Committee appointed by the Prime Minister under the chairmanship of Lord Robbins, 1961–63*. The Robbins Report. Cmnd 2154. London: Her Majesty's Stationery Office.

D'Aveni, R. (2001) *Strategic Supremacy*. New York: The Free Press.

Department for Education and Skills (DfES) (2003) *The Future of Higher Education*. Cm 5735. London: Her Majesty's Stationery Office.

Dill, D. (1997) 'Higher education markets and public policy'. *Higher Education Policy*, 10 (3/4), 167–85.

Dill, D., Teixeira, P., Jongbloed, B., and Amaral, A. (2004) 'Conclusion'. In Teixeira, P., Jongbloed, B., Dill, D., and Amaral, A. (eds) *Markets in Higher Education: Rhetoric or reality?* Dordrecht: Kluwer Academic Publishers.

DiMaggio, P. and Powell, W. (1991) 'Introduction'. In Powell, J. and DiMaggio, P. (eds) *The New Institutionalism in Organizational Analysis*. Chicago: University of Chicago Press, 1–38.

Dutton, J., Dukerich, J., and Harquail, C. (1994) 'Organizational images and member identification'. *Administrative Science Quarterly*, 39 (2), 239–63.

Hall, P. and Taylor, R. (1996) 'Political science and the three new institutionalisms'. *Political Studies*, 44 (5), 936–57.

Helfat, C. (1997) 'Know-how and asset complementarity and dynamic capability accumulation: The vase of R&D'. *Strategic Management Journal*, 18 (5), 339–60.

Heracleous, L. (2004) 'Boundaries in the study of organization'. *Human Relations*, 57 (1), 95–103.

Hopkins, D. and Massy, W. (1981) *Planning Models for Colleges and Universities*. Stanford, CA: Stanford University Press.

James, E. (1986) 'How nonprofits grow: A model'. In Rose-Ackerman, S. (ed.) *The Economics of Nonprofit Institutions*. New York: Oxford University Press.

Johnes, G. (1993) *The Economics of Education*. London: Macmillan.

Jongbloed, B. (2003) 'Marketisation in higher education, Clark's triangle and the essential ingredients of markets'. *Higher Education Quarterly*, 57 (2), 110–35.

Kogut, B. (2000) 'The network as knowledge: Generative rules and the emergence of structure'. *Strategic Management*, 21 (3), 405–25.

Le Grand, J. and Bartlett, W. (1993) *Quasi-Markets and Social Policy*. London: Macmillan.

March, J. and Olsen, J. (2009) 'The logic of appropriateness'. ARENA Working Papers, WP 04/09. Online. www.sv.uio.no/arena/english/research/publications/arena-publications/workingpapers/working-papers2004/wp04_9.pdf (accessed 12 April 2016).

Massy, W. (ed.) (1996) *Resource Allocation in Higher Education*. Ann Arbor: University of Michigan Press.

Massy, W. (2003) *Honoring the Trust: Quality and cost containment in higher education*. Bolton, MA: Anker Publishing Company.

— (2004) 'Markets in higher education: Do they promote internal efficiency?' In Teixeira, P., Jongbloed, B., Dill, D., and Amaral, A. (eds) *Markets in Higher Education: Rhetoric or reality?* Dordrecht: Kluwer Academic Publishers.

Meyer, J., Ramirez, F., Frank, D., and Schofer, E. (2007) 'Higher education as an institution'. In Gumport, P. (ed.) *Sociology of Higher Education: Contributions and their contexts*. Baltimore, MD: Johns Hopkins University Press.

National Committee of Inquiry into Higher Education (1997) *Higher Education in the Learning Society*. The Dearing Report. London: Her Majesty's Stationery Office.

Neave, G. and van Vught, F. (eds) (1994) *Government and Higher Education Relationships across Three Continents: The winds of change*. London: Pergamon Press.

Papadopoulos, G. (1994) *Education 1960–1990: The OECD perspective*. Paris: OECD.

Pechman, J. (ed.) (1989) *The Role of the Economist in Government: An international perspective*. New York: Harvester Wheatsheaf.

Pfeffer, J. and Salancik, G. (1978) *The External Control of Organizations. A resource dependence perspective*. New York: Harper and Row.

Rostow, W. (1990) *Theorists of Economic Growth from David Hume to the Present*. New York and Oxford: Oxford University Press.

Santos, F. and Eisenhardt, K. (2005a) 'Constructing markets and organizing boundaries: Entrepreneurial action in nascent fields'. Working paper. Fontainebleau: INSEAD.

— (2005b) 'Organizational boundaries and theories of organization'. *Organization Science*, 16 (5), 491–508.

Schultz, T. (1963) *The Economic Value of Education*. New York: Columbia University Press.

Teixeira, P. (2005) 'The human capital revolution in economic thought'. *History of Economic Ideas*, XIII (2), 129–48.

— (2009) 'Economic imperialism and the ivory tower: Economic issues and policy challenges in the funding of higher education in the EHEA (2010–2020)'. In Huisman, J., Stensaker, B., and Kehm, B. (eds) *The European Higher Education Area: Perspectives on a moving target*. Rotterdam: Sense Publishers.

Teixeira, P. and Dill, D. (2011) (eds) *Public Vices, Private Virtues? Assessing the effects of marketization in higher education*. Rotterdam: Sense Publishers.

Teixeira, P., Jongbloed, B., Dill, D., and Amaral, A. (eds) (2004) *Markets in Higher Education: Rhetoric or reality?* Dordrecht: Kluwer Academic Publishers.

Williams, G. (1972) 'What educational planning is about'. *Higher Education*, 1, (4), 381–90.

— (1992) *Changing Patterns of Finance in Higher Education*. Buckingham: SRHE/Open University Press.

— (1996) 'The many faces of privatisation'. *Higher Education Management*, 8 (3), 39–57.

— (1997) 'The market route to mass higher education: British experience 1979–1996'. *Higher Education Policy*, 10 (3/4), 275–89.

— (1998) 'Advantages and disadvantages of diversified funding in universities'. *Tertiary Education and Management*, 4 (2), 85–93.

— (2004) 'The higher education market in the United Kingdom'. In Teixeira, P., Jongbloed, B., Dill, D., and Amaral, A. (eds) *Markets in Higher Education: Rhetoric or reality?* Dordrecht: Kluwer Academic Publishers.

— (2009) 'An economic view of higher education theory'. Paper presented at the SHRE Conference, Newport, South Wales, 8–10 December.

— (2011) 'Will higher education be the next bubble to burst?' In *The Europa World of Learning 2011*. Online. www.educationarena.com/pdf/sample/sample-essay-williams.pdf (accessed 15 April 2016).

— (2012) 'Some wicked questions from the dismal science'. In Temple, P. (ed.) *Universities in the Knowledge Economy: Higher education organisation and global change*. Abingdon: Routledge.

Winston, G. (1999) 'Subsidies, hierarchy and peers: The awkward economies of higher education'. *Journal of Economic Perspectives*, 13, 13–36.

Wolf, C. (1993) *Markets or Governments: Choosing between imperfect alternatives*. Cambridge, MA: MIT Press.

Zemsky, R. and Massy, W. (1995) 'Expanding perimeters, melting cores, and sticky functions: Toward an understanding of our current predicaments'. *Change*, 27 (6), 40–9.

Chapter 2

The idea of the market in financing English higher education

Paul Temple

I first began to learn about higher education finance as a topic for study – as distinct from my experience of managing it as a university planner – from Gareth Williams on my MA course on higher education. Gareth later helped with my doctoral work, and later still I became a colleague of his at the Institute of Education in London. As well as learning from him about the economics and finance of higher education, I also absorbed his views about academic life more generally: when supervising my own doctoral students, I often recall his dictum that, at a certain point, doctoral work becomes a conspiracy between the student and the supervisor to outwit the examiners. I am glad to say that I have been able to put Gareth's wisdom into practice on a number of occasions.

Introduction: From the plan to the market

Gareth Williams's book, *Changing Patterns of Finance in Higher Education* (1992), set a benchmark for the study of higher education finance in the UK and more widely. Nearly a quarter of a century later, the copies of this book on the shelves of the Institute of Education Library are still regularly borrowed. In the book, he argues that the 1980s in Britain marked a major shift in the funding philosophy for higher education as well as for other public services:

> [T]he idea of higher education as a publicly provided service ... [was giving way to] the introduction of market incentives and forms of organization ... national funding agencies now see themselves as 'buying services' from universities and colleges on a contractual basis, rather than subsidising them.
>
> (Williams, 1992: 136)

Since he wrote that, the market idea has become a central feature of thinking about public sector planning and organization in the UK and more widely.

This chapter will focus on how the market idea has come to be applied in financing English higher education, and the extent to which this is a particular instance of a broader trend. The shift from the central planning methods developed during the Second World War and in the immediate post-war period (culminating perhaps in the UK with the publication of *The National Plan* (1965)) towards market-based methods was both historically rapid and a striking late-twentieth-century development. As one historian of the period put it, 'Just as it later became difficult, even on the [political] Left, to question a market approach, so in the 1960s it became hard, even on the Right, to doubt the wisdom of some form of planning' (Pimlott, 1992: 276). What I intend to do is to explore how this changed basis for understanding the organization of public services arose.

In thinking about markets in education, and especially in the financing of higher education, there are two separate yet related matters to keep in mind. The higher education landscape contains, on the one hand, institutions that require incomes, and on the other hand, individual students who wish to benefit from this institutional provision. In this respect, conceptualizations of higher education finance appear broadly similar to those found in health service finance (universities/students, hospitals/patients), but dissimilar to the financing of, say, defence (where there are institutions, but no individual beneficiaries – though of course there are plenty of employees) or social welfare (where there are beneficiaries, but no particular institutions to be maintained). In order to work, the financing of higher education thus has to consider the needs of both institutions and individual students. In recent years, policy in England has swung in a way that might fairly be described as revolutionary (though Scott suggests that the revolutionary effect is most likely to arise from unintended consequences of current policies (2013: 54)). It has moved, as far as teaching costs are concerned, from concentrating on the needs of institutions to an almost exclusive focus on the needs of students.

The development of market approaches to university finance

Historically, the British approach to university finance – in common with most other European and many other countries – was one of providing from public funds the resources (or at least a proportion of them) considered necessary for universities to carry out a broadly defined set of functions to acceptable standards. At most periods, in most places, not much further elaboration of this approach – perhaps various performance indicators were used to guide allocations between universities – was apparently felt to be necessary. From the 1920s, this approach was implemented in Britain through what was known as quinquennial planning, where, in essence, universities submitted their plans for the next five years, which were agreed to a greater or lesser extent by the University Grants Committee (UGC) acting on behalf of the government to allocate funds. The UGC also acted from time to time as a planning body, by providing special ('earmarked') funding to develop or to restructure particular academic areas: this was a significant part of its work in the immediate post-war years (Berdahl, 1983: 86). (During this period, a non-university higher education sector also developed, separately funded, leading to the creation of the polytechnics in the 1960s and 1970s.) But the UGC's generally accepted essential function was to act as a 'buffer', keeping the government and its politics at arm's length from the universities, something widely regarded as a brilliant, and uniquely British, policy process: 'The basis of [the UGC's] undoubted success as a constitutional device is that throughout the fifty years of its history it has earned and still enjoys the confidence of both the government and the universities' was one typically congratulatory 1960s analysis (Mountford, 1966: 157). The quinquennial funding method continued in use until the national 'oil shock' financial crisis of the early 1970s cut government spending in many areas, including higher education (Shattock, 2012: 109). It never returned.

Instead, the quinquennial method was replaced in piecemeal fashion during the 1980s by the idea that the government's role should be to purchase services from universities (teaching and research separately), with the UGC and its successor agencies acting as a purchasing agent on behalf of the public. 'The transformation has been dramatic ... Funding formulae were developed between 1988 and 1993 that explicitly linked finance to student numbers and research output' (Williams, 1995: 177). (Parallel developments in the English National Health Service led to the division of a unified service into purchasers of health care on behalf of patients, and providers of it – mostly hospitals.) As I shall discuss later, it is significant that Britain elected a new Conservative government in 1979, led by Margaret Thatcher, with ideas about the management of the public sector – and the economy generally – that differed markedly from the post-war consensus.

For higher education, the first hesitant step in developing a new financial relationship with government was through the imposition of 'cash limits', a device introduced by the Labour government in 1975 (Shattock, 2012: 111) and then revived in sharper form by the new Conservative government in 1981. The aim was to combat inflation by forcing a wide range of public sector organizations to operate within fixed cash budgets, regardless of the inflationary environment in which they were operating.

'Long-term planning was replaced by short-term expediency' (Shattock, 2012: 113). In effect, the UGC found itself buying university outputs for a fixed cash sum, regardless of the state of individual university budgets – just as a normal customer of a firm would. I have no evidence that cash limits were seen at the time as the thin end of a marketization wedge (the notion was not then current), but with the benefit of hindsight it seems reasonable to see them in this way. Interestingly, Margaret Thatcher, as a new prime minister, noted that cash limits were seen in the early 1980s as being 'apparently technical but [she believed them to be] of great significance' (Thatcher, 1993: 137).

As time went on, under the Conservative governments of the 1980s and into the 1990s, 'Across Whitehall producer-led financing was being replaced by ... the ideas embodied in public choice economics' (Shattock, 2012: 153). That is to say, government was moving from being a provider of *input* funding for public services to being a purchaser of *outputs* on the public's behalf, and seeking value for money in the process. Viewed in that light, the financial position of any one provider becomes of limited interest to the purchaser. This is conceptually different to even current ideas on performance funding, where allocations are guided by various performance indicators but where the objective is the more effective provision of input funding (Claeys-Kulik and Estermann, 2015).

By the early 1990s, as Williams noted above, university funding for teaching was being allocated by a method involving 44 'funding cells'. Each cell represented an academic subject group by mode of study (full-time or part-time) and by level (undergraduate or postgraduate). The amount of money that HEFCE had decided to allocate for each cell was then divided by the number of students that the cell represented (full-time postgraduates studying chemistry, say), which gave the 'average unit of Council funding', the AUCF, for that cell. This enabled a competitive element to be introduced into the funding process: 'The major part of the funds available for growth is distributed through competition based on institutions' recent performance ... The institutions with the lowest AUCF in each funding cell will receive the highest percentage rate of growth' (HEFCE, 1993: 20). That is to say, a quasi-market – 'when governments fund institutions *as if* procuring services for their constituents' (Massy, 2004: 15; italics original) – had been created. When the national picture for university funding deteriorated, this changed to 'cheaper universities (those with lower AUCFs) will be rewarded by receiving a smaller downward adjustment', that is, a smaller cut in grant (HEFCE, 1995: 12). This is what Williams later described as the 'manipulation of the small print of the formulae [through which] government policy is put into practice' (Williams, 2004: 249). Let us call this approach, with the government agency buying outputs from competing (at least, theoretically) providers on behalf of the public, Market 1. The approach remained, however, one of paying money to institutions rather than to individual students: although now, crucially, the UGC's central task was no longer one of funding particular institutions as such.

For most people working in universities, little seemingly had changed: public money (if less of it) still arrived at the university in the form of a block grant, for the university to spend (up to a point) as it chose. However, the Market 1 approach, aimed at reducing the overall publicly funded costs of higher education by directing funding to the cheapest producers, was the exact opposite of the previous long-standing UGC policy of 'protecting the unit of resource'. This had meant that, for example, when overall funding was cut by the new Conservative government in 1981, the UGC's response had been to require universities to cut student numbers in order to protect the unit of resource: that is, to maintain, rather than to reduce, the cost per student – which was seen as a key measure of academic standards (Shattock, 2012: 95).

The biggest change in this period, as far as most academic staff were concerned, was the introduction of 'selectivity' in research funding – concentrating activity at the apparently most productive university locations – following the first Research Assessment Exercise (RAE) in 1986. This might also be considered as introducing market methods but by a different route – 'the differentiation of universities successful in the RAE from the rest … [the RAE was later] deliberately used to reinforce institutional rather than subject differentiation' (Shattock, 2012: 182). In other words, rather than being used simply to identify and categorize research quality – the original purpose of the RAE – it came to be used to create, or at least reinforce, an institutional hierarchy. The results of successive RAEs then fed into commercially produced rankings tables, aimed at influencing student choices, thus solidifying the hierarchy and giving a further turn to the marketization ratchet, as it became a matter of vital financial concern to institutions to maintain or improve their rankings. Academic research outputs, as well as teaching work, had become commodities (with 'star' research performance becoming tradeable) in the higher education marketplace. That said, different considerations apply to the funding of teaching and research in England. The latter is today a competitive activity (at individual, institutional, and national levels) aimed at producing research outputs of the highest quality achievable; whereas, as we have seen, competitive pressures applied to teaching have been intended to minimize costs while maintaining acceptable levels of quality.

The other, related, but far more controversial use of market ideas – the one informing the 2011 White Paper on higher education (BIS, 2011) – is that students-as-customers should be the foundations on which university financing rests. This, then, was the shift from funding institutions to funding individuals. Unlike with the Market 1 changes, even academic staff wholly uninterested in the details of their university's finances could hardly fail to notice the change, which led, in the words of one commentator, to a 'pervasive sense of malaise, stress and disenchantment' among university academics (Collini, 2013). The 2011 proposals from the Coalition Government built on the Labour Government's 2006 changes to the tuition fee regime (Temple *et al.*, 2005), but with the difference that the greater part of central funding for university teaching (but not research) would be progressively removed, with universities being required to make up the shortfall from the new, higher, tuition fees they were able to charge. From a figure of £4.3 billion in 2011/12 (the year before the new fee regime began), the HEFCE grant for teaching was planned to fall to £1.4 billion in 2015/16 (by which time nearly all undergraduates would have come under the new fee system). This reduced sum was intended to support the teaching of high-cost subjects and also to fund universities' work on widening undergraduate access and improving retention (HEFCE, 2015).

As the government intended, this change has shifted power away from central bureaucracies – even those operating in Market 1 mode – towards the intended beneficiaries of the whole process, the students. This is the approach often referred to as 'cost-sharing', promoted by the World Bank from the 1990s as a way of financing higher education in low- and middle-income countries (World Bank, 1994: 41), and often associated with the work of a distinguished contributor to the present volume, D. Bruce Johnstone (see, for example, Johnstone, 2004). The rationale for cost-sharing, notes Johnstone, 'focuses on the presumed greater efficiency brought about when there is a charge ... that reflects (even with a substantial taxpayer subsidy) at least some of the real costs and the trade-offs involved [in undertaking higher education]' (2004: 39). The English funding model of 2012 broadly follows this approach, with its claim (noted later) that students would as a result be 'driving teaching excellence'. We may call this approach Market 2.

It is this Market 2 approach to the funding of English higher education (other parts of the UK have taken different approaches) that has drawn criticism from commentators such as Brown, who considers it a deeply flawed idea because (to mention just a few of his criticisms) it fails, at least potentially, to take account of the public 'spillover' benefits of higher education, and does not address the inevitable information asymmetry between producers and so-called customers. Issues around the distorting effects of the seeking of prestige and/or reputation by institutions, and the drift towards 'institutional isomorphism' with a resulting loss of diversity, are also said to be linked to the Market 2 approach (Brown, 2011). An even more trenchant critique of the current English funding model claims that 'our flirtation with a market-based approach has led us into a terrible muddle, unmatched anywhere in the world. The present arrangements are philosophically, economically and socially untenable' (Bekhradnia, 2013).

Nevertheless, the 2012 fee regime in England has, it appears, caused a cultural change inside universities, with different universities responding in different ways, but broadly with a new emphasis on improving the management of 'the student experience', and directing more resources to it; and often with students asserting what they see as their new-found rights: the student-as-customer rather than the student-as-academic apprentice. Some universities have responded to these new pressures generally within the framework of their existing, broadly collegial, management processes. Others, however, appear to be introducing new top-down management arrangements in order to provide greater uniformity in what students might experience. It would seem reasonable to claim that the 2012 changes and the cost-sharing Market 2 model that these ushered in have affected how perhaps most English universities now relate to their students (Temple *et al.*, 2014). It is probably too early to assess the balance of the benefits and disbenefits that are arising, but the extent and direction of change are unmistakeable.

It remains to be seen whether or not England has reached the high-water mark of market methods in higher education finance – or whether the tide will rise still higher, stay at the current level, or ebb. Even before the current fee system was introduced, the UK ranked just below Chile and South Korea as the countries with the highest private contributions to the costs of tertiary education: 70 per cent for the UK, compared with an OECD 2011 average of 31 per cent (OECD, 2014: 240). However, this UK figure, and equivalent post-2012 data, need the caveat that what the OECD assumes to be private payments of tuition fees may turn out in substantial part to be public payments, as possibly up to 45 per cent of government loans for students' fees may not be repaid (McGettigan, 2015: 38). Even so, current arrangements certainly represent a more radically marketized picture than the ones described by Williams in 1992 and 1995. Writing more recently, Williams suggests that the economically justifiable limits of marketization may now have been reached, due to the extent of externalities involved in higher education, questions of equity, and other points about higher education's character as a public good, mentioned above (2013: 66). That is to say, the potential benefits of higher education go beyond those accruing to individual students, but as its financing becomes more market-based, it becomes less likely that these wider benefits will be maximized.

It should be noted that the shift in the 1980s and early 1990s to what I have called the Market 1 model was, seemingly, little remarked on at the time beyond the circle of those professionally involved with university planning and funding – and a few analysts such as Williams – presumably because the changes appeared to be of a dry, technical nature. I suggest, though, that these changes represented a greater conceptual leap – breaking with a tradition dating back to the beginning of the twentieth century as to how public financing of higher education should be conceived and planned for – than did the much more controversial 2012 move to the cost-sharing Market 2 model.

Before the market: Improving decision making in government

Twenty-one years before Gareth Williams wrote *Changing Patterns of Finance in Higher Education*, Sir Richard Clarke, a retiring British civil service permanent secretary (that is, the chief official of a government department) – and, incidentally, whose son, Charles Clarke, became Education Secretary in 2002 – gave a series of lectures published under the title *New Trends in Government* (Clarke, 1971). These lectures offer a wide-ranging set of reflections on various aspects of the machinery of government, covering amongst other matters the structuring of government departments, the (then new) annual cycle for determining public expenditure, and the allocation of resources across government. They also give an insight into a lost world of British government, where the organization and operation of nationalized industries – coal, steel, electricity, gas, telecommunications, railways, ports, airlines, and airports, to name only the largest among them – were major preoccupations. What, to a reader today, is conspicuously missing from Clarke's thinking is any suggestion that the idea of the market, in any form, could provide a useful basis for organization and decision making in government. Clarke is certainly concerned to improve the effectiveness and efficiency of central government, but his approach is essentially one of improving organizational structures and internal processes, and more smoothly articulating political ideas with official decision making. Better structures and processes, Clarke seems to suggest, must lead to better decisions about the use of resources.

However, at around the time that Clarke was writing, a good deal of thought was being given in government circles, both national and local, as to how decision making could be improved by the use of new techniques, not simply by changing structures and processes. As a contemporary government-sponsored study of cost–benefit analysis put it, 'by marshalling data systematically, putting it in quantitative terms wherever appropriate, and rendering it as commensurable as possible, [cost–benefit analysis] lays bare the considerations relevant to a complex decision' (Walsh and Williams, 1969: 3). I have discussed elsewhere how the technique known as PPBS (Planning, Programming, and Budgeting System), developed by the US government in the 1960s, had somewhat similar aims in allowing decision makers to make more rational[1] choices, by understanding the full costs, direct and indirect, of activities and how the organization was allocating its resources to pursue them (Temple, 2014: 31). Operational research (OR) was another quantitative technique in vogue (Bane, 1968), as was statistical decision theory (Peston and Coddington, 1968): both intended to give precision to the factors involved in decisions. It was thought, then, at this point, that public sector decisions could be made more rational by technical means – by collecting more and better data, and analysing them in more sophisticated ways, and presenting the results to policymakers.

These approaches could be considered as substituting analytical techniques to reach conclusions that in certain cases or other circumstances might have been reached through the use of market mechanisms. But investment decisions on transport infrastructure, say, cannot sensibly be reached purely through the use of market data, even where they exist (rail passenger demand, for example), because the large externalities which such projects typically generate – changes in property prices, reduced business costs, changes in CO_2 emissions, for example – will not be captured in the financial accounts of (say) the rail companies. As noted above, this failure to take externalities into account is a current objection to market methods in higher education funding, although quantifying externalities is notoriously difficult in any circumstances. But it was perhaps the failure of these analytical techniques to show convincingly that they could lead to better (however defined) decisions, and the consequent frustration of decision makers, that opened the way to the use of actual (or at least, quasi-) markets in public decision making. One historic failure was the Roskill Commission's massive 1970 study to select a site for a third London airport[2], which valiantly, if misguidedly, attempted to place financial values on intangibles – such as the cultural worth of medieval churches – as part of its cost–benefit analysis (Mishan, 1970).

Another example of thinking at the time about the management challenges facing the UK's public sector is given by Desmond Keeling's book, *Management in Government* (1972). Keeling was a senior civil servant with an academic background in economics who had worked in the Treasury, and whose book examines approaches to public sector resource allocation in some detail, including cost–benefit analysis, methods taken from welfare economics, and the then-novel idea of objective (rather than subjective) budgeting. In a section headed 'The Contrast Between Public Service and Business Management', Keeling argues that the differences lie in the public service need 'to secure consistency and conformity, the political environment, problems of measuring inputs and outputs, accountability' and other matters (1972: 157). What he does not mention as being of significance – which would surely be a central feature in a similar account today – is the extent to which markets are relevant in the two sectors.

There was, then, in the later 1960s and the 1970s, in British central and local government, a widespread sense that decision making should, and could, be improved through the use of data-based analytical techniques. New approaches were being sought actively. What did not apparently feature in thinking at the time – surprisingly, in the light of contemporary academic debates, to which I will refer in a moment – was the use of market-based methods. This was about to change.

'Putting the world to rights'[3]

My father's background as a grocer is sometimes cited as the basis for my economic philosophy. So it was ... My father was both a practical man and a man of theory. He liked to connect the progress of our corner shop with the great complex romance of international trade which ... ensure[d] that a family in Grantham could have on its table rice from India, coffee from Kenya, sugar from the West Indies ... I knew from my father's accounts that the free market was like a vast sensitive nervous system, responding ... to meet the ever-changing needs of peoples ... I had been equipped at an early age with the ideal mental outlook and tools of analysis for reconstructing an economy ravaged by state socialism.

(Thatcher, 1993: 11)

Thus, Margaret Thatcher, who became Britain's Prime Minister in May 1979, in the introduction to her political memoirs, *The Downing Street Years*. It is a long step, certainly, from her father, Alderman Roberts, pointing (we may imagine) to a sack of coffee beans and inviting his young daughter to consider its journey from the highlands of Kenya to a Lincolnshire market town – to the 2010–15 Coalition Government's higher education plans in which students would operate as consumers in a higher education marketplace, thereby 'driving teaching excellence' (BIS, 2011: 25). A long step, but not, perhaps, an impossible one.

Although discussions of markets as such do not figure largely in the Thatcher memoirs, they do provide a basis for her antipathy to the British trade unions of the period, which she saw as distorting labour markets with 'their preference for monopoly and protection' (Thatcher, 1993: 101), and preventing British firms from operating efficiently: 'Producers want a protected market for their products. That is the union demand. But the same trade unionists, as consumers, want an open market. They cannot both win. But they can both lose' (from a speech made in November 1979: ibid: 102). One of her close advisers, Patrick Minford, has written that, as far as a 'guiding vision' is concerned, 'she has never been so unprofessional as to write it down or describe it too precisely ... [but it] is of a world in which small businesses could compete freely for the favours of the individual family consumer' (Minford, 1988: 94). It is, then, a vision of markets familiar to her from her childhood.

Towards the end of her premiership, around 1990, Thatcher was viewing higher education in a similar way to other apparently underperforming British industries:

> By exerting financial pressure [on universities] we had increased administrative efficiency ... A shift of support from university grants [that is, direct funding of universities] to the payment of tuition fees [on behalf of students] would lead in the same direction of greater sensitivity to the market.
>
> (Thatcher, 1993: 598)

But even more radical plans – never implemented – were in her mind: 'a scheme to give the leading universities much more independence. The idea was to allow them to opt out of Treasury financial rules ... it would have represented a radical decentralization of the whole system' (ibid: 599). (This section of the memoirs seems to show a misunderstanding of the status of UK universities, with the suggestion that the proposed changes would lead to universities 'owning their assets': they already did.)

The attractions of introducing what became known as 'top-up fees' for students (although universities did charge tuition fees at this period, they were normally paid on UK students' behalf by their home local authorities) as a solution to university funding problems had not always seemed so straightforward to the Prime Minister, however. When Sir Keith Joseph, her Education Secretary, had proposed introducing means-tested 'top-up' tuition fees in 1985, a revolt by Conservative MPs, concerned about how this would be received by their constituents with university-aged children, killed off any idea of a cost-sharing model, not only for the rest of the Thatcher administration but for the succeeding Conservative Government as well (Shattock, 2012: 161). It would be left to a Labour government to introduce this crucial change in 1999.

Throughout the 1980s, despite the Prime Minister's apparent preferences, market-based solutions to public sector funding problems made little apparent headway, although, deep down, change was beginning. A senior civil servant in the Education Department, writing of the 1980s, says:

> ... perhaps there was a guiding philosophy, which ministers brought to the feast and to which they and civil servants together gave effect ... The obvious candiate [*sic*] for consideration is promotion of some sort of 'market' whose functioning compels greater attention to the customer. For my own part, I have always found it hard to discern any clarity of theme or practice which would justify an assertion that a 'market approach' ... was being pursued.
>
> (Bird, 1994: 83)

Nevertheless, that was the result. It seemed though, to some observers, that what was lacking as this change took place was a sophisticated appreciation of the limitations of markets – 'it is the coarseness with which Thatcherism conceives of market economies that is one of its prime and dangerous failings. This is most glaring ... in its failure to grasp the special case of public goods' (Hahn, 1988: 123) – of which higher education (at least, aspects of it), as noted, is a good example.

Through the 1980s and 1990s, one study finds that there were 'continuing pressures within the Conservative Party to dismantle this institutional structure [that is, university funding provided through a block grant from a funding agency] and for the state to encourage a much closer relationship between the universities and their clients ... this could mean giving students vouchers with which they could purchase directly their higher education' (Salter and Tapper, 1994: 201). This thinking was possibly influenced by the work of Milton Friedman, whose 1962 book, *Capitalism and Freedom*, provided the 'classic modern statement on the importance of markets in (higher) education … [proposing] the use of market mechanisms in many activities for which this was unusual, especially in education' (Teixeira *et al.*, 2004: 5). One historian of the period concludes, though, that the 'links between Friedman and British Conservatives were in fact fairly limited' (Vinen, 2009: 108). Certainly, there seems no clear evidence of Friedman's thinking influencing Thatcher in any specific way – although she was pleased to discover on a visit to the Soviet Union in 1990 that the Mayor of Moscow, Gavriil Popov, was apparently 'a devotee of Milton Friedman and the Chicago School of Economics' (Thatcher, 1993: 804). It seems likely that the corner shop in Grantham was a more important source of her own ideas about markets.

Friedman was not, however, the first economist to apply economic analysis to the problems of education finance. A few years earlier, Jack Wiseman, a leading figure at the time in British applied economics, had proposed the provision of vouchers:

> … to be 'spent' by the parents at schools of their own selection … At university level, the scheme would require the replacement of the University Grants Committee by an increase in size of the awards made to 'qualified' students: the remainder of university finance would come from … additional charges that particular universities find themselves in a position to make …
>
> (Wiseman, 1959: 58)

In other words, there could be variable tuition fees, as introduced in England in 2006 with its 2012 variant, but with students being given grants, rather than loans, to cover the basic fee. In a rejoinder to criticisms of his paper, Wiseman questioned why economists were apparently unwilling to apply:

> … the logic of choice … [in the context of] a 'social service' … [The value of choice], here as elsewhere, is as a means of setting out the relevant considerations for policy decisions … What is the nature of the objection to a diversity of interests offering education facilities (subject to ability to meet the state's minimum standards) …?
>
> (Wiseman, 1960: 76)

Other than the fact that the UGC's successor body is still with us (not least because the public interest in higher education goes beyond its teaching function), Wiseman's scheme, and the arguments surrounding it, after half a century, map closely onto the current debate in England.

Conclusions: Theory into practice

Ideas from economic theory involving the role of markets underlay, I suggest, the development by the UGC in the late 1980s and early 1990s of what I have called the Market 1 method – a quasi-market approach of making grants determined by metrics of student numbers and types, and research outputs, rather than by the traditional method of assessing university needs and attempting to fund them, perhaps with a planning role as in the quinquennial method, or supported by the use of performance indicators. These new methods allowed, their supporters argued, better control of costs in higher education, and the ability to improve quality in both teaching and research. They also helped meet a contemporary demand for transparency in decision making: although subjectivity is inevitable in metrics-based processes (which metrics? how are they defined and weighted?), there is at least a formal process to point to, unlike with the previous opaque method. The 1979 Thatcher Government, Salter and Tapper claim, regarded the UGC as 'a lobby on behalf of universities' (1994: 200) and wanted to decrease the reliance of universities on financial support from the UGC and its successor bodies by using public money in a different way to create a 'managed market' (ibid: 212) – the Market 1 idea, although perhaps pointing towards Market 2.

The new tuition fee arrangements introduced by a Labour government in 2006 were in a sense a halfway-house between the Market 1 and Market 2 models. They shifted substantially the balance of universities' incomes from block grants to tuition fees: as the later Browne report put it, the 2006 changes 'helped to address the investment challenge but [did not meet universities' needs] in full' (Browne, 2010: 21). A substantial Market 1-style block grant for teaching – as we noted earlier, £4.3 billion in the year before the 2012 fee regime began – remained. What the 2006 changes did do, however – and the strong personal commitment of the then Prime Minister, Tony Blair, must be acknowledged here (Blair, 2011: 490) – was, as Browne put it, to change the national debate as far as contributions from graduates for their educations – cost-sharing – were concerned (Browne, 2010: 20). Before the 2004 legislation which led to the 2006 fee regime, cost-sharing on anything more than a token scale was highly controversial; afterwards, it became an accepted part of the higher education landscape. The debate then centred on the level of contribution, not the principle of it. This opened the way for the Market 2 model from 2012, with greatly reducing block grant funding and a commensurate increase in tuition fees supported by a student loan system to channel funding to universities.

The 20 years from 1993 to 2013 have seen an avalanche of changes, piling on top of one another, in the financing of English higher education. By contrast, the previous three-quarters of a century showed slow, evolutionary change, with long periods of no significant change in policy at all. This modern political hyperactivity is independent of governing parties and national economic peaks and troughs. What is consistent is the ever-growing belief that market methods, of various kinds, will lead to improved public sector outcomes.

Notes
[1] I am using 'rational' in a positive, rather than normative, sense, to mean the systematic organization of resources to achieve defined ends.
[2] Forty-five years later, in July 2015, the government-appointed Airports Commission reported on the need for additional runway capacity in the London area, unchanged since Roskill's day. This impasse should perhaps cause us to view Roskill's difficulties sympathetically.
[3] Chapter title in *The Downing Street Years*.

References
Bane, W. (1968) *Operational Research, Models and Government*. CAS Occasional Paper. London: Her Majesty's Stationery Office.

Bekhradnia, B. (2013) 'Higher education in the UK: Punching above our weight. Really?' HEPI 2013 Annual Lecture. Oxford: Higher Education Policy Institute.

Berdahl, R. (1983) 'Co-ordinating structures: The UGC and US state co-ordinating agencies'. In Shattock, M. (ed.) *The Structure and Governance of Higher Education*. SRHE/Leverhulme Series, 9. Guildford: Society for Research into Higher Education.

Bird, R. (1994) 'Reflections on the British government and higher education in the 1980s'. *Higher Education Quarterly*, 48 (2), 73–85.

Blair, T. (2011) *A Journey*. London: Arrow Books.

Brown, R. (2011) 'The impact of markets'. In Brown, R. (ed.) *Higher Education and the Market*. New York: Routledge.

Browne, J. (2010) *Securing a Sustainable Future for Higher Education: An independent review of higher education funding and student finance*. Online. http://tinyurl.com/jyro5f2 (accessed 11 April 2016).

Claeys-Kulik, A.-L. and Estermann, T. (2015) *DEFINE Thematic Report: Performance-based funding of universities in Europe*. Brussels: European University Association. Online. http://tinyurl.com/hbmha88 (accessed 12 April 2016).

Clarke, R. (1971) *New Trends in Government*. London: Her Majesty's Stationery Office.

Collini, S. (2013) 'Sold out'. *London Review of Books*, 24 October, 35 (20), 3–12. Online. www.lrb.co.uk/v35/n20/stefan-collini/sold-out (accessed 16 April 2016).

Department for Business, Innovation, and Skills (BIS) (2011) *Higher Education: Students at the heart of the system*. Cm 8122. London: BIS.

Hahn, F. (1988) 'On market economies'. In Skidelsky, R. (ed.) *Thatcherism*. London: Chatto and Windus.

HEFCE (1993) *Annual Report, 1992/93: Promoting quality and opportunity*. Bristol: Higher Education Funding Council for England.

— (1995) *A Guide to Funding Higher Education in England: How the HEFCE allocates its funds*. Bristol: Higher Education Funding Council for England.

— (2015) *Recurrent Grants for 2015/16*. Circular 2015/05. Bristol: Higher Education Funding Council for England.

Johnstone, B. (2004) 'Cost-sharing and equity in higher education'. In Teixeira, P., Jongbloed, B., Dill, D., and Amaral, A. (eds) *Markets in Higher Education: Rhetoric or reality?* Dordrecht: Kluwer Academic Publishers.

Keeling, D. (1972) *Management in Government*. London: Royal Institute of Public Administration/George Allen and Unwin.

McGettigan, A. (2015) *The Accounting and Budgeting of Student Loans*. HEPI Report 75. Oxford: Higher Education Policy Institute.

Massy, W. (2004) 'Markets in higher education: Do they promote internal efficiency?' In Teixeira, P., Jongbloed, B., Dill, D., and Amaral, A. (eds) *Markets in Higher Education: Rhetoric or reality?* Dordrecht: Kluwer Academic Publishers.

Minford, P. (1988) 'Mrs Thatcher's economic reform programme: Past, present and future'. In Skidelsky, R. (ed.) *Thatcherism*. London: Chatto and Windus.

Mishan, E. (1970) 'What is wrong with Roskill?' *Journal of Transport Economics and Policy*, 4 (3), 221–34.

Mountford, J. (1966) *British Universities*. London: Oxford University Press.

OECD (2014) *Education at a Glance 2014: OECD indicators*. Paris: OECD.

Peston, M. and Coddington, A. (1968) *Statistical Decision Theory*. CAS Occasional Paper. London: Her Majesty's Stationery Office.

Pimlott, B. (1992) *Harold Wilson*. London: HarperCollins.

Salter, B. and Tapper, T. (1994) *The State and Higher Education*. London: The Woburn Press.

Scott, P. (2013) 'The coalition government's reform of higher education: Policy formation and political process'. In Callender, C. and Scott, P. (eds) *Browne and Beyond: Modernizing English higher education*. London: IOE Press.

Shattock, M. (2012) *Making Policy in British Higher Education 1945–2011*. Maidenhead: McGraw Hill/Open University Press.

Teixeira, P., Jongbloed, B., Amaral, A., and Dill, D. (2004) 'Introduction'. In Teixeira, P., Jongbloed, B., Dill, D., and Amaral, A. (eds) *Markets in Higher Education: Rhetoric or reality?* Dordrecht: Kluwer Academic Publishers.

Temple, P. (2014) *The Hallmark University: Distinctiveness in higher education management*. London: IOE Press.

Temple, P., Farrant, J., and Shattock, M. (2005) *New Variable Fee Arrangements: Baseline institutional case studies for the Independent Commission*. DfES Research Report. London: Department for Education and Skills.

Temple, P., Callender, C., Grove, L., and Kersh, N. (2014) *Research Report: Managing the student experience in a shifting higher education landscape*. York: Higher Education Academy.

Thatcher, M. (1993) *The Downing Street Years*. London: HarperCollins.

The National Plan (1965) Cmnd 2764. London: Her Majesty's Stationery Office.

Vinen, R. (2009) *Thatcher's Britain: The politics and social upheaval of the Thatcher era*. London: Simon and Schuster.

Walsh, H. and Williams, A. (1969) *Current Issues in Cost–Benefit Analysis*. CAS Occasional Paper. London: Her Majesty's Stationery Office.

Williams, G. (1992) *Changing Patterns of Finance in Higher Education*. Buckingham: SRHE/Open University Press.

— (1995) 'The "marketization" of higher education: Reform and potential reforms in higher education finance'. In Dill, D. and Sporn, B. (eds) *Emerging Patterns of Social Demand and University Reform: Through a glass darkly*. Oxford: IAU Press/Pergamon.

— (2004) 'The higher education market in the United Kingdom'. In Teixeira, P., Jongbloed, B., Dill, D., and Amaral, A. (eds) *Markets in Higher Education: Rhetoric or reality?* Dordrecht: Kluwer Academic Publishers.

— (2013) 'A bridge too far: An economic critique of marketization of higher education'. In Callender, C. and Scott, P. (eds) *Browne and Beyond: Modernizing English higher education*. London: IOE Press.

Wiseman, J. (1959) 'The economics of education'. *Scottish Journal of Political Economy*, 6 (1), 48–58.

— (1960) 'Rejoinder'. *Scottish Journal of Political Economy*, 7 (1), 75–6.

World Bank (1994) *Higher Education: The lessons of experience*. Washington, DC: The World Bank.

Chapter 3

Financing British higher education: The triumph of process over policy

Michael Shattock

It is generally claimed that a distinctive characteristic of British higher education is the autonomy of its universities. In one sense this is confirmed by the European Universities' Association's Autonomy Scorecard, which showed British universities as the most autonomous in Europe (Estermann *et al.*, 2011). What is not always as generally recognized is that this institutional autonomy has been exercised since the early 1960s within a very tightly drawn national policy envelope, which has been in great part determined not by pressure from within higher education itself nor by 'blue ribbon' committees of inquiry into its future, nor by ministers (though there have been exceptions to this), but by the processes required to regulate and control public expenditure. Policy on higher education might have been expected to be internally generated or driven by arguments about the way its development contributed to public policy issues. In practice, however, it has been much more about how it could be accommodated within an overstretched economy.

The Thatcher Government's statement in 1980 that public expenditure was 'at the heart of Britain's present economic difficulties' (HM Treasury, 1980) could have been a text for Osborne's budget statements in 2010 and 2015, and in practice these were foreshadowed in government policy as far back as the oil crisis of 1973–4. Increasingly this has put the Treasury, rather than the spending department, as the arbiter of policy towards higher education. The process by which it has trimmed the education department's bids for new money, demanded cuts in other parts of the department's budget to obtain release for necessary new expenditures, or simply reduced budget provision has had a far greater policy impact than almost any secretary of state has exercised over higher education.

Historically, since 1945, the key policy determinants have been the growth in student demand for entry to higher education and how this is to be paid for with, since the mid-1980s, the incorporation of a third consideration, the contribution of research to the Innovation agenda, now an important element in national economic policy. The research and teaching funding streams are now determined at source without reference to one another, leaving universities to adapt themselves to the consequences. The growth in student demand and the political need to provide finance to meet it represented a constant challenge to a resource allocation process that could only be met at the expense of justifiable bids from other areas of public expenditure or by reducing the funding per student. By the late 1990s this latter approach was recognized to have been taken about as far as it would go, and the position was ameliorated by the adoption of what was generally regarded as the neoliberal policy of charging tuition fees to students, beginning at £1,000 in 2000, rising to up to £3,000 in 2006 and to up to £9,000 in 2012, the last increase eliminating the requirement for a recurrent grant for teaching altogether except in some scientific and technological fields where special costs were involved.

In itself the move to charging 'full-cost' tuition fees supported by a government loan scheme marked a radical shift in funding methodology, but it was followed by a further step that is having an equal impact on the higher education system as a whole. From 1945 the universities were funded by the state against student number targets determined by the University Grants Committee (UGC), though the local authority higher education institutions were not funded in this way until 1981. (No one at the time seemed to regard this UGC control of student numbers as representing any diminution of university autonomy.) Following the 1992 Act, common controls linking funding to numerical targets were made to apply to the whole sector. However, from 2015, the cap on numbers was removed and universities were free to accept as many students, and in whatever fields (except medicine), as they wished. The two sets of decisions marked a decisive change not only in the relationship of universities with the state, but also in the relationships between universities and their students and the state. The questions this chapter will explore are how much these changes were brought about by individually determined policy and how much they were driven by the processes endemic in the funding mechanisms adopted by the Treasury to regulate and control public expenditure. My argument will be that the latter has consistently been a more important driver of policy, and that the effect of having two Chancellors of the Exchequer (Brown and Osborne) who have sought to extend their reach across the whole public sector of the economy, albeit for different reasons, has been to enhance the role of the Treasury over the responsible department in the determination of higher education policy.

The establishment of the Public Expenditure Survey Committee (PESC)

It is, of course, possible to exaggerate the role of the Treasury in government affairs (especially when writing in the period of austerity following the financial crisis of 2008–9). But from Gladstone's time the Treasury has occupied a central position within the machinery of government. Standing Order 78 of the House of Commons, dating back to 1713, prescribes that no MP may put forward a bill or propose an amendment that would cost the Treasury money without the government's consent, giving it a headlock on opportunist bids for new expenditure. In 1884, it was agreed that any proposal for new expenditure or any new service, whether or not it required additional expenditure by the department concerned, must have Treasury sanction, thus reinforcing its ability to sink initiatives that might have longer-term expenditure implications. In 1924, the requirement was added that no memorandum which proposed additional expenditure could be circulated to the Cabinet without discussion first with the Treasury (Brittan, 1964). The Treasury had always been powerful within government in its exercise of control over the purse strings: until 1939 it controlled directly the staffing establishment of every government department, and right up to 1957 it exercised the right of approval for all capital works put up for departments by the Ministry of Works costing more than £1,000. Before the Plowden Report of 1961 the Treasury had not, however, been able to exercise systematic control over routine bids for new public expenditure. The dangers implicit in this were highlighted in the report commissioned by the Prime Minister, Harold Macmillan, *Future Policy Study,* presented in 1960, which contained the following warning:

> In the next five years ... there are no declining public programmes to make room for the expanding ones. The defence and overseas claims are expanding; public investment is expanding; education and health and public services generally are expanding. These are all good claims and recently there have been a succession of new ones, such as a greatly expanded road programme.
>
> (quoted in Hennessey, 2006)

The Plowden Report of 1961, *Control of Public Expenditure*, sought to answer the problem by recommending:

> that arrangements should be introduced for making surveys of public expenditure for a period of years ahead and that all major decisions involving future expenditure should be taken against

the background of such a survey and in relation to prospective resources.

(quoted in Shattock, 2012)

The report proposed a standing Cabinet Expenditure Committee, chaired by the Prime Minister, which would determine spending priorities, but this was rejected in favour of a new ministerial post, Chief Secretary to the Treasury, later accorded membership of the Cabinet. But perhaps the most important reform, reflecting the close linkage of public expenditure with government borrowing requirements and tax policy, was the decision that prior to the bidding process for new expenditure the Cabinet itself would decide the percentage of GDP that would be permitted. This set a ceiling beneath which bids for new expenditure had to compete and put the Treasury in the driving seat in establishing priorities within the various departmental bids. This changed the Treasury's role as coordinator and regulator of public expenditure to something much more proactive and determinist. Policy development on higher education became a product of negotiation between the Treasury through the Public Expenditure Survey Committee (PESC) or later PES (because the idea of a Committee was soon reduced to a team of Treasury officials) and the spending department over the spending bids they had submitted. The impact on universities was immediate when the Chief Secretary had to report to Parliament that in 1962, the first year of the PESC process, it had not been possible to meet the UGC's bid for additional resources to match its forecast of rising demand for student places. This provoked a major political row in both Houses and was the prime reason for the Government accepting Robbins's forecasts so quickly a year later (Shattock, 2012).

The PES methodology

Higher education policy was particularly at risk under PES because the increasing pressure imposed by continued expansion required resourcing additional to compensation for inflation or modernization. Increased resources for higher education could only be achieved at the expense of some other public service, a fact that secretaries of state for education tried hard to impress on the universities. Moreover, the format of the PES negotiations left higher education vulnerable: they were conducted not by the UGC (or by a representative of the local authority controlled sector of higher education), but by a senior civil servant designated as 'principal finance officer' in the Department of Education and Science (DES) whose task was to represent the totality of the Department's budget, not just that of higher education. The Treasury's first response in such negotiations across the board of public expenditure, according to Thain and Wright (1995), was to ask what the Department was prepared to cut out to pay for any additional resources. This left higher education peculiarly at risk to 'deals' within the totality of the education budget, where expenditure on primary or secondary education could be protected at the expense of higher education. (In 1967, Anthony Crosland, then Secretary of State, was offered the choice of charging for school meals or increasing the tuition fees for overseas students. In opting for the latter he opened a Pandora's box of protest and negotiation between the Committee of Vice-Chancellors and Principals (CVCP) and the Department extending over more than a decade.) Negotiations at officer level were normally concluded with a statement of issues and possible solutions and were followed by the secretary of state appearing before the Chief Secretary to the Treasury accompanied by appropriate Treasury officials. Negotiations at this level were political as well as financial and the secretary of state's success depended a great deal on his or her negotiating skills. Sir Keith Joseph, for example, was the despair of his officials because, being a firm believer in reducing public expenditure, he was likely to offer up budget reductions even before they had been pressed for by the Treasury. His successor, Kenneth Baker, however, illustrated another aspect of the process as described by John Major, an apparently very effective Chief Secretary:

> [Baker] would bound in full of enthusiasm and with lots of ideas all of which he assured me would be hugely popular with the electorate and would guarantee another election victory ... When detailed questioning on costs were put to Ken he was often poorly briefed. His spending plans were grossly inflated and it never took long to reduce the padding. At the end of our negotiations Ken bounded out as cheerfully as he had come in, but with much less money than he had sought.
>
> (Major, 1999: 103)

Thus, individual competence could become a factor. Kenneth Clark was a great deal more robust, but used restructuring to engineer a significant concession to the Treasury. By 1990 the joint CVCP/Committee of Directors of Polytechnics (CDP) working party had come to the conclusion that unless there was a change in Treasury thinking, the only real source for reversing the fall in unit costs was the introduction of fees. The 1991 White Paper was notable for proposing the merger of the two sectors, but what was not so obvious was that this involved a merger of funding systems in a situation where the non-university sector had much lower unit costs for undergraduate teaching. When these were rationalized across the two sectors, significant savings were achieved. The real beneficiary of the ending of the binary line was the Treasury.

Where a secretary of state and the Chief Secretary found it impossible to reach agreement the Cabinet appointed a special committee, known sometimes as the Star Chamber, to hear the case. Where this device failed to reconcile positions the secretary of state had the right to appeal to the whole Cabinet. Only one Secretary of State for Education (Gillian Shephard) has ever attempted this option and apparently lost on the Prime Minister's casting vote.

Over the years the process of bidding for new funding has been refined but not fundamentally changed. Departments are required to follow a process outlined in the Treasury Green Book (HM Treasury, 2013) whose purpose is stated to be to raise questions such as: are there better ways to achieve this objective or are there better uses for these resources? The methodology applied is not sympathetic to the assessment of a bid from higher education. Although the Green Book emphasizes the need to take into account the wider social costs, it nevertheless requires departments to attribute monetary values wherever possible to the impacts of any proposed policy, project, or programme. Every spending proposal must follow the Treasury's standard 'five case model' of presenting a strategic, an economic, a commercial, a financial, and a management case.

What the methodology emphasizes is how much the PES system has become a process, and one that is designed to be applicable to activities drawn from across the whole of the public sector rather than to the priorities for higher education.

The PES process in action 1963–2000

Unsurprisingly, 1962 was the only occasion that the government felt it necessary to report to Parliament that it had failed to allocate resources to match UGC (or later the Higher Education Funding Council for England's [HEFCE's]) demands. But the influence of the PES process over policy development remained considerable. Apart from the policy impact of the three great crises in public expenditure, the oil crisis of 1973–4, the Thatcher/Howe budgets of 1979–80, and the 2010 Comprehensive Spending Review, all of which were mediated through the PES process and had long-term policy implications for higher education development, changes in the PES process itself forced significant changes in higher education policies. The first of these was the change from 'volume' planning to resourcing via cash limits. One of the attractive features of the Plowden settlement, from the universities' point of view, was the provision that the allocation to a spending department for the first year of the funding period was extended in programmatic terms for the further years. The levels of inflation that followed the oil crisis pushed the level of public expenditure from 44 per cent of GDP in 1964 to 58.5 per cent in 1975–6 and had to be curbed. In 1974–5, departmental spending plans based on approved programmes rose by £9 billion more than could be accounted for by their published expenditure plans (Middleton, 1996). The decision in 1976 was to replace programmatic ('volume') planning with a requirement that each year should be subject to a cash limit imposed in the PES round. This removed the relative security of planning for university expansion, which, in principle at least, had been provided by the quinquennial funding system. In particular, it rendered planning, essential in a period of Robbins's forecast expansion, vulnerable because building costs could easily escalate above any pre-planned cash figure. Thain and Wright concluded that 'from 1982–83 all public expenditure decisions were taken solely in cash' (Thain and Wright, 1995: 54). One consequence was that arguments based on formulae or the preservation of certain levels of units of resource were likely to be rejected. The UGC's management of the budget cuts in 1981 was regarded as mistaken in Whitehall, not only because in cutting back student numbers it was exposing the Government to a political storm not unlike that which its predecessor had faced 20 years previously, but also because its rationale for cutting student numbers to regain a previous level of unit of resource was linked to notional student:staff ratios that conflicted with the new Treasury resource allocation model.

However, the abandonment of student:staff ratio or unit of resource formulae as a kind of gold standard for funding allocations was to have long-term policy consequences. In his autobiography, Baker echoed the Treasury's view in his condemnation of the traditional defence of the universities' budget:

> The UGC had developed an ingenious system where a unit of resource was established which represented the amount needed to teach one student. This formula became sacrosanct and meant that if student numbers were to be increased then the amount paid through the unit of resource had to be increased *pro rata*.
>
> (Baker, 1993: 233)

His alternative, he said, was a 'system where expansion would be determined by demand' (ibid). In his 1989 Lancaster speech he claimed to be putting a bomb under the Treasury by allowing the age participation to rise from 18.5 per cent to one-third by the year 2000 but, in encouraging growth without matching finance, he was precipitating the crisis in 1995–6, by which time the unit of resource had fallen by 45 per cent since 1980.

A further example of the impact of the PES process can be found in the Financial Management Initiative launched in 1982. This was a cross-Whitehall exercise under the leadership of Lord Rayner, chairman of Marks and Spencer, where 'scrutiny teams' were established to review efficiency in government departments as part of the continuing need to reduce public expenditure. The exercise was based in the public sector branch of the Treasury and was seen as a more wide-ranging approach to restructuring than could easily be achieved as a product of the regular round of PES negotiations. Both sides of the binary line submitted themselves to scrutiny, having been advised informally that not to do so would jeopardize PES bids later in the year. CVCP evidence suggests that acceptance of the Jarratt Committee was seen as a way of deflecting the Treasury from pursuing the abolition of tenure (Shattock, 2012).

The university sector exercise was overseen by a committee headed by Sir Alex Jarratt, a former civil servant, now chairman and managing director of Reed International. The scrutiny teams examined six case study institutions and found little to comment on, but the Committee itself issued a report (Jarratt, 1985) that had far-reaching recommendations on university governance designed to prepare universities for a decreasing dependence on government finance. Thirty years later, any attempt within a university to simplify committee structures risks being described as the institution being 'Jarrattized'.

The Treasury's impact on major inquiries into higher education

One consequence of the short-termism in policy bred by the two-year cycle of the PES process (to be extended to three years from 1997) was that from time to time the Government commissioned external inquiries to break policy deadlocks. Four such exercises stand out as being intended to resolve contentious issues and propose long-term policies. These were the Committee on Higher Education (1963) known as the Robbins Committee, the National Committee of Inquiry into Higher Education (1997) known as the Dearing Committee, the Clarke Working Party (producing *The Future of Higher Education*: DfES, 2003), and the Browne Committee (Browne, 2010). In the case of Robbins, Dearing, and Browne the decision was taken to establish committees that were to be seen as outside the normal processes of policymaking and detached from immediate departmental (including the Treasury's) concerns. In the case of Clarke the decision was taken to attempt the exercise in house, both to circumvent Treasury involvement (essentially the views of the Chancellor) and to produce a report that was politically directed. In the cases of Robbins, Dearing, and Clarke the dominant incentive to set the process in motion was to break a policy log jam. For Robbins, it was to determine authoritatively the scale and timing of the increased demand for higher education, and how it was to be accommodated and financed. For Dearing, it was how to come up with a politically acceptable scheme for financing higher education in response to the CVCP's proposal to charge top-up fees. For Clarke, it was to update the Dearing proposal on tuition fees in the light of the Prime Minister's acceptance of the argument that Britain was in danger of falling behind other competitor countries in its level of investment in higher education. Of all the reports, the Browne Report was the most radical. A review after three years of the effect of the new level of tuition fees had been promised and the Browne Report could have fulfilled its brief by offering reassurances about the apparent absence of negative effects of the new fee levels coupled with a modest increase to maxima of £5–6,000. Instead it offered a set of proposals that removed the cap on student numbers, thus creating an open market, permitted institutions to charge tuition fees up to £12,000 subject to a levy being paid to the government on any figure over £6,000, and guaranteed a loan system (also covering living expenses) financed by government which would ensure that entry to higher education remained free at the point of entry, with repayment only after graduation. The Browne Report effectively changed the basis of debate on how higher education was to be financed.

While the external view and the long-term perspective on policy are undoubtedly valuable to governments and to higher education itself, the true test of a report must be the extent to which its recommendations are implemented. In each case, however, key recommendations were frustrated or overturned by Government process, usually exercised through PES. The Robbins Report provides a good example. On the one hand, its forecast of future student demand up to 1980–1 was regarded as a key policy indicator both for the Treasury and for higher education, and PES negotiations were consistently based on estimates of how far the actual numbers matched the forecast figures. On the other hand, the shape of the higher education system that Robbins recommended to accommodate the numbers was significantly restructured by the finance made available. Robbins's vision of the expansion being concentrated in the university sector, with non-university institutions being upgraded to join it as appropriate, was deferred until 1992.

The fate of the Dearing Report was equally brutal. The Report was primarily established to resolve the financial issue of 'top-up' fees and its chapter on finance and its recommendations admirably answered the question. However, the effect of its recommendation, implemented in 2000, that students should contribute a £1,000 fee funded on an income-contingent loan, was negated by the Chancellor's decision to adhere to his predecessor's budget, which had included a further reduction in the higher education estimates of a figure almost exactly the same as the income to be derived from the new tuition fees. The result was that the additional funding envisaged in Dearing appeared to be clawed back by the Treasury.

Implicit in the 2003 White Paper was the feeling that Dearing had not gone far enough, and its recommendation that universities should be enabled to charge tuition fees of up to £3,000 was explicit in claiming 'to deal with student finance for the long term' (DfES, 2003: 3). Yet within four years of the White Paper's implementation the Browne Report and the 2010 Comprehensive Spending Review had overturned its central recommendation. The problem was two-fold: the increase in institutional income remained insufficient to recover the lowering of the unit of resource that had occurred during the 1990s, and the national economic picture had changed significantly so that the PES exercise in 2010, which itself significantly watered down Browne, was looking for a 25 per cent cut in the budget of the Department of Business, Innovation, and Skills (BIS). In the no doubt electric atmosphere of drastic budget reductions to be made in ten days, a scheme which in public expenditure terms reduced BIS's budget by 25 per cent by apparently reducing higher education's budget painlessly by 40 per cent was bound to be attractive. Whether this was a Treasury idea which David Willetts, the minister responsible for higher education, laid claim to, or whether it was wholly a Willetts contribution to policy, it is clear that its acceptance and implementation has entrenched the Treasury in the higher education policy driving seat, a fact emphasized by the Chancellor rather than the responsible minister announcing the removal of the cap on student numbers in 2014 and reinstating the Browne recommendation.

The Treasury as a policy actor in higher education

Bearing in mind its position at the fulcrum of policymaking in higher education, it is legitimate to ask whether the Treasury itself had policies in relation to higher education that it wished to influence the Department to follow. The evidence available suggests it did not, and that its concern remained primarily with how to balance the books in a situation where the total bids from spending departments always exceeded the agreed target for public expenditure. On the other hand, it had a view about the development of the national economy and had a consistent agenda of financial economies that it regularly wheeled out when reductions in the higher education budget were sought.

Thus, historically, the Treasury had always been interested in the extent to which higher education could contribute to the economy. Its concern about the need to produce a sufficient number of scientists and technologists extended right back to the Barlow Committee of 1946 (Barlow was himself a Treasury man). It is no surprise that a Chancellor of the Exchequer, Gordon Brown, should have set up a review of Business–University Collaboration (the Lambert Review, 2003) or that, when Prime Minister, he should have transferred higher education out of the DfES into a Department of Industry, Universities and Skills (DIUS) (later transmuted into the Department of Business, Innovation and Skills (BIS). The Treasury had a close interest in the Innovation agenda and, as a consequence, in the introduction of research selectivity, and it was Brown who announced the introduction of 'impact' into the Research Excellence Framework (REF) criteria. (One reason for the transfer of higher education out of the DfES into DIUS was that it was thought that the DfES was ineffective in prosecuting the Innovation agenda.) It could not be said, however, that the Treasury ever took a narrowly economic view of higher education.

The only occasion where the Treasury publicly intervened in higher education policy was in its evidence to the Robbins Committee. There its concern was primarily over the financial implications of alternative scenarios for student number forecasts and their distribution amongst different institutional structures. Treasury files show the intensity of the debate within the Treasury as to these issues and the public evidence passed through many drafts before final submission. The evidence showed that the Treasury fully accepted the argument that the expansion of higher education represented an investment for the future, but it offered a clear warning as to the vulnerability of any generous settlement in the light of competition from other sectors of the economy:

> There is likely to be a large expansion of public expenditure in the next decade and it can reasonably be forecast that governments will continue to limit the rate of growth of each service in order to keep the aggregate within tolerable limits. The development of all publicly financed services is therefore bound to depend upon the Government's choice of priorities between a large number of objectives, all desirable in themselves but not simultaneously practicable.
>
> (Committee on Higher Education, 1963: Pt 1 Vol F para 58)

It went on to suggest a number of ways of ameliorating the costs of the programme that became a Treasury litany throughout the next three decades. The most important of these, based on the argument that higher education brought a private as well as a public benefit, was to introduce student loans to cover part of the cost of a first degree. A second was to raise the issue of overseas students paying tuition fees at the heavily subsidized rate charged to local authorities for home students. (This was to be revisited first, in the 1967 PES round, when Crosland was persuaded to raise tuition fees for overseas students by £180 and second, in 1980, when the Government removed the subsidy altogether.) The evidence ended with a list of major claims across education as a whole that would compete with higher education: abolishing class sizes of 40 in primary schools, raising the secondary school leaving age to 16, and extending part-time education in technical education.

Seven years later in 1969, the then Minister for Higher Education, Shirley Williams, issued her '13 points'. These were clearly derived from Treasury advice because the occasion for their first unveiling was a meeting between the Minister, the UGC, and the CVCP, devoted to finding ways of reducing the costs of expansion in the 1972–7 quinquennium and was clearly intended as the preliminary to a PES round. The list of points included loans for maintenance grants, loans for tuition fees, voluntary reductions in the numbers of overseas students admitted, worsening student:staff ratios, introducing distance learning, and two-year degrees.

Further evidence of Treasury thinking in regard to value for money can be seen in the early 1980s in respect of the costs of university research. The UGC estimated that 43 per cent of its recurrent grant to universities was spent on research activity, but the Treasury argued that the UGC's 1981 cuts programme had demonstrated its view that research was unevenly pursued across the sector and that a 'black hole' existed in unjustifiable research monies being granted to some universities. The issue was one, it said, of lack of accountability; the first research selectivity exercise was the direct result.

The consistency of Treasury thinking is evident in a paper that the former Prime Minister, Edward Heath, addressed to the Society for Research into Higher Education as a basis for a discussion about higher education policy with the Society in 1983. His choice of questions included:

> How far should the labour market determine the shape of higher education? Are research and teaching indivisible in higher education if standards are to be maintained – is it better to have a few research institutions or many, given financial constraints? …

> Are the links between higher education and industry poor by comparison with other major countries? What are the merits of shorter courses – two years for liberal arts or for vocational subjects?
>
> (Heath, 1983)

These points must have come straight from a Treasury briefing: the question about research costs was live in the Treasury, relations between higher education and industry was a recurrent theme, and two-year degrees had been a Treasury fallback as an economizing measure as far back as Williams' '13 points'. It was to continue on the Treasury's agenda until David Blunkett accepted the challenge in his announcement of the introduction of Foundation Degrees in 1999.

The Treasury's task over this period was not to make policy, although that was a natural consequence of the outcome of PES negotiations, but to keep the lid on public sector financial commitments. Although there were exceptions – Crosland and the polytechnic policy, Baker and expansion, and Clarke and the abolition of the binary line – the freedom of action of most secretaries of state was so limited by the Treasury that policy initiatives from the Department on any scale were reduced to relatively minor changes of detail. It was only when the introduction of student contributions through tuition fees broke the financial log jam (except in Scotland) that new opportunities for policy initiatives, not universally welcomed in higher education, became available, but these had the effect of making the Treasury even more dominant in policy than it had been before.

Process reinforced: The implications of the post-2012 funding structure

The funding structure that has emerged from the 2011 White Paper drives policymaking in higher education yet further into the orbit of financial process rather than of seeking to match the needs of higher education itself. The financial structure of the student loan arrangements is complex, but has usefully been discussed in four contributions, the first by Willetts (2015), the second and third by McGettigan (2015a, 2015b), and the fourth by Thompson and Bekhradnia (2015). These point to the fact that many of the most significant decisions, certainly those on the fundamental financing of the system, may in the future be taken entirely on purely financial criteria, the level of interest rates, and the condition of financial markets, and the interests of higher education may be entirely excluded. Financial policy issues will dominate the process.

The situation arises because approximately 80 per cent of higher education funding, the element devoted to teaching, is funded by the Government, in effect the Treasury, via loans through the Student Loans Company. The Treasury borrows the money by issuing gilts, which it then lends to BIS, which lends it to the Student Loans Company, which lends it to individual students. The loan to BIS forms part of the allocation following a PES spending review and includes a special element to cover the anticipated losses on loans to students made each year. This figure is ring-fenced, so it may not be allocated to other purposes without Treasury approval. This is termed the resource accounting and budget (RAB) charge. The Treasury loan to BIS does not count as public spending because, theoretically at least, there is an obligation for it to be repaid, and in government accounting terms it is regarded as an asset, albeit one which may only be fully realized after 30 years. However, the borrowing necessary to sustain the loan arrangements counts against total government borrowing but, according to McGettigan, not against the Public Sector Net Debt, the standard measure of government borrowing, because the Office for National Statistics considers student loans to be an illiquid asset (McGettigan, 2015a: 18). The key issue for negotiation between BIS and the Treasury is the RAB charge, that is, the extent to which the student loan is not repaid. In 2013, the Treasury set a target of 36 per cent, although more recent estimates have been made of 45 per cent. However, as Willetts (2015) argues, these are at this stage only estimates, which can only be finalized in 30 years' time. (One variable is that the Treasury assumes that its cost of borrowing is 2.2 per cent above inflation, a rate that applies across all government borrowing, so that in a period of historically low interest rates the actual RAB charge may turn out to be lower.) Moreover, since the Treasury's stated intention is to sell the loan book, the return on loans may be correspondingly increased. But the Treasury remains concerned about the size of the RAB and, according to McGettigan, is 'creating new incentives for BIS to improve loan performance' (2015b). BIS has responded with a consultation document suggesting that the income threshold below which graduates are not required to repay their loans, which was previously frozen at £21,000 from 2016 for five years, could be varied not only for future students, but also for graduates who took out loans under earlier terms (Thompson and Bekhradnia, 2015).

In a situation, therefore, where higher education is funded primarily by student fees on borrowed resources the key decisions will revolve around interest rates, income thresholds, discount rates, and borrowing requirements. The creation of a student market where there is no cap on student numbers has transferred the fundamental decisions away from either the Funding Council or BIS to the Treasury, where judgements must be based on financial criteria. Policies towards higher education have substantially been replaced by the interaction of financial processes, government accounting principles, and fiscal markets: issues affecting access and the level of demand, potentially the level of entry standards, the future of postgraduate study, the viability of institutions, and the shape of the sector, could be determined on financial criteria remote from the operation of the higher education system. While this new policy environment offers potentially greater freedoms to at least some universities to engage in policy initiatives of their own, unfettered by restrictions on the growth of their student population and uncertainties regarding funding targets, it seriously weakens the concept of a system of higher education that subscribes to common educational goals.

Process and policy: The changing role of financial processes in the development of British (English) higher education

Gareth Williams in *Changing Patterns of Finance in Higher Education* (Williams, 1992) argued that up to the early 1970s it was widely accepted that the expansion of higher education should be funded publicly on grounds of equity and efficiency. There were, he wrote, three arguments for state funding: first, the state needed to influence and control an activity that prepared citizens for leading positions; second, an efficiency argument was that 'unless the state ... plays an active part there will be a less than socially optimal amount of investment into higher education'; and finally, that with the cost of higher education rising it was unfair to impose heavier burdens on the economically disadvantaged (ibid: 136). The latter point was reinforced by Robbins's argument about the pool of untapped talent. Robbins's own answer to the question of how, in a world of competitive bidding for public sector resources, investment to the level the Committee was proposing could be achieved, was that 'the communities that have paid most attention to higher studies have in general been the most obviously progressive in respect of income and wealth' (Committee on Higher Education, 1963: para 626) and that:

> if in any country educational investment in general and investment in higher education in particular falls appreciably behind what is being undertaken elsewhere, then, in the long run, general earning power is liable to be affected far beyond anything that may have

been foregone in the way of pecuniary return on investment in the individuals concerned.

(ibid: para 629)

These arguments about broad human capital and its contribution to the public good sustained higher education's position, though not its funding levels, up to the end of the 1980s, but by the beginning of the 1990s, when Williams's book was published, the consensus was beginning to break down and arguments for greater marketization were beginning to take hold. (It might be said that higher education institutions had only themselves to blame for this in the light of their readiness to engage in the market for overseas students.)

The reasons for the change of heart were not philosophical, however, but severely practical. The Robbins formula was based on the expectation of a continued growth in GDP that would have provided space to satisfy the demands not only of higher education expansion, but of the public sector of the economy at large. The country's economic development did not provide this. The situation was compounded by a sudden spurt in student demand, stimulated either by the open door offered by Baker, or by the high levels of youth unemployment, so that numbers rose by 50 per cent between 1989 and 1994. The Treasury, it was rumoured, believed that a 30 per cent participation rate was optimum for the maintenance of the economy. (The Blair target of 50 per cent never received official Treasury blessing.) The 1990s and up to 2010 represented, therefore, a search for a new funding paradigm which Browne essentially provided, though its proposed funding model was refined by the 2011 White Paper.

Thus, Gareth Williams's career has seen a revolution in the funding structure of higher education and, in consequence, of the fundamentals of how policy is made. Having cut his academic teeth when the state was most closely identified with the development of higher education, he has lived to see a situation where the state has, in one sense, sought to resile from its role and transfer policymaking to the market. Such a statement must, of course, be heavily qualified, because the cross-over from a direct to an indirect funding role through complex student loan processes leaves the true drivers of the system dependent on the operation of financial mechanisms that remain entirely within the state's control. The implication must be that while the old system was aimed at the public good, the new system is weighted much more heavily towards the private good. That was perhaps inevitable.

One result of this has been to change the locus of policymaking. As this chapter has sought to show, the operation of financial processes has always exercised a considerable influence on how higher education policy is made, much more than most people engaged in policy have been prepared to admit. The new, post-2012 funding system represents the culmination of a trend current since 2000 of transferring direct state funding to funding via a student market supported by indirect funding from the state. In doing so policymaking is likely to become much less transparent because so many of the variables interlock with Treasury processes. Higher education policymaking has in the past involved a network of consultations with a variety of bodies from the Funding Councils, Universities UK, professional bodies, and the universities themselves. This will not be the case when, for example, fresh estimates of the RAB drive up interest rates on student loans, with potential consequences for access rates. Questions of public accountability will seem remote if policy decisions are derived from the interpretation of government accounting conventions. On the one hand, the new market funding model pushes policymaking much more down to the institutions and the strategies they adopt to respond to the market forces that have been unleashed, but on the other, at the system level, it redirects it away from what have been conventional sources of policy towards an enclosed world where financial rather than educational criteria hold sway. The 2010 Comprehensive Spending Review may have preserved higher education from deep cuts, but it consigned it to a new and untried financial framework, which neither the Treasury nor higher education may find sustainable.

References

Baker, K. (1993) *The Turbulent Years: My life in politics*. London: Faber and Faber.

Brittan, S. (1964) *The Treasury under the Tories 1951–64*. London: Secker and Warburg.

Browne, J. (2010) *Securing a Sustainable Future for Higher Education: An independent review of higher education funding and student finance*. Online. http://tinyurl.com/jyro5f2 (accessed 11 April 2016).

Committee on Higher Education (1963) *Higher Education: Report of the Committee appointed by the Prime Minister under the chairmanship of Lord Robbins, 1961–63*. The Robbins Report. Cmnd 2154. London: Her Majesty's Stationery Office.

Department for Education and Skills (DfES) (2003) *The Future of Higher Education*. Cm 5735. London: Her Majesty's Stationery Office.

Estermann, T., Nokkal, T., and Steinal, M. (2011) *University Autonomy in Europe*, II. Brussels: European Universities Association.

Heath, E. (1983) SRHE Archive MSS 323/1/4 Modern Records Centre, University of Warwick.

Hennessey, P. (2006) *Having It So Good: Britain in the fifties*. London: Allen Lane.

HM Treasury (1980) *The Government's Expenditure Plans 1980–81*. Cmnd 7746. London: Her Majesty's Stationery Office.

— (2013) *The Green Book Appraisal and Evaluation*. London: The Stationery Office.

Jarratt, A. (1985) *Report of the Steering Committee for Efficiency Studies in Universities*. The Jarratt Report. London: Committee of Vice-Chancellors and Principals.

McGettigan, A. (2015a) *The Accounting and Budgeting of Student Loans*. HEPI Report 75. Oxford: Higher Education Policy Institute.

— (2015b) 'Impaired drivers'. *Times Higher Education*, 2 July, 28.

Major, J. (1999) *The Autobiography*. London: HarperCollins.

Middleton, R. (1996) *Government Versus the Market*. Cheltenham: Edward Elgar.

National Committee of Inquiry into Higher Education (1997) *Higher Education in the Learning Society*. The Dearing Report. London: Her Majesty's Stationery Office.

Shattock, M. (2012) *Making Policy in British Higher Education 1945–2011*. Maidenhead: McGraw Hill/Open University Press.

Thain, C. and Wright, M. (1995) *The Treasury and Whitehall: The planning and control of public expenditure 1976–93*. Oxford: Clarendon Press.

Thompson, J. and Bekhradnia, B. (2015) 'What price trust?' *Times Higher Education*, 30 July, 26.

Willetts, D. (2015) 'It's a winning formula, just adjust the variables'. *Times Higher Education*, 18 June, 40–3.

Williams, G. (1992) *Changing Patterns of Finance in Higher Education*. Buckingham: SRHE/Open University Press.

Chapter 4

Performance indicators and rankings in higher education

Jill Johnes

Introduction

Publicly funded sectors are under pressure to use resources efficiently, and awarding funds on the basis of performance is one approach to trying to achieve a more efficient use of taxpayers' money.[1] Resource allocation to the UK higher education sector has long followed such a policy. The 1980s funding cuts to UK higher education prompted rapid development of performance indicators as a means of encouraging accountability:

> ... higher education policy was dominated by two main concerns: to help reduce public expenditure; and to increase efficiency by encouraging institutions to 'earn' a larger proportion of their income from both government and non-government sources, and to be explicitly accountable for it.
>
> (Williams, 1992b: 3–4)

This observation strongly resonates with the current situation in English higher education.[2]

The performance of a traditional firm is relatively straightforward to measure since it is typically assumed to have the objective of profit maximization. The firm's accounts therefore provide an indication of how well the firm is performing against this benchmark. Any firm where the assumption of profit maximization is not applicable cannot have its performance assessed in this manner. Non-profit institutions like universities fall into this category and a conventional approach is inappropriate. In the UK, the need for performance indicators in the higher education sector has long been recognized (DES, 1985). Proposed performance indicators initially focused on a particular output or operation (Jarratt, 1985) and were at best simple ratios, such as the proportion of students with 'good' degrees or the cost per student. Media interest in these performance indicators was also stimulated and the performance of universities in certain key areas of interest to both taxpayers and prospective students was put under the spotlight:

for example, labour market destinations (Dixon, 1985), completion rates (Dixon, 1989), and achievement rates (Dixon, 1976).

It is a simple step to go from performance indicators to rankings and league tables. We should highlight at the outset the distinctions between performance indicators and university rankings: the differences revolve around the presentation and usage of the two. The former are usually a set of quantitative data on the performance of higher education institutions (HEIs) typically used by policymakers in assessing whether resources are being used efficiently. The latter are lists of HEIs, often produced by commercial publishers, ranked in descending order of performance according to a set of quantitative data and presented in the format of a league table (Usher and Medow, 2009). Rankings draw attention to relative performance, and have largely been aimed at the general public, in particular prospective students and their parents, to help them make an informed choice about their university. The first serious media rankings of universities and colleges (at the institution level) appeared in *US News and World Report* in 1983 (Dill, 2009)[3], and since 1994 the publication of university league tables based on various individual measures of performance has become commonplace in the UK, the USA, and elsewhere (Yorke, 1997). Distinctions between performance indicators and rankings are blurred by the fact that official performance data often underpin the rankings produced by the media. Moreover, interest and usage of rankings has widened to universities themselves (as an internal auditing and resource allocation tool) and to governments, especially with the recent development and regular publication of global rankings of universities across the world (for example, the 'Shanghai rankings', or the rankings of the *Times Higher Education*).

HEIs are multi-product firms with complex production processes, so that indicators based on simple ratios (and rankings which utilize these ratios) are unlikely to capture the true picture of performance. My own PhD thesis, for which Gareth Williams was external examiner, represents an early attempt to address these issues and to suggest ways of measuring the value-added rather than raw outputs of HEIs (Johnes and Taylor, 1990b). In the ensuing 30 years, as techniques have developed to capture performance in a multi-output, multi-input production framework, it has become possible to develop more sophisticated indicators. There is a trade-off, however, between simplicity and complexity: between providing indicators that are easy to construct and interpret, and computing performance measures that more closely capture the production process but whose construction is poorly understood by the layperson. The continued interest in media rankings suggests that simplicity is the current winner. But the simple approach can provide a misleading picture of performance with adverse consequences for institutional behaviour, as will be explored further in the following sections.

This chapter examines the development and use of performance indicators and rankings in the context of higher education, from the use of individual indicators and their amalgamation into a composite measure, to the construction of efficiency measures from an economist's perspective of universities as multi-product firms. The potential effects of these indicators and rankings on national policy and institutional behaviour are then considered together with proposals for an alternative way forward. The chapter ends with final conclusions. While the ideas and methodological approaches are of general application and interest, illustrative examples are typically from the UK.

Developing measures of performance in higher education: A simple approach

Higher education in the UK and elsewhere often receives funding from government. This can be potentially problematic, as the objectives of those funding higher education and those running universities may not be in alignment, leading to a classic principal–agent problem (Johnes, 1992). The government that provides the funds (the principal) can only imperfectly observe the actions of those running the HEIs (the agents) and so resorts to performance indicators to ensure that its own goals are being met. This raises the question of how to construct meaningful performance indicators.

One approach to performance measurement involves deriving various indicators and using these (or a subset) for a particular purpose. For example, funding for a particular activity can be given on the basis of performance in that area, or prospective students might examine performance in areas that are of particular relevance to their own interests. In arriving at a set of appropriate performance indicators, two main issues need to be initially addressed:

i.   *Level of analysis*: what are the entities being measured?
ii. *Dimensions*: what are the dimensions by which performance should be measured?

The separate performance indicators produced by official agencies such as the Higher Education Funding Council for England (HEFCE) and the Higher Education Statistics Agency (HESA) in the UK are used (often by the media) to produce rankings of universities that purport to highlight the relative performance of HEIs over a spectrum of dimensions. Thus, a third issue that needs to be addressed is:

iii. *Weights*: how can individual dimensions be aggregated into one composite index?

We will consider each of these in turn.

Level of analysis

Within higher education, we might want to measure the performance of individual academics, departments, academic programmes, institutions, or even the whole sector (against higher education sectors in other countries). The level of analysis depends on the target audience and the purpose of evaluation. The opening statement of HESA on their performance indicators, which they have published since 2002/03 (prior to which these were published by HEFCE), makes it clear that the entity in which they are interested is the higher education provider, i.e. the university.[4] Lower-level performance (e.g. of departments), however, might be of interest to managers within institutions, and country-level performance to governments interested in the performance of the domestic higher education sector relative to those of global competitors.

Dimensions

The dimensions by which we measure university performance depend, like level of analysis, on the target audience and the purpose of evaluation. In the context of government monitoring of university performance, the dimensions should relate closely to the outcomes from higher education most valued by society (Dill, 2009). Research and teaching are two obvious dimensions of interest. HEFCE undertakes a periodic review of UK universities' research on behalf of all the funding councils. The most recent review was the Research Excellence Framework (REF), the results of which were published in 2014.[5] This was preceded by various Research Assessment Exercises (RAEs) undertaken in 1986, 1989, 1992, 1996, 2001, and 2008. The greater part of funds distributed by the funding councils to universities for research purposes has been allocated on the basis of REF/RAE results (Harman, 2011), and there is a clear link between funding and measured performance. The UK is not alone in funding research in this way (Dill, 2009); Australia, for example, uses similar performance-based schemes to fund research and research training.[6]

The UK has no analogous mechanism for funding teaching, where student numbers drive allocations. Student numbers determine resources in two ways: through the university tuition fee; and through HEFCE resourcing, which is currently linked to student numbers by subject.[7] The latter is therefore not performance related, and the former is linked to teaching performance only insofar as students might choose their university and programme on the basis of teaching reputation. In practice, of course, this requires reliable indicators to inform potential students. A Teaching Excellence Framework (TEF) to mirror the REF is therefore currently being mooted in the UK as a means of linking funding to teaching performance, with the explicit aim of improving teaching quality and assuring students and taxpayers of efficient use of resources.[8]

There may be more than two dimensions of interest, however, and a variety of performance indicators can be found. Jarratt (1985) provided an early attempt at suggesting performance indicators that could provide useful information to stakeholders. The development of performance indicators has steadily progressed in the UK since then, with numerous indicators now being published annually (Pollard *et al.*, 2013), and the media compile their own rankings from these official sources, as well as any additional data that they have collected.

It is not difficult to find data on all aspects of university activities. HESA provides a huge amount of data on UK higher education including indicators relating to widening participation rates, non-continuation rates, module completion rates, research output, and graduate employment.[9] The media address the requirements of prospective students whose interests lie with feedback from current students, the reputation of the institution, or simply with the facilities at each institution. *The Complete University Guide*, for example,[10] examines ten aspects of activity likely to be of interest to prospective students: entry standards, student satisfaction, research assessment, research intensity, graduate prospects, student:staff ratio, academic services spend, facilities spend, good honours, and degree completion.[11]

Numerous dimensions can pose problems of interpretation if performance varies across different measures. Indeed there is no reason to expect that a university that is good in one area will necessarily be good in another. Take the rankings from *The Complete University Guide*. A simple rank correlation of the ten measures in the most recent ranking (2015–16) illustrates the point (Table 4.1). While the majority of indicators are highly correlated, 17 pairs have a correlation coefficient below 0.4.[12] This means that a university's position in the ranking changes dramatically depending on which indicator is used: one HEI, for example, is ranked top on academic services, second on research intensity, but bottom on facilities, and amongst the bottom ten universities on student satisfaction. Indeed the student satisfaction indicator generally appears to provide a noticeably different picture compared with the other measures. This result should perhaps come as no surprise since, in contrast to the other variables, it is based on perceptions and opinions.

Table 4.1: Rank correlations of ten indicators from
The Complete University Guide

	1	2	3	4	5	6	7	8	9
1. Entry standards									
2. Student satisfaction	0.17								
3. Research assessment	0.84*	0.14							
4. Research intensity	0.73*	0.27*	0.73*						
5. Graduate prospects	0.79*	0.29*	0.67*	0.61*					
6. Staff:student ratio	0.73*	0.22*	0.77*	0.69*	0.59*				
7. Academic services spend	0.57*	0.11	0.60*	0.54*	0.53*	0.62*			
8. Facilities spend	0.21*	0.11	0.27*	0.27*	0.23*	0.21*	0.29*		
9. Good honours	0.86*	0.23*	0.78*	0.76*	0.75*	0.68*	0.54*	0.15	
10. Degree completion	0.76*	0.33*	0.68*	0.62*	0.77*	0.63*	0.48*	0.27*	0.75*

Notes: * = significant at the 5% significance level. Note that *The Complete University Guide* uses student:staff ratio (indicator 6) and this has been reversed for the purposes of the correlation table to ensure that a higher value is consistent with more favourable performance.

Source: Calculated using data from *The Complete University Guide 2015–16.*

The complexities of interpreting performance measures are surely apparent. If, like the media rankings, the objective is to use the quantitative data to produce a composite index of overall performance, then these disparate measures need to be combined into a meaningful aggregate index. This is not an insignificant problem.

Weights

The purpose of a single index derived from information across multiple indicators is to summarize information across dimensions and to provide an indicator that is easier to interpret than a set of many separate measures (Saltelli *et al.*, 2005). This means that all parts of society can use the indicators, from policymakers to the general public, and this promotes accountability. Comparisons can be made not just amongst the group of entities being assessed but also over time (assuming calculation is consistent over time). Deriving a single index requires a set of weights in order to aggregate the separate measures.

The easiest approach is to apply an equal weighting across all indicators;[13] alternatively, different weightings can be assigned. *The*

Complete University Guide assigns weightings of between 0.5 and 1.5 to the ten individual measures (Table 4.2). Different publications use different weightings (and underlying indicators). Publishers of media rankings generally do not explain why they have chosen these weightings, or the fact that other weightings could be equally legitimate and potentially provide different rankings (Usher and Medow, 2009).

Table 4.2: Weightings used to produce an overall performance indicator in *The Complete University Guide* and rank correlation between the overall ranking and its components

	Weight	Correlation
1. Entry standards	1.0	0.91
2. Student satisfaction	1.5	0.35
3. Research assessment	1.0	0.86
4. Research intensity	0.5	0.78
5. Graduate prospects	1.0	0.83
6. Staff:student ratio	1.0	0.82
7. Academic services spend	0.5	0.64
8. Facilities spend	0.5	0.34
9. Good honours	1.0	0.89
10. Degree completion	1.0	0.85

Source: Weights from www.thecompleteuniversityguide.co.uk/
league-tables/methodology/ (accessed 29 June 2015);
correlation own calculation.

Ideally, weightings should reflect the preferences of the target audience, but deriving preferences for a group from the preferences of the individuals within that group is notoriously difficult. To construct a meaningful overall index is therefore fraught with difficulties. Is any purpose served by computing a composite index? The danger is that the apparent ease of interpretation provided by a composite index conceals the fact that the picture of performance that it represents is misleading, particularly if a) it is unrepresentative of all the dimensions that it purports to cover and b) inappropriate weightings are used. This in turn can lead, for example, to inappropriate policy development or unsuitable choice of university by potential students.

To illustrate these points, consider again *The Complete University Guide* where rankings from the overall indicator are strongly correlated with those from all the separate indicators, *with the exception of* those relating to student satisfaction and facilities spend (Table 4.2). Stakeholders for whom these dimensions are of particular interest would appear to be poorly served by the overall ranking.

In the absence of information on the relative importance of each dimension (and hence of an appropriate weighting system), it might still be possible to reduce numerous indicators to a manageable number of dimensions using such techniques as principal components analysis, data envelopment analysis (in particular, the 'benefit of the doubt' approach introduced by Cherchye *et al.*, 2007), the analytic hierarchy process, or co-plot (Johnes, 2015). Details and a critique of these techniques can be found elsewhere (Johnes, 2015; Saltelli *et al.*, 2005). We can illustrate the potential advantages of using one of these techniques (principal components analysis) in the context of *The Complete University Guide* data. The objective of a principal components analysis is to explain as much of the variation in the original data (the ten dimensions in *The Complete University Guide*) with as few variables as possible. More details regarding principal components can be found in Saltelli *et al.* (2005).

The weightings for each of the ten principal components calculated from *The Complete University Guide* data are displayed in Table 4.3 along with the associated percentage variation accounted for by each principal component. If we use the Kaiser criterion (Saltelli *et al.*, 2005) to select the principal components that are adequate to represent the data, we are left with the first two principal components. The weights (Table 4.3) of these two principal components suggest that the first principal component is mainly a combination of all dimensions *apart from* those reflecting student satisfaction and facilities spend, while the second principal component largely represents the combined dimensions of student satisfaction and facilities spend. This should come as no real surprise given the rank correlations already presented in Table 4.1.

Table 4.3: Weightings for the ten principal components (PC) associated with *The Complete University Guide* data

	Principal components									
The Complete University Guide dimensions	PC1	PC2	PC3	PC4	PC5	PC6	PC7	PC8	PC9	PC10
1. Entry standards	0.39	−0.05	0.01	−0.07	−0.11	−0.09	−0.18	0.28	0.24	−0.81
2. Student satisfaction	0.13	0.65	−0.59	0.37	0.25	0.02	0.03	0.07	0.07	−0.02
3. Research assessment	0.35	−0.09	−0.00	−0.28	0.40	−0.40	0.66	0.14	−0.07	0.06

	Principal components									
The Complete University Guide dimensions	PC1	PC2	PC3	PC4	PC5	PC6	PC7	PC8	PC9	PC10
4. Research intensity	0.36	0.07	0.04	−0.21	0.35	−0.13	−0.43	−0.68	−0.20	−0.04
5. Graduate prospects	0.36	0.06	−0.06	0.10	−0.47	−0.39	−0.22	0.28	−0.54	0.25
6. Staff:student ratio	0.35	−0.21	0.07	0.07	0.37	0.66	−0.13	0.37	−0.29	0.12
7. Academic services spend	0.27	−0.35	0.19	0.80	0.02	−0.13	0.13	−0.24	0.19	0.05
8. Facilities spend	0.07	0.61	0.77	0.07	0.05	−0.00	0.02	0.11	0.07	0.05
9. Good honours	0.38	−0.02	−0.09	−0.24	−0.13	0.01	−0.22	0.10	0.68	0.50
10. Degree completion	0.34	0.16	−0.05	−0.11	−0.51	0.45	0.46	−0.39	−0.07	−0.08
% variation	58.1	10.8	9.4	6.1	5.2	2.9	2.5	2.0	1.9	1.1

Source: Data used to derive the principal components from
The Complete University Guide 2015–16.

A plot of the first two principal components is displayed in Figure 4.1. Universities in the top right of the plot score highly on both principal components and therefore have good performance across all ten dimensions. The converse is true of universities located to the bottom and left of the plot. The leading diagonal quadrants represent mixed performance. Numbers next to the plotted points in Figure 4.1 are the rankings obtained in the composite measure (using the weightings as described above) of *The Complete University Guide*, with 1 representing top performance.[14] Both the top- and bottom-ranked universities are in the top right and bottom left quadrants of the principal components plot, suggesting that the composite ranking and the principal components provide a similar message. There are, however, many instances where the messages from the composite ranking and the principal components plot are mixed. For example, the university ranked 113th in *The Complete University Guide* appears in the bottom right-hand quadrant of the scatter plot: while it performs badly on eight of the indicators, it is amongst the top five universities on the basis of the second principal component (reflecting student satisfaction and facility spend). Conversely, the university ranked 13th is in the top left-hand quadrant but is amongst the bottom five on the basis of the second principal component (reflecting student satisfaction and facility spend).

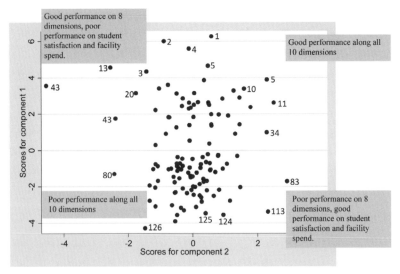

Figure 4.1: Plot of first two principal components

Source: Data used to construct the principal components
from *The Complete University Guide 2015–16*.

The rank correlations between the first two principal components and the overall ranking (Table 4.4) confirm that performance across all ten dimensions is adequately captured *neither* by the first principal component *nor* the composite ranking. A single indicator is insufficient to capture all the information contained in these ten measures. This finding is in line with results of a similar analysis of university rankings from *The Guardian* and the *THES* (see HEFCE, 2008, Appendix C). The general message is that, in trying to give a simple overview of performance, composite indicators can be misleading. As they sacrifice information which may be of interest or policy relevance to users of the performance assessment, little is gained from their construction.

Table 4.4: Rank correlations between the first two principal components and the university ranking

	1	2
1. University ranking		
2. Principal component 1	0.98	1.00
3. Principal component 2	0.15	0.08

Source: Data used in calculations from
The Complete University Guide 2015–16.

Methods for measuring performance: An economist's perspective

Let us now return to the basic idea underpinning performance indicators, namely as tools for government to assess the efficiency with which HEIs use publicly provided resources. The simple approach to efficiency measurement already discussed derives separate indicators that at best reflect reputation and resources but do not adequately capture the *efficiency of resource use*. Efficiency requires a knowledge of the outputs of universities, the inputs going into those outputs, and the production relationship between them (Johnes and Taylor, 1990b). This invokes the idea of 'value added' or, from an economist's perspective, 'technical efficiency'.

HEIs are multi-product organizations and produce (in simple terms) teaching, research, and third mission (the last reflecting universities' wider social engagement). Initial attempts to derive measures of value added applied Ordinary Least Squares (OLS) regression methods[15] to separate measures of universities' outputs (Johnes and Taylor, 1990b). At a time when proposed performance indicators included degree completions, classes of degrees, destinations of graduates, and unit costs (Jarratt, 1985), such analyses proved useful in demonstrating that these suggested measures were affected by characteristics of the HEI. Thus, much of the inter-university variation in unit costs was shown to be a consequence of subject mix, student mix, and the ratio of students to staff (Johnes, 1990; Johnes and Taylor, 1990b). Similarly, much of the inter-university variation in the percentage of graduates gaining employment was explained by subject mix, along with factors such as the academic ability of students on intake and location of the HEI (Johnes and Taylor, 1989a; Johnes and Taylor, 1989b; Johnes and Taylor, 1990b). The percentage of students gaining firsts and upper seconds and non-completion rates were also strongly related to the academic ability of students recruited by universities as well as factors such as library facilities, the percentage of students living in halls, and type of university (Johnes, 1997; Johnes and Taylor, 1989c; Johnes and Taylor, 1990a; Johnes and Taylor, 1990b; Johnes and Taylor, 1990c).

The problem with these analyses is that they separately examine the production of each output, which raises the difficulty of interpreting multidimensional information (Johnes, 1996). Another problem is that the approach ignores synergies that surely exist in the university production process (Chizmar and McCarney, 1984; Chizmar and Zak, 1984). The reason that universities produce, for example, undergraduate and postgraduate teaching alongside research and interaction with business is that these are all joint products: there are savings from producing these within one production unit rather than separately. A simple portrayal of the higher education production relationship is provided in Figure 4.2.

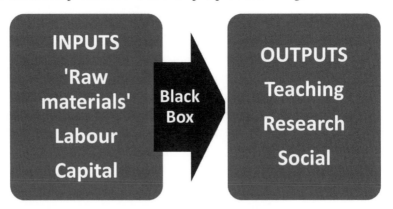

Figure 4.2: A production framework for universities

The idea of linking resource allocation to performance is that universities that are efficient at transforming inputs into outputs should receive more resources than those which are inefficient. Performance indicators should ideally represent the efficiency with which universities transform inputs into outputs. We are interested, for example, in how much more output universities could produce from given inputs (known as an output-oriented approach), or how many fewer inputs could be used to produce given outputs (known as an input-oriented approach). Consider a visual presentation of the first of these questions. Let us assume that universities produce two outputs (say, graduates and research) from one input (say, staff). For the sector as a whole there will be a production possibility frontier (PPF), which represents the maximum outputs that can be achieved from given input with current technology (Figure 4.3).

We can use this frontier as a benchmark against which the production of an individual university can be measured. In Figure 4.3, the observed production point of university F (i.e. the combination of research/staff and teaching/staff) lies inside the PPF and so it is clearly less efficient than it could be. One way of measuring that inefficiency is to take a ray from the origin through point F, and projecting it on to the PPF at point F'. The technical efficiency (TE) of university F is then measured as the ratio TE = OF/OF'.

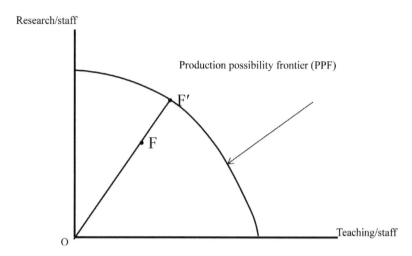

Figure 4.3: Measuring technical efficiency of a university

The problem is how to estimate the PPF (Figure 4.3). OLS regression is clearly an unsatisfactory approach to estimating a frontier because it estimates an average vector *through* the data rather than a *frontier*. Resulting efficiency ratios will therefore be calculated against an incorrectly estimated PPF. Furthermore, efficiency ratios derived from an OLS function are based on OLS regression errors.[16] Two frontier estimation techniques have been developed that overcome these problems, and which help in the construction of performance indicators: data envelopment analysis (DEA) and stochastic frontier analysis (SFA). We will briefly consider each of these approaches.

DEA (Banker *et al.*, 1984; Charnes *et al.*, 1978; Charnes *et al.*, 1979) is a non-parametric frontier estimation technique[17] which can handle a production situation with both multiple outputs and multiple inputs, and does not require *a priori* specification of a functional form. It estimates using linear programming methods a piecewise linear PPF (see Figure 4.4) which allows the performance of each institution to be measured *relative to institutions with similar missions or objectives*. This makes DEA attractive in the context of higher education where missions and objectives can differ substantially. An additional merit of DEA is that it provides benchmark information to those institutions which are performing inside the frontier. In Figure 4.4, point F' represents a more efficient virtual production point to which university F should aspire. Since point F' is a linear combination of the outputs (relative to input) of universities B and C, target input and output levels can be derived, to which university F should aspire.

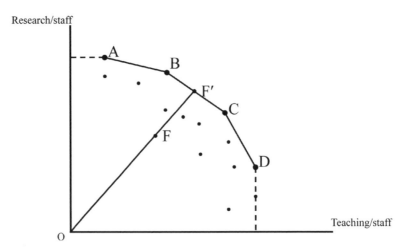

Figure 4.4: The PPF estimated by DEA

There are many examples of empirical studies which have applied DEA (and related non-parametric techniques) to measuring the efficiency of universities (Beasley, 1990; Beasley, 1995; Duh *et al.*, 2014; Fandel, 2007; Flegg and Allen, 2007; Flegg *et al.*, 2004; Giménez and Martínez, 2006; Glass *et al.*, 2006; Johnes, 2006; Johnes, 2008; Johnes, 2014b; Thanassoulis *et al.*, 2011). DEA studies of UK universities tend to find that average efficiency across the sector as a whole is fairly high (typically 80 per cent or above), but the specific findings depend on the sample used (the more restricted the sample, the higher the average efficiency) and the time period covered. DEA has also been used to assess the efficiency of individual academic departments or programmes within an institution (Casu *et al.*, 2005; Colbert *et al.*, 2000; Kao and Hung, 2008; Kao and Liu, 2000; Moreno and Tadepalli, 2002; Ray and Jeon, 2008), central administration, or services across universities (Casu and Thanassoulis, 2006; Simon *et al.*, 2011), and to make efficiency comparisons across different national education systems (Giménez *et al.*, 2007).

DEA is a deterministic non-parametric approach, with the disadvantages that random fluctuations in the data are not allowed for, there are no conventional tests of significance or methods for drawing inference, and efficiency estimates are particularly affected by sample size. This means that great care should be taken in choosing the variables to represent the inputs and outputs in any DEA model; the model specification should be consistent with the higher education production process. In addition, DEA has not been extended to address specific issues of modelling in a panel data context. In its favour, recent developments in DEA include the incorporation of bootstrapping techniques[18] to produce confidence intervals and bias-corrected estimates of efficiency, and the development of hypothesis tests to assess the significance of specific inputs and/or outputs (Banker, 1996; Johnes, 2006; Pastor *et al.*, 2002).

SFA is a parametric frontier estimation method, which allows for stochastic errors in the data (Figure 4.5) and provides parameter estimates and associated significance tests (Aigner *et al.*, 1977; Meeusen and van den Broeck, 1977). Following Jondrow *et al.* (1982), SFA also allows the estimation of technical efficiency for each university. These features of SFA make it an attractive methodological tool which has frequently been used particularly in studies relating to policy development (Abbott and Doucouliagos, 2009; Johnes *et al.*, 2008; Johnes and Schwarzenberger, 2011; Johnes, 2014b; McMillan and Chan, 2006; Stevens, 2005).

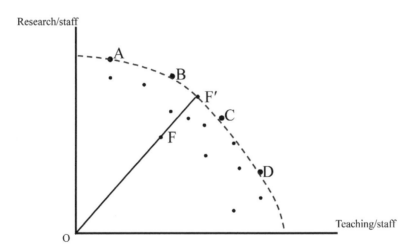

Figure 4.5: The PPF estimated by SFA

Many of the SFA empirical studies relate to the context of university costs where SFA lends itself to the framework of a single left-hand side variable (costs) and multiple right-hand side variables. Average efficiency levels for the English higher education sector are estimated to be around 70 per cent and there is considerable variation around this mean (Johnes *et al.*, 2005; Johnes *et al.*, 2008). The parameters of the SFA cost function can be used to estimate the presence of economies of scale (reduction in cost per unit from increasing output) and economies of scope (reduction in costs from producing two or more outputs jointly); recent evidence reveals that typically economies of scale are exhausted and that there are diseconomies of scope in English higher education (Izadi *et al.*, 2002; Johnes *et al.*, 2005; Johnes *et al.*, 2008; Johnes and Johnes, 2009). This suggests that, for the HEI of average size, there are no further opportunities for economies of scale from expansion in size. Moreover, the existence of diseconomies of scope suggests that the opportunities for economies from sharing resources across different outputs have been exhausted (indeed HEIs may already be producing too many outputs simultaneously).

An exception to these SFA empirical studies of costs is one by Johnes (2014b) who examines technical efficiency in a multi-input, multi-output framework. Average efficiency levels for the English higher education sector are estimated to be around 70 to 80 per cent, and the estimated parameters provide insights into potential input substitutability: there is least scope for substituting between academic staff and administrative inputs, whilst academic staff and capital are the inputs with the greatest potential for substitution. Perhaps of greater interest (particularly from a policy viewpoint) is that universities which ultimately merge typically have greater flexibility in terms of input substitution than those which do not (Johnes, 2014a).

The downside of the SFA approach is that the assumptions which underpin it (regarding the distribution of efficiencies and the stochastic error, as well as the functional form of the function being estimated) are often made for ease of analysis; results can be biased as a consequence. SFA is not a benchmarking tool and provides no precise information on how managers of an institution can alter inputs and/or outputs to improve their efficiency.

In comparisons of DEA and SFA applied to higher education, SFA generally provides lower efficiency estimates than DEA, and rank correlations of efficiencies derived from the two methods are positive but very low (Johnes, 2014b; Kempkes and Pohl, 2010). Policymakers and users of performance indicators should be aware that the relative position of universities is not consistent across methodological approaches.

Potential effects of performance indicators and rankings

We consider in this section the effects on subsequent efficiency of measuring performance using the simple and frontier approaches.

Measuring performance using individual indicators or a composite index

The problem with the simple approach stems directly from what might seem its main advantage: transparency, of the method and the data used.

While this makes it easy for an HEI to see its strengths and weaknesses and alter its behaviour accordingly, it also means that rankings are open to manipulation and gaming. According to Goodhart's 'law', a variable which is used to measure performance is open to manipulation by those whose performance is being measured (Johnes, 1992; Pollard *et al.*, 2013). Changing behaviour is a desirable consequence of performance measurement *only* if the changed behaviour genuinely improves *performance* rather than simply *rank*.

Rankings are important to individual institutions. National and global rankings can be used by other institutions to identify suitable collaborative partners; they can be used by students to inform their choice of university; by prospective academic employees seeking new posts; and by employers for recruitment (Hazelkorn, 2015; Saisana *et al.*, 2011). This means that a university has an incentive to change its behaviour in response to the rankings, but changed behaviour may not benefit performance.

Many popular measures of performance are under the control of the HEI. Graduation rates, for example, can be improved by more effective teaching delivery – the desired effects of university performance assessment – or by lowering standards (so-called 'grade inflation'), on which there is mixed evidence in the UK and the USA (Bachan, 2015; Johnes, G. 2004; Johnes and Soo, 2015; Popov and Bernhardt, 2013). More generally, there is confirmation of concern from senior managers of universities that some measures in league tables are vulnerable to 'cheating' behaviour (Rolfe, 2003), and evidence that universities are manipulating, or influencing, data in order to raise their rankings (Hazelkorn, 2015). There have been claims, for example, that students have been pressured to provide favourable responses to the National Student Survey in the UK (Newman, 2008). Gaming behaviour by universities is unlikely to achieve the efficiency objective of performance assessment:

> The pernicious effect of this competitive pursuit of academic prestige is that it is a highly costly, zero-sum game, in which most institutions as well as society will be the losers, and which diverts resources as well as administrative and faculty attention away from the collective actions within universities necessary to actually improve student learning ...
>
> (Dill, 2009: 6)

Gaming behaviour can mislead those using university rankings. National policy towards higher education, for example, can be based on fallacious information: a policy of merging HEIs is being rolled out in France, Russia, and China, in the belief that global rankings of domestic HEIs can be favourably affected (Shin and Toutkoushian, 2011). Merger policy has also been promoted in the UK in the belief that greater size leads to greater visibility in the world rankings as well as greater efficiency (Jump, 2014). Given the problems with rankings, however, much more research into the wider likely effects of any policy initiative should be undertaken: in the case of merger policy, there has been little statistical research into the benefits of merging universities and this is an area that should be explored further (Johnes, 2014b).

Even if gaming behaviour is not a serious problem, by focusing on improvement of the components that underpin the media rankings, HEIs are in danger of becoming much more homogeneous. For example, the underlying components of the rankings are often biased towards research activity, particularly to research in the sciences (Dill, 2009), and this could lead to an HEI altering its mission to scientific research activity even though it might formerly have pursued teaching excellence (Shin and Toutkoushian, 2011). In addition, the highly ranked elite universities become the benchmarks for the lower-ranked HEIs to mimic, thereby ensuring a reduction in diversity between universities (Morphew and Swanson, 2011). Yet diversity in higher education is desirable because it stimulates a dynamic sector, giving more choice to students (HEFCE, 2012), and reducing this choice might be socially undesirable because of the negative impact on student access caused by imperfect geographical mobility (De Fraja and Valbonesi, 2012; Kelchtermans and Verboven, 2010).

Finally, university rankings suggest a precision which is unlikely to be supported by detailed examination of the data: the methodology is such that differences in rankings, which can appear large, conceal the fact that there are only very small differences in the scores from which the rankings have been derived (Longden, 2011).[19] It is therefore important to know whether or not the differences in rankings between HEIs are 'real' or significant in a statistical sense. Little work has focused on this aspect in the context of individual measures or composite indexes. An exception is work by Smith *et al.* (2000) who examine the performance of HEIs in the UK on the basis of the first destinations of graduates, and find that the differences in performance are significantly different only for the top ten and the bottom ten institutions. Thus, rankings not only leave the higher education sector open to undesirable behaviour and consequences, but these effects may be based on rankings that have little meaning. This point is pursued further below.

Performance measures based on frontier estimation techniques

Deriving efficiency scores using DEA or SFA involves complex procedures such that the end-user loses direct engagement with the data. The advantage is that it becomes more difficult to alter behaviour merely to affect a *position* in the rankings, so these approaches are less likely to incite gaming behaviour. However, the availability of managerial information on benchmarks which inefficient universities should use to improve their performance means that HEIs still have the opportunity genuinely to improve their *efficiency*.

This might lead one to suppose that rankings based on frontier estimation techniques are more reliable than the simple rankings based on aggregating individual measures. There are two *caveats* to this. First, the production relationship in higher education is extremely difficult to model, and incorporating quantity and quality of all aspects of a university's activities can challenge the estimation methods. Second, as with the simple approach, point estimates of each university's relative position are highly suspect. The estimation of confidence intervals around efficiency estimates derived from both SFA and DEA suggests that there is considerable overlap in performance between many universities (Johnes, 2014b).

Groupings rather than point estimates

Point estimates of rankings are misleading since there is likely no significant difference in efficiency between many universities, and are possibly even damaging if they result in undesirable gaming behaviour. How can we gain some idea of the performance of universities whilst avoiding these problems? One idea is that performance *groupings*, rather than point estimates, would be more appropriate (Bougnol and Dula, 2006).

This raises the question of how to construct the groups. One suggestion by Barr *et al.* (2000) is to use DEA to produce tiers of universities (known as 'peeling the DEA onion'): the first application of DEA to the data produces a set of efficient universities which are removed to form the top tier. DEA is then applied to the truncated data set, and the efficient universities removed to form the second tier. This process, or 'peeling', continues until all universities are assigned to a tier (Figure 4.6).

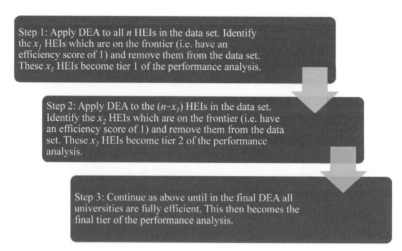

Step 1: Apply DEA to all n HEIs in the data set. Identify the x_1 HEIs which are on the frontier (i.e. have an efficiency score of 1) and remove them from the data set. These x_1 HEIs become tier 1 of the performance analysis.

Step 2: Apply DEA to the $(n-x_1)$ HEIs in the data set. Identify the x_2 HEIs which are on the frontier (i.e. have an efficiency score of 1) and remove them from the data set. These x_2 HEIs become tier 2 of the performance analysis.

Step 3: Continue as above until in the final DEA all universities are fully efficient. This then becomes the final tier of the performance analysis.

Figure 4.6: Peeling the DEA onion

The advantage of DEA is that it can be applied in either context: producing a composite index from a number of performance indicators or the production approach relating inputs to outputs. In the former case, the 'benefit of the doubt' version of DEA is used whereby the indicators are classified as 'outputs' and the single 'input' is equal to one for all universities (Cherchye *et al.*, 2007). This therefore constructs a composite index using objectively derived weightings which differ for each university and are constructed to show each HEI in its best possible light. In practice this means that each university is measured against universities with a similar mission or objectives, and hence diversity in the sector is preserved.

We illustrate the peeling method using the data from *The Complete University Guide 2015–16* and applying the DEA 'benefit of the doubt' model to the data. The peeling approach yields four groupings of universities (shown in Table 4.5: universities are ordered alphabetically within group). Alongside the HEIs in each tier is the ranking assigned in *The Complete University Guide 2015–16*. The average of the rankings of the universities in each tier is very broadly in line with the tiers produced, in that the average for the first tier is the lowest, and so on. But there are some big differences between ranking and tier for some universities. This might arise because of the calculation of the weightings in DEA, but it is possible to restrict the weighting assigned to each measure if this were desired.

Table 4.5: Groupings of universities produced by the peeling approach applied to data from *The Complete University Guide 2015–16*

Tier 1 (Average ranking 42.15)	Rank	Tier 2 (Average ranking 54.85)	Rank	Tier 3 (Average ranking 69.53)	Rank	Tier 4 (Average ranking 98.71)	Rank
Bath	11	Abertay	95	Aberdeen	40	Bedfordshire	110
Birmingham	18	Aberystwyth	86	Anglia Ruskin	115	Bolton	121
Bishop Grosseteste	117	Aston	32	Arts University Bournemouth	57	Brighton	76
Bristol	15	Bangor	58	Bournemouth	54	Canterbury Christ Church	106
Brunel University London	49	Bath Spa	70	Central Lancashire	91	Derby	94
Buckinghamshire New	113	Birmingham City	88	Chester	93	London Metropolitan	126
Cambridge	1	Bradford	63	Chichester	77	London South Bank	119
Cardiff	31	City	41	De Montfort	54	Manchester Metropolitan	73
Cardiff Metropolitan	79	Cumbria	111	Dundee	42	Newman	120
Coventry	48	East Anglia	16	Edge Hill	82	Northumbria	60
Durham	5	Falmouth	70	Edinburgh	20	Plymouth	90
East London	124	Glasgow	30	Edinburgh Napier	92	Portsmouth	59
Essex	34	Glasgow Caledonian	83	Gloucestershire	80	Salford	96
Exeter	10	Glyndwr	123	Greenwich	107	Southampton Solent	122
Heriot-Watt	37	Goldsmiths, University of London	50	Huddersfield	74	Staffordshire	103
Imperial College London	4	Harper Adams	60	Hull	63	Teesside	98
Loughborough	11	Hertfordshire	75	Kingston	104	Worcester	105
Middlesex	89	Keele	46	Leeds Beckett	114		
Northampton	83	Kent	22	Lincoln	51		
Oxford	2	King's College London	23	Liverpool	39		
Queen's, Belfast	36	Lancaster	9	Manchester	28		
Royal Agricultural University	85	Leeds	19	Nottingham	25		
St Andrews	5	Leeds Trinity	101	Nottingham Trent	53		
St George's, University of London	43	Leicester	24	Oxford Brookes	54		
Strathclyde	38	Liverpool Hope	97	Queen Margaret	78		

Tier 1 (Average ranking 42.15)	Rank	Tier 2 (Average ranking 54.85)	Rank	Tier 3 (Average ranking 69.53)	Rank	Tier 4 (Average ranking 98.71)	Rank
Surrey	8	Liverpool John Moores	68	Queen Mary, University of London	33		
		London School of Economics	3	Reading	29		
		Newcastle	26	Royal Holloway, University of London	34		
		Robert Gordon	63	Sheffield Hallam	72		
		Roehampton	66	SOAS, University of London	43		
		Sheffield	27	South Wales	102		
		Southampton	14	St Mary's, Twickenham	109		
		Sussex	21	Stirling	47		
		Trinity Saint David	125	Sunderland	116		
		Ulster	66	Swansea	45		
		University College London	13	University for the Creative Arts	52		
		University of the Arts, London	80	West London	108		
		Warwick	7	West of Scotland	118		
		West of England, Bristol	62	Westminster	100		
		York	17	Winchester	86		

Source: Data used to do calculations and to compile table from *The Complete University Guide 2015–16*.

This analysis is offered purely as an example of how a tiered approach to performance assessment might work in practice. Alternative approaches should also be explored and evaluated. It seems, however, that a move away from specific rankings can only have beneficial effects on the performance of the higher education sector.

Conclusions

This chapter summarizes approaches to performance assessments and rankings of universities particularly over the last 30 to 40 years. Various approaches – ranging from individual indicators through composite indexes to the technical efficiency approach permitted by recent developments in frontier estimation techniques – have been presented and compared. The chapter ends with the suggestion that the potentially pernicious and self-seeking effects of the commonly applied simple approach to performance measurement could be reduced by adopting a tiered performance approach, using frontier estimation, to produce groupings rather than specific rankings. Throughout, the possible approaches have been illustrated using data from recent media rankings in the UK. It is apparent that different approaches deliver different conclusions and the user of performance indicators and rankings should beware: university rankings should come with a serious health warning and be handled with care. Indeed, the words of Gareth Williams from more than 20 years ago continue to be relevant today: 'Like all quantitative performance indicators these figures raise more questions than they answer' (Williams, 1992a: 147).

Notes

[1] I am grateful to Gerry Steele (Lancaster University) for comments on an earlier draft.

[2] See HEFCE, www.hefce.ac.uk/funding/efficient.

[3] There were some rankings of US HEIs produced prior to 1983. But these were produced *ad hoc* and do not follow the methodology of many of today's media rankings.

[4] See HESA, www.hesa.ac.uk/pis.

[5] See www.ref.ac.uk.

[6] See https://education.gov.au/research-block-grants.

[7] See www.hefce.ac.uk/lt/howfund.

[8] See www.gov.uk/government/speeches/teaching-at-the-heart-of-the-system.

[9] Source: www.hesa.ac.uk/pis (accessed 29 June 2015).

[10] Source: www.thecompleteuniversityguide.co.uk/league-tables/methodology (accessed 29 June 2015). Note that this particular university guide is chosen purely for illustrative purposes; conclusions from any analysis presented here can be generalized across all university guides.

[11] An additional environmental ranking, derived from a 2014 report from the Higher Education Academy (Drayson *et al.*, 2014), is also provided for those interested in the 'green' credentials of universities.

[12] A rank correlation value close to 1 represents a strong positive correlation while a value close to 0 indicates no relationship between the variables.

[13] Performance indicators are usually standardized to produce a z-score before calculating an overall ranking. This ensures that the composite index is not affected by the units of measurement of the components underlying it.

[14] Note that some rankings appear twice because of tied values.

[15] OLS regression is a common method for estimating a linear relationship between observations of a variable Y (university output in this case) and an explanatory variable X (or explanatory variables $X_1,...,X_K$). In the case of one explanatory variable it therefore provides estimates of the coefficients (or parameters) a and b in the linear relationship $Y = a + bX$. OLS regression relies on certain underlying assumptions in order for the parameter estimates to have desirable statistical properties.

[16] An underlying assumption of OLS regression is that the errors are randomly distributed, hence estimated efficiencies are highly unsatisfactory (Johnes, 1996).

[17] Non-parametric estimation means that the technique does not rely on any underlying assumptions such as the data being distributed in a certain way.

[18] In statistics, bootstrapping is a method which relies on random sampling (with replacement) of the original data in order to estimate a sampling distribution of a required statistic. In the context of DEA, bootstrapping techniques can, for example, generate a sampling distribution for the efficiency score which then allows estimation of a confidence interval around the score. See Johnes, J. (2004) for more detail.

[19] Related to this is the problem of the volatility of rankings over time, which might be due to changing methodology or might have alternative explanations. This idea is explored elsewhere (Longden, 2011: 96–9).

References

Abbott, M. and Doucouliagos, C. (2009) 'Competition and efficiency: Overseas students and technical efficiency in Australian and New Zealand universities'. *Education Economics*, 17 (1), 31–57.

Aigner, D., Lovell, C., and Schmidt, P. (1977) 'Formulation and estimation of stochastic frontier production models'. *Journal of Econometrics*, 6, 21–37.

Bachan, R. (2015) 'Grade inflation in UK higher education'. *Studies in Higher Education*, 40, 1–21.

Banker, R. (1996) 'Hypothesis tests using data envelopment analysis'. *Journal of Productivity Analysis*, 7 (2–3), 139–58.

Banker, R., Charnes, A., and Cooper, W. (1984) 'Some models for estimating technical and scale inefficiencies in data envelopment analysis'. *Management Science*, 30 (9), 1078–92.

Barr, R., Durchholz, M., and Seiford, L. (2000) *Peeling the DEA Onion: Layering and rank-ordering DMUs using tiered DEA*. Dallas, TX: Southern Methodist University.

Beasley, J. (1990) 'Comparing university departments'. *Omega*, 18 (2), 171–83.

— (1995) 'Determining teaching and research efficiencies'. *Journal of the Operational Research Society*, 46 (4), 441–52.

Bougnol, M.-L. and Dula, J. (2006) 'Validating DEA as a ranking tool: An application of DEA to assess performance in higher education'. *Annals of Operations Research*, 145 (1), 339–65.

Casu, B. and Thanassoulis, E. (2006) 'Evaluating cost efficiency in central administrative services in UK universities'. *Omega*, 34 (5), 417–26.

Casu, B., Shaw, D., and Thanassoulis, E. (2005) 'Using a group support system to aid input–output identification in DEA'. *Journal of the Operational Research Society*, 56 (12), 1363–72.

Charnes, A., Cooper, W., and Rhodes, E. (1978) 'Measuring the efficiency of decision making units'. *European Journal of Operational Research*, 2 (4), 429–44.

— (1979) 'Measuring the efficiency of decision making units: A short communication'. *European Journal of Operational Research*, 3 (4), 339.

Cherchye, L., Moesen, W., Rogge, N., and van Puyenbroeck, T. (2007) 'An introduction to "benefit of the doubt" composite indicators'. *Social Indicators Research*, 82 (1), 111–45.

Chizmar, J. and McCarney, B. (1984) 'An evaluation of "trade-offs" implementation using canonical estimation of joint educational production functions'. *Journal of Economic Education*, 15 (1), 11–20.

Chizmar, J. and Zak, T. (1984) 'Canonical estimation of joint educational production functions'. *Economics of Education Review*, 3 (1), 37–43.

Colbert, A., Levary, R., and Shaner, M. (2000) 'Determining the relative efficiency of MBA programs using DEA'. *European Journal of Operational Research*, 125 (3), 656–69.

De Fraja, G. and Valbonesi, P. (2012) 'The design of the university system'. *Journal of Public Economics*, 96 (3–4), 317–30.

Department of Education and Science (DES) (1985) *The Development of Higher Education into the 1990s*. Cmnd 9524. London: Her Majesty's Stationery Office.

Dill, D. (2009) 'Convergence and diversity: The role and influence of university ranking'. In Kehm, B. and Stensaker, B. (eds) *University Rankings, Diversity, and the new Landscape of Higher Education*. Rotterdam: Sense Publishers.

Dixon, M. (1976) 'Careers: More means better'. *The Financial Times*, 28 February.

— (1985) 'Jobs column: What happened to universities' graduates?' *The Financial Times*, 14 November.

— (1989) 'Jobs column: Benefits, and risks, of trying for a degree'. *The Financial Times*, 19 April.

Drayson, R., Bone, E., Agombar, J., and Kemp, S. (2014) *Student Attitudes towards and Skills for Sustainable Development*. York: Higher Education Academy.

Duh, R., Chen, K., Lin, R., and Kuo, L. (2014) 'Do internal controls improve operating efficiency of universities?' *Annals of Operations Research*, 221 (1), 173–95.

Fandel, G. (2007) 'On the performance of universities in North Rhine-Westphalia, Germany: Government's redistribution of funds judged using DEA efficiency measures'. *European Journal of Operational Research*, 176 (1), 521–33.

Flegg, T. and Allen, D. (2007) 'Does expansion cause congestion? The case of the older British universities, 1994–2004'. *Education Economics*, 15 (1), 75–102.

Flegg, T., Allen, D., Field, K., and Thurlow, T. (2004) 'Measuring the efficiency of British universities: A multi-period data envelopment analysis'. *Education Economics*, 12 (3), 231–49.

Giménez, V. and Martínez, J. (2006) 'Cost efficiency in the university: A departmental evaluation model'. *Economics of Education Review*, 25, 543–53.

Giménez, V., Prior, D., and Thieme, C. (2007) 'Technical efficiency, managerial efficiency and objective-setting in the educational system: An international comparison'. *Journal of the Operational Research Society*, 58 (8), 996–1007.

Glass, J., McCallion, G., McKillop, D., Rasaratnam, S., and Stringer, K. (2006) 'Implications of variant efficiency measures for policy evaluation in UK higher education'. *Socio-Economic Planning Sciences*, 40, 119–42.

Harman, G. (2011) 'Competitors of rankings: New directions in quality assurance and accountability'. In Shin, J., Toutkoushian, R., and Teichler, U. (eds) *University Rankings: Theoretical basis, methodology and impacts on global higher education*. Dordrecht: Springer.

Hazelkorn, E. (2015) 'How the geo-politics of rankings is shaping behaviour'. *Higher Education in Russia and Beyond*, 2 (4), 6–7.

HEFCE (2008) *Counting What is Measured or Measuring What Counts? League tables and their impact on higher education institutions in England*. Bristol: Higher Education Funding Council for England.

— (2012) *Collaborations, Alliances and Mergers in Higher Education: Consultation on lessons learned and guidance for institutions*. London: Higher Education Funding Council for England.

Izadi, H., Johnes, G., Oskrochi, R., and Crouchley, R. (2002) 'Stochastic frontier estimation of a CES cost function: The case of higher education in Britain'. *Economics of Education Review*, 21 (1), 63–71.

Jarratt, A. (1985) *Report of the Steering Committee for Efficiency Studies in Universities*. The Jarratt Report. London: Committee of Vice-Chancellors and Principals.

Johnes, G. (1992) 'Performance indicators in higher education: A survey of recent work'. *Oxford Review of Economic Policy*, 8 (2), 19–34.

— (2004) 'Standards and grade inflation'. In Johnes, G. and Johnes, J. (eds) *International Handbook on the Economics of Education*. Cheltenham: Edward Elgar, 462–83.

Johnes, G. and Johnes, J. (2009) 'Higher education institutions' costs and efficiency: Taking the decomposition a further step'. *Economics of Education Review*, 28 (1), 107–13.

Johnes, G. and Schwarzenberger, A. (2011) 'Differences in cost structure and the evaluation of efficiency: The case of German universities'. *Education Economics*, 19 (5), 487–99.

Johnes, G. and Soo, K.T. (2015) 'Grades across universities over time'. *The Manchester School*. Online. http://onlinelibrary.wiley.com/doi/10.1111/manc.12138/abstract (accessed 9 May 2016).

Johnes, G., Johnes, J., and Thanassoulis, E. (2008) 'An analysis of costs in institutions of higher education in England'. *Studies in Higher Education*, 33 (5), 527–49.

Johnes, G., Johnes, J., Thanassoulis, E., Lenton, P., and Emrouznejad, A. (2005) *An Exploratory Analysis of the Cost Structure of Higher Education in England*. Research Report 641. London: Department for Education and Skills.

Johnes, J. (1990) 'Unit costs: Some explanations of the differences between UK universities'. *Applied Economics*, 22 (7), 853–62.

— (1996) 'Performance assessment in higher education in Britain'. *European Journal of Operational Research*, 89, 18–33.

— (1997) 'Inter-university variations in undergraduate non-completion rates: a statistical analysis by subject of study'. *Journal of Applied Statistics*, 24 (3), 343–61.

— (2004) 'Efficiency measurement'. In Johnes, G. and Johnes, J. (eds) *International Handbook on the Economics of Education*. Cheltenham: Edward Elgar, 613–742.

— (2006) 'Data envelopment analysis and its application to the measurement of efficiency in higher education'. *Economics of Education Review*, 25 (3), 273–88.

— (2008) 'Efficiency and productivity change in the English higher education sector from 1996/97 to 2004/05'. *The Manchester School*, 76 (6), 653–74.

— (2014a) 'Efficiency and input substitutability in English higher education 1996/97 to 2008/09'. INFORMS Annual Meeting, 9–12 November, San Francisco, CA.

— (2014b) 'Efficiency and mergers in English higher education 1996/97 to 2008/9: Parametric and non-parametric estimation of the multi-input multi-output distance function'. *The Manchester School*, 82 (4), 465–87.

— (2015) 'Operational research in education'. *European Journal of Operational Research*, 243 (3), 683–96.

Johnes, J. and Taylor, J. (1989a) 'An evaluation of performance indicators based upon the first destination of university graduates'. *Studies in Higher Education*, 14 (2), 219–35.

— (1989b) 'The first destination of new graduates: Comparisons between universities'. *Applied Economics*, 21 (3), 357–73.

— (1989c) 'Undergraduate non-completion rates: Difference between UK universities'. *Higher Education*, 18 (2), 209–25.

— (1990a) 'Determinants of student wastage in higher education'. *Studies in Higher Education*, 15 (1), 87–99.

— (1990b) *Performance Indicators in Higher Education*. Buckingham: SRHE/ Open University Press.

— (1990c) 'Undergraduate non-completion rates: A reply'. *Higher Education*, 19 (3), 385–90.

Jondrow, J., Lovell, C., Materov, I., and Schmidt, P. (1982) 'On the estimation of technical inefficiency in the stochastic frontier production function model'. *Journal of Econometrics*, 19 (2–3), 233–8.

Jump, P. (2014) 'Cut 50% of universities and bar undergraduates from Oxbridge'. *Times Higher Education*, 25 June.

Kao, C. and Hung, H. (2008) 'Efficiency analysis of university departments: An empirical study'. *Omega*, 36 (4), 653–64.

Kao, C. and Liu, S. (2000) 'Data envelopment analysis with missing data: An application to university libraries in Taiwan'. *Journal of the Operational Research Society*, 51 (8), 897–905.

Kelchtermans, S. and Verboven, F. (2010) 'Program duplication in higher education is not necessarily bad'. *Journal of Public Economics*, 94 (5–6), 397–409.

Kempkes, G. and Pohl, C. (2010) 'The efficiency of German universities: Some evidence from nonparametric and parametric methods'. *Applied Economics*, 42 (16), 2063–79.

Longden, B. (2011) 'Ranking indicators and weights'. In Shin, J., Toutkoushian, R., and Teichler, U. (eds) *University Rankings: Theoretical basis, methodology and impacts on global higher education*. Dordrecht: Springer.

McMillan, M. and Chan, W. (2006) 'University efficiency: A comparison and consolidation of results from stochastic and non-stochastic methods'. *Education Economics*, 14 (1), 1–30.

Meeusen, W. and van den Broeck, J. (1977) 'Efficiency estimation from Cobb-Douglas production functions with composed error'. *International Economic Review*, 18 (2), 435–44.

Moreno, A. and Tadepalli, R. (2002) 'Assessing academic department efficiency at a public university'. *Managerial and Decision Economics*, 23 (7), 385–97.

Morphew, C. and Swanson, C. (2011) 'On the efficacy of raising your university's ranking'. In Shin, J., Toutkoushian, R., and Teichler, U. (eds) *University Rankings: Theoretical basis, methodology and impacts on global higher education*. Dordrecht: Springer.

Newman, M. (2008) 'Students urged to inflate national survey marks to improve job options'. *Times Higher Education*, London. 15 May, 7.

Pastor, J., Ruiz, J., and Sirvent, I. (2002) 'A statistical test for nested radial DEA models'. *Operations Research*, 50 (4), 728–35.

Pollard, E., Williams, M., Williams, J., Bertram, C., and Buzzeo, J. (2013) *How Should We Measure Higher Education? A fundamental review of the performance indicators. Part 2: The evidence report*. Brighton: Institute for Employment Studies.

Popov, S. and Bernhardt, D. (2013) 'University competition, grading standards, and grade inflation'. *Economic Inquiry*, 51 (3), 1764–78.

Ray, S. and Jeon, Y. (2008) 'Reputation and efficiency: A non-parametric assessment of America's top-rated MBA programs'. *European Journal of Operational Research*, 189 (1), 245–68.

Rolfe, H. (2003) 'University strategy in an age of uncertainty: The effect of higher education funding on old and new universities'. *Higher Education Quarterly*, 57 (1), 24–47.

Saisana, M., d'Hombres, B., and Saltelli, A. (2011) 'Rickety numbers: Volatility of university rankings and policy implications'. *Research Policy*, 40 (1), 165–77.

Saltelli, A., Nardo, M., Tarantola, S., Giovannini, E., Hoffman, A., and Saisana, M. (2005) *Handbook on Constructing Composite Indicators: Methodology and user guide*. Paris: OECD.

Shin, J. and Toutkoushian, R. (2011) 'The past, present, and future of university rankings'. In Shin, J., Toutkoushian, R., and Teichler, U. (eds) *University Rankings: Theoretical basis, methodology and impacts on global higher education*. Dordrecht: Springer, 1–18.

Simon, J., Simon, C., and Arias, A. (2011) 'Changes in productivity of Spanish university libraries'. *Omega*, 39 (5), 578–88.

Smith, J., McKnight, A., and Naylor, R. (2000) 'Graduate employability: Policy and performance in higher education in the UK'. *Economic Journal*, 110 (464), 382–411.

Stevens, P. (2005) 'A stochastic frontier analysis of English and Welsh universities'. *Education Economics*, 13 (4), 355–74.

Thanassoulis, E., Kortelainen, M., Johnes, G., and Johnes, J. (2011) 'Costs and efficiency of higher education institutions in England: A DEA analysis'. *Journal of the Operational Research Society*, 62 (7), 1282–97.

Usher, A. and Medow, J. (2009) 'A global survey of university rankings and league tables'. In Kehm, B. and Stensaker, B. (eds) *University Rankings, Diversity, and the New Landscape of Higher Education*. Rotterdam: Sense Publishers.

Williams, G. (1992a) 'British higher education in the world league'. *Oxford Review of Economic Policy*, 8 (2), 146–58.

— (1992b) *Changing Patterns of Finance in Higher Education*. Buckingham: SRHE/Open University Press.

Yorke, M. (1997) 'A good league table guide?' *Quality Assurance in Education*, 5 (2), 61–72.

Part Two

A changing academic life

Managerialism, garbage cans, and collegial governance: Reflections on an economic perspective of university behaviour

David Dill

Introduction

Throughout his career Gareth Williams has applied an economic perspective to higher education policy and organization.[1] In a now classic early analysis, Williams (1984) noted the seminal insights Adam Smith contributed to the field, but stressed that contemporary economic research on higher education had emphasized Smith's 'macroeconomic' insight on university behaviour, what is now termed 'human capital theory' (e.g. Becker, 1994). As a consequence Williams suggested the 'microeconomic' insight also advocated by Smith, which, examining the influence on university behaviour of the different means of allocating finance to and within universities, had received much less emphasis and study. In subsequent analyses Williams contributed to this neglected area of research from an economic perspective (1995, 1997, 2004).

With the reforms associated with the 'massification' of higher education (i.e. expansion of participation to the majority of the relevant age group) in most developed and developing countries over the last quarter of a century, the impacts of finance on the policymaking behaviour of institutions of higher education has become a much more significant as well as controversial area of study. Because many within the academic profession perceive the impacts of these policy changes in negative terms, economic perspectives on university organization and governance themselves have sometimes been criticized, if not seriously contested. But similar to other areas of public regulation, it is important to distinguish between the insights of economic research and the design of implemented public policies. As with any public policy issue dealing with regulation, policymakers and economists may not agree on the necessary elements of the most effective policy options. Therefore, in the analysis to follow I explore the research on university decision-making behaviour, attempting to suggest how an economic perspective, appropriately applied, may continue to provide useful insights into the design of university governance.

One of the earliest applications of a modern economic perspective to university behaviour is Garvin's (1980) study of American research universities. At the outset of his empirical study Garvin reviewed the alternative models of university behaviour drawn from other disciplines as well as from academic tradition itself: the bureaucratic model, the political model, the 'organized anarchy' model, and the academic collegial model. To provide a clearer understanding of the insights to be drawn from an economic perspective, I briefly examine these alternative models of university behaviour, still widely applied and debated in contemporary research on higher education (Huisman *et al.*, 2015), contrasting them where appropriate to generalizations drawn from relevant economic research.

The bureaucratic model

The bureaucratic or 'command and control' perspective on university behaviour was typically applied in the past to less developed university systems such as Eastern Europe, Latin America, and Africa; however, aspects of the bureaucratic model have also always been associated with US higher education. Its tradition of corporate independence among colleges and universities, and its pattern of dual or 'shared governance', combined collegial control with aspects of administrative hierarchy (Dill, 2014). The bureaucratic model assumes and justifies greater influence and control by university administrators through more top-down forms of academic governance and decision making. Because the massification of higher education systems worldwide in recent decades has been associated with growing concerns among policymakers about the efficiency and effectiveness of university systems, the bureaucratic model of university governance and administration has increasingly influenced the design of national higher education financing and regulatory policies in many developed nations as well. These new policies are viewed by many in the university community as an effort to empower academic administrators, imposing an inappropriate and ineffective 'managerialism' on university behaviour. This view is particularly espoused in the professorially guided university systems of the Westminster countries and some EU nations.

These managerially oriented policies for higher education have often been justified by policymakers using concepts drawn from the New Public

Management (NPM), a term first attributed to Christopher Hood (1991). However, because the concept of NPM is not systematically defined, it has become an 'umbrella' concept associated with policy reforms that vary significantly from country to country. That is, they are path dependent, shaped by the particular history and institutions of each nation. But some of the NPM-related reforms appear to have been influenced by core assumptions of the new institutional economics (Weimer and Vining, 1996).

For example, the principal–agent assumption that transaction costs, including monitoring the self-interested behaviour of professionals, can be minimized through better specified contracts has led to national policies tying university research funding to clearly defined indicators of university output. But as previously suggested, economic research (Weimer and Vining, 1996) raises questions about the effectiveness of applying simplistic principal–agent conceptions to organizations as complex as universities. For example, the principal–agent model is likely to be inefficient for organizations with the goals of research universities because of the difficulties and high costs of validly measuring complex outputs, such as academic education and research. In addition, the principal–agent model predicts difficulties in effectively controlling cross-subsidies in professional organizations with multiple outputs, such as universities, which are engaged in teaching, research, and public service. The costs, continual adjustments in measures, and identified impacts upon university behaviour of the former Research Assessment Exercise (RAE) in the UK provide some evidence in support of these points (Dill, 2015).

NPM policies have similarly been associated with government efforts to reshape university governance, encouraging greater executive authority for administrators and diminishing the collegial influence in university decision making of academic staff. But an economic perspective also suggests an emphasis on managerial authority in universities is likely less efficient for society than well-designed collective or collegial processes of governance and decision making, because long-term academic staff are more likely to provide truly independent judgements on critical university decisions than are shorter-term administrators, who may personally benefit from the decisions made (McPherson and Schapiro, 1999). As Williams observed with regard to dishonest management in the UK university sector:

> In any economic or social organization there is always a risk of corruption, as some people in positions of influence use their power for their own advantage rather than for that of the organization or society to which they owe allegiance. ... In a

competitive market system those in positions of authority are particularly susceptible to temptation, especially if they promote entrepreneurial behaviour where success is measured largely in terms of effective innovations, which often means bending the rules, sometimes to breaking point. However, the adoption of market values and financial incentives greatly increases the temptation. ... Certain British universities have been fined considerable sums for over-recruiting on student target numbers and occasionally for submitting misleading statistical returns about numbers of students and course completions.

(2013: 67–9)

Furthermore, consistent with an economic perspective, research on university governance in the USA indicates administrators and academic staff members pursue different goals and interests (Kaplan, 2004). Consequently, a recent economic behavioural model of shared governance (Carroll *et al.*, 2012), which controlled for the degree of faculty participation in US higher education, discovered that decisions made primarily by administrators led to an overinvestment in university 'non-academic quality', such as athletics, amenities for student life, and residential facilities. Administrator-controlled decisions also led to increased undergraduate enrolments and to higher total costs for undergraduate students. In contrast, decisions reflecting greater faculty participation in governance led to lower investments in non-academic quality and to higher levels of graduate enrolment, to greater sponsored funding, and to increased academic quality as measured by the scope and rigour of academic programme offerings, as well as faculty qualifications. Based upon their measures of impacts, the authors concluded that when compared with greater administrative authority, increased faculty participation in academic governance, particularly in tight fiscal times, yields more socially optimal outcomes.

At the same time it is important to distinguish between national policies promoting managerialism within universities, understood as increased executive authority and centralized decision making, and collective actions by universities themselves designed to improve the management of instruction, research, and public service. For example, the increased emphasis on 'national innovation' among the OECD nations has stimulated reforms in academic research funding that have led to experimentation with new means of managing academic research and technology transfer within universities. Research (Dill and van Vught, 2010) suggests some of these new university processes have improved both the productivity of academic research and scholarship as well as their benefits for the larger society.

The political model

The 'political model' of university behaviour, well-articulated in the USA by Baldridge (1971), emphasizes the variations in university goals and policies among administrators, students, and faculty members, as well as differences among faculty members in different disciplines regarding educational matters. However, in contrast to the bureaucratic model, emphasizing increased executive authority and centralized decision making, the political perspective focuses on the distribution of power among all constituencies of the university, as well as the governance structures and processes employed to resolve internal conflicts. Therefore, the political perspective is often associated with models advocating a more inclusive or 'democratic' form of academic governance.

Research on university behaviour employing a political perspective expanded in the latter part of the twentieth century, because of the changes in university governance made in the USA and Europe in response to the student demonstrations of the 1960s and 1970s. In the USA, this led for a period of time to much greater student representation in university governance, while in Northern Europe, related national reforms led to longer-lasting democratic forms of university governance involving not only students but also representatives of non-academic staff and external lay groups (Kogan, 1984).

In the USA, contemporary research (Kezar and Eckel, 2004) employing the political perspective on university behaviour argues that the academic tradition of 'shared governance' among administrators and faculty members rarely functions effectively in practice, slows necessary decision making, and impedes needed university reorganization and strategic change. However, much of this research, as Garvin (1980) originally noted, fails to control for academic performance, is often based upon case studies, and, given its perspective, tends to underemphasize if not diminish the tradition of collegial or guild control of academic processes. In contrast, Kaplan's (2004) national survey of academic governance in the USA, which replicated a survey by the American Association of University Professors (AAUP) in 1970, discovered the same institutions reported striking increases in faculty control over decision making in the traditional areas of faculty authority. Kaplan's survey responses, which included faculty representatives and administrators from each institution, also provided little evidence that shared governance posed widespread problems to effective academic management. Furthermore, reports of encroachments on the tradition of shared governance or the ineffectiveness of the process represented a clear minority of cases in his survey. Kaplan's research also reaffirmed the hierarchical nature of academic authority in the US system of higher education identified by Clark (1987) and other researchers. That is, the highest rated and most productive research universities and liberal arts colleges reported greater influence of faculty authority and higher levels of faculty participation in academic governance.

In a later critique of the collected academic research on academic governance in the USA, Kaplan (2006) argued it has too often reflected a political focus on the 'hard' institutions of rules, procedures, and decision structures in academic governance and underemphasized the 'soft' institutions by which universities communicate the attitudes and norms about how governance decisions ought to be made. Kaplan's criticism is given empirical support by recent intensive case studies of leading international universities (Paradeise and Thoenig, 2013), which included the public University of California, Berkeley and the private Massachusetts Institute of Technology in the USA, which focused on the collegial form of 'internal governance' by which these institutions attain standards of excellence in instruction and research. Like Kaplan, the authors concluded that academic quality was primarily sustained through the social interactions that occur within and between academic subunits and among academic staff at the host university. These collegial processes play a major role in building shared identities, developing valuable common knowledge in instruction and research among academic staff members, as well as generating and communicating communal norms and values through socialization and internal regulation. Finally, these processes legitimate certain decision-making criteria within academic institutions and have an impact as well on the distribution of authority and power within the university.[2]

The 'organized anarchy' model

The 'organized anarchy' model and the related 'garbage can model' of decision making articulated by Cohen *et al.* in 1972 have been continually influential in organizational research and are still widely cited as particularly descriptive of university behaviour (Huismann *et al.*, 2015). Cohen and March as well as Olsen (Cohen *et al.*, 2012) were engaged in separate studies of higher education in the USA before they collaborated in the development of these models. Cohen and March (1986) also subsequently utilized these models as a conceptual cornerstone of their influential national survey of US academic leadership and decision making.

The 'garbage can model' assumes decision making is a process in which decisions are generated by the random intersection of independent 'streams' of problems, solutions, participants, and choice opportunities. Thus, choice opportunities are 'garbage cans' in which the resulting decisions, if any, depend on whatever mixtures the intersecting streams generate. As a consequence, choices often just happen and solutions have no clear connection to problems. But garbage can decision making requires an 'organized anarchy', a setting characterized by problematic preferences, unclear technology, and fluid participation – conditions of ambiguity readily recognizable within universities. While some of the conceptual underpinnings of these two models can be related to economic theory, the unpredictable if not irrational nature of the garbage can decision-making model appears to undercut traditional economic concepts of rational choice. The models therefore are often cited by those who criticize the relevance to higher education of current 'managerially oriented' policies.

However, many scholars citing and generalizing from these models, particularly in the field of higher education, have been inattentive to their derivation and conceptual components. For example, the original models, while inspired by observations from American universities, were not based upon an empirical study or test, but were supported by the results of a computer simulation included with the published article. A retest of this simulation by respected scholars in the USA (Bendor *et al.*, 2001) revealed that it did not support many of the components of the accompanying verbal model, and they therefore called for a needed reformulation and retesting of the core concepts. In response, one of the original authors (Olsen, 2001) objected that the 'garbage can' and 'organized anarchy' concepts were never intended to be 'testable models', but rather were better understood as 'metaphors' to help shape and guide thinking about organizational behaviour. Possibly in response to this theoretical dispute a major conference on the 'garbage can model' was subsequently held featuring recent studies applying the concepts to organizational behaviour (Lomi and Harrison, 2012). While this new research may have helped refurbish the reputation of the original 'models', it is worth noting that in contrast to the initial studies by Cohen and March, and those by Olsen that gave birth to the concepts, none of the new studies was based upon or included a sample from higher education.

More useful for comprehending the value of an economic perspective on university behaviour are two often neglected components of these original 'metaphors'. The irrational behaviour of garbage can decision making was argued to be contingent upon an exogenous variable, 'organizational slack', defined to include the amount of money and other resources provided to an organization by the external environment. Cohen *et al.* (1972) noted, in an analysis based upon the computer simulation that also appeared almost verbatim in Cohen and March's (1986) subsequent study of higher education decision making, that slack in higher education declines during periods of financial adversity. As the financial adversity continues, Cohen *et al.*'s (1972) model predicts for all schools a very significant improvement in decision making: a substantial reduction in problem activity and decision time as well as a substantial increase in decisions by resolution. This apparently positive relationship between the degree of rationality in organizational decision making and the competitiveness of financial support would of course be quite consistent with an economic perspective regarding the impact of competitive markets on university behaviour.

It is especially worth noting, and little observed in the related literature on higher education, that the 'metaphors' of both organized anarchy and garbage can decision making were originally derived from observations of US higher education in the late 1960s. This period is generally described (Geiger, 1993) as part of the 'golden age' of American governmental support for colleges and universities, in which publicly provided financial resources for higher education grew precipitously and were loosely related to institutional behaviour. By contrast many developed countries, including the USA and the UK, have experienced over the last quarter of a century declining public support for universities. During the current period of greater market competition for financial resources there has also been some evidence of a corresponding increased rationality and efficiency in university governance and decision making, particularly with regard to research (Dill and van Vught, 2010).

Finally, as noted, the original Cohen *et al.* (1972) model required organized anarchy as a necessary structural condition for garbage can decision making. Organized anarchy was particularly characterized by 'uncertain technology'. This assumed that in certain organizations or circumstances the technology or technique for converting inputs to outputs and/or for making strategic decisions was unclear if not unknowable. This condition is relevant to the structure of universities where the technology of research and scholarship is constantly changing and assumed to be improving. But the uncertainty of technology has been particularly observable in teaching and student learning, where there have been long-standing debates and disagreements within universities regarding appropriate technique, and where the norms of academic freedom offer professorial staff opportunities to avoid or resist organizational attempts to promote educational efficiency.

But similar to the nature of market competition, technology is also subject to change, and this is clearly occurring in higher education, as innovations in information technology are now significantly influencing traditional techniques of teaching and student learning.

The noted economist and former President of Princeton University William Bowen (Bowen *et al.*, 2014) recently conducted a rigorous study comparing the productivity of a traditional university course in statistics and a hybrid version of the same course utilizing online instruction. Bowen is well known as the co-author in the 1960s of the 'cost disease' concept (Baumol and Bowen, 1966). Following this concept wages in certain labour-intensive professions such as the performing arts and higher education necessarily rise at a rate greater than their growth in productivity, because technical efficiencies are difficult to achieve in these fields. However, Bowen now argues that productivity growth in higher education instruction has become both technically feasible and necessary.

Bowen underscores the need for systematic evaluations of different approaches to online learning, in different subject fields, and in different academic settings. However, his research study led him to call both for openness to new means of instruction by traditional institutions of higher education and for needed reforms in our conventional models of academic governance and decision making:

> … if wise decisions are to be made in key areas, such as teaching methods, it is imperative that they be made by a mix of individuals from different parts of the institution – including faculty leaders but also others well-positioned to consider the full ramifications of the choices before them. There are real dangers in relying on the compartmentalized thinking that too often accompanies decentralized modes of organization to which we have become accustomed.
>
> (Bowen, 2013: 64)

The academic collegial model

The traditional model of university behaviour explored in the literature of higher education is the 'collegial' model of internal university governance most prevalent in the USA and the UK (Shattock, 2010). This focus on peer control of organizations has received some theoretical support from sociologists such as Hage (1974) and Mintzberg (1979), and most recently in an insightful study by Lazega (2001). But for the most part the literature in higher education has ignored these theoretical contributions and based

David Dill

the collegial model upon descriptive analyses of academic organizations. For example, Tapper and Palfreyman's (2010) recent attempt to clarify the academic collegial model employs the English tradition of the 'collegiate university', characteristic of Oxford and Cambridge, which they define as autonomous residential colleges emphasizing undergraduate education. Consequently, Tapper and Palfreyman's analysis of collegial governance in US higher education focuses exclusively on the collegial structure of liberal arts colleges and consortial arrangements among these colleges, but completely ignores the collegial governance processes for instruction, research, and public service characteristic of the best US research universities.[3] As a consequence this particular 'federal' conception of academic collegiality is of limited assistance in understanding the internal academic governance of universities in other countries, including the USA, which are not organized according to the English tradition of the collegiate university.

Within all universities there is always a tension between the academic authority granted particular roles, for example the significant influence traditionally awarded to individual professors in European university systems, and collegial or collective academic authority. Clark (1987) therefore highlighted the US academic department as a powerful mechanism not only for protecting the professional control of academic work, but also for providing a means of constraining excessive individual authority. Academic departments in the best US universities do acknowledge the importance of faculty seniority and experience by requiring the chair of a department to be a senior or full professor and by assigning to full professors responsibility for all appointments and promotions to full professor, as well as for the award of academic tenure. But on most other departmental matters, voting is by 'one person, one vote', which includes junior members of the academic staff, and thereby acts as a collegial brake on the authority of senior professors. As Clark observed:

> National systems that do not have [academic departments] seem to evolve toward [them] to tame the more narrow inclinations of individual specialists and to bring collegial principles to the fore.
>
> (1987: 155)

Consistent with Clark's view, many EU universities are now for the first time adopting departmental structures and also reforming the traditional 'master–apprentice' model of doctoral training, based upon the substantial authority historically awarded to individual professors. Instead they are developing a university-wide culture of shared values and commitment to research doctoral education featuring new governance structures 'with defined

116

processes that enhance quality and aim at coordinating individual efforts' (Byrne *et al.*, 2013: 13). These changes in EU university internal governance were not made in response to external policy directives or 'managerialist' incursions, but rather illustrate the types of voluntary collegial adaptations viewed as crucial for assuring and improving academic quality in the more competitive global environment of higher education.

The new structures implemented by EU universities (Byrne *et al.*, 2013) include doctoral schools, often a university-wide unit similar to a US graduate school. In the USA a graduate school is a collegial governance structure engaging the collective academic staff of an institution in developing and implementing policies designed to assure the academic standards of each of a university's research doctoral programmes. Similarly, in a number of EU universities the collective faculty has been significantly involved in creating new university-wide rules and guidelines for doctoral supervision. These new rules include the adoption of doctoral committees to augment the expertise of the traditional thesis supervisor, the creation of university-level admissions committees for research doctoral education, as well as the creation of 'institutional spaces' for the exchange of experiences and good practices among thesis supervisors via informal peer-learning groups and training opportunities.

The adoption by many EU universities of departmental and graduate school structures as well as university-wide policies governing research doctoral education represents necessary adjustments in the distribution of academic authority within institutions, a shift to a more balanced system featuring collegial or collective academic authority over research doctoral and instructional programmes. These changes in university governance and decision making appear largely voluntary, not influenced by government incentives or directives, and responsive to ongoing changes in the universities' environment.

The perspective of organizational economics

Over the last several decades the use of economic logic and methods to understand the existence, nature, design, and performance of managed organizations has matured into the field of organizational economics (Colombo and Delmastro, 2008; Gibbons and Roberts, 2013). Several generalizations from this field, which is based primarily upon studies of organization in business and industry, may be used to summarize a number of the points noted above regarding organizational behaviour in higher education. First, organizational design and performance is significantly influenced by the character and competitiveness of the markets in which organizations operate. Second, the nature of relevant technologies has independent effects on organizational design and performance. Third, as a consequence of changes in markets and technologies, historical studies of organizational design (Colombo and Delmastro, 2008) reveal an evolution from the early hierarchical 'M-form' to the more contemporary and leaner 'J-form' of organizational structure. The M-form was characterized by a deep organizational hierarchy, vertical coordination and control, highly centralized decision making, and measurable data upon which the organization's strategies were based. The more contemporary J-form reflects the demands of global market competition and is characterized by decreased bureaucratization, larger spans of control, decentralized decision making to encourage more innovative approaches to complex and less quantifiable tasks, as well as greater reliance on the management of human resources to achieve needed coordination. Strikingly the more modern J-form of organizational design evolving in the business sector has many similarities to recent research on the governance and structure of effective universities (Paradeise and Thoenig, 2013).

As noted in the preceding review of organizational behaviour in higher education, greater market competition, some but not all induced by new forms of government financing and regulation, as well as significant changes in technologies relevant to university research, teaching, and resource allocation are requiring universities worldwide to make adjustments in their organizational design. Reflecting the recent research on organizational economics, some economists (Aghion *et al.*, 2010) have argued national policy reforms for higher education are most efficient for society when they emphasize merit-based competition for university research funding and allocate greater authority to universities. This autonomy permits universities to control the use of their budgets independently, to choose compensation for their faculty, and to hire whichever academic staff they most prefer, processes associated with socially beneficial research performance.

While these types of deregulatory policies are being implemented in a number of countries, as previously indicated, policymakers in some developed nations including the UK and the USA are also advocating increased 'managerialism' in university governance and decision making. This is being pursued through regulations promoting greater executive authority, more centralized governance of university strategy, and diminished influence of academic staff over teaching and research policy. From an economic perspective this type of managerialism appears to be applying an outdated and increasingly inappropriate organizational design to academic work.

The 'commons' model

The forces of increased market competition and changing technology will require significant changes in university behaviour. Additionally, in countries where institutional governance was significantly influenced by the policies of educational ministries and/or by the collective academic profession, universities are now being awarded greater autonomy, transforming them into strategic actors able to define their own policies and to implement them through internal organizational processes. In this new and challenging environment, how is the organizational design of universities best conceptualized and studied? A potentially more valuable framework for exploring organizational behaviour in universities is the 'commons' model thoughtfully articulated by the Nobel laureate in Economics Elinor Ostrom (2005). In her Nobel Prize lecture Ostrom (2010) argued that neither market forces nor the rules of the state are the most effective institutional arrangements for governing, managing, and providing complex public goods. Instead, she has attempted to identify universal design principles that permit individuals in self-governing organizations to address collective action dilemmas effectively.

Although she received the Nobel Prize in Economic Sciences, Ostrom's work has often been viewed as marginal to economic theory. For example, the recent authoritative *Handbook on Organizational Economics* (Gibbons and Roberts, 2013) cites her work only once. In part this is because rather than statistically testing formal economic models, she attempted to build her commons model from empirical analyses of actual collective goods problems in the field. But Ostrom's commons perspective is not inconsistent with much economic theory, as she incorporated concepts of rational choice, transaction costs, and game theory into her perspective on self-governance.

More to the point, Ostrom argued a commons perspective is most applicable in circumstances where more effective cooperation and integration among independent individuals is critical to performance, clearly and increasingly the case in contemporary university instruction, research, and service. Her commons perspective is also most appropriate when the organization's members share common values, when the organization is a self-organizing community, when the organization possesses a 'nested' structure with multiple levels of rule-making (e.g. the 'federal' model of academic governance), and when the organization is of a size to facilitate the active participation and interaction of its members. All of these characteristics apply to most established universities around the world. Finally, the external governance of universities in the USA and many developed countries including the UK has traditionally assigned the *collective* faculty or academic staff of an institution primary responsibility for the quality of academic degree offerings, the content of the curriculum, the evaluation of teaching and research, as well as for the rules and norms governing instruction, research, and public service (Dill, 2014). Indeed in one of her last publications Ostrom (Ostrom and Hess, 2007) applied her commons framework to universities and argued they are best understood as humanly constructed, self-organizing, 'knowledge commons'.

From research utilizing her model Ostrom (2005) has developed several principles of 'commons design'. The first principal requires public confirmation of the professional autonomy and responsibility of commons members to govern their own institutions. Implementing this design principle could strengthen the commons members' motivation and commitment to invest the necessary time and effort in collective actions required to address contemporary challenges to assuring effective performance. Research relevant to this principle would explore the 'external governance' of higher education, particularly the impacts on university behaviour of government policies. With regard to internal university governance and decision making, additional 'commons' design principles emphasize collective actions by commons members:

1) to develop more valid and reliable information for improving professional performance;
2) to enhance members' ability to learn new means of improving professional activities from one another; and
3) to develop more effective governance processes.

Systematic research on these types of university practices, employing as in Ostrom's approach careful field studies and/or as in the traditional economic approach, testable formal models of the efficiency and impacts of these types of processes, would be more consistent with the emerging perspective of organizational economics.

Conclusion

Over the many centuries of their existence, universities have been continually adjusting and adapting their internal governance and decision-making processes. As publicly supported or subsidized organizations, universities have necessarily been conscious of and responsive to legitimate government directives as well as resource allocation policies. But changes in the processes of instruction, research, and public service and their respective management within universities have also occurred over time, often without government influence. While dramatic changes in basic university instruction have been less common, even in the UK the development of the residential college system at Oxford and Cambridge, the adoption of the tutorial system, and in the nineteenth century the implementation of laboratory instruction all represented a significant change and arguably led to improvements in student learning. As previously suggested, the thoughtful adoption and implementation of ICT in student instruction within universities can potentially further improve student learning.[4] In the case of university research and scholarship, changes in methods, measures, and instruments over time have been continual, increasingly rapid, and significantly beneficial in improving academic knowledge and understanding. As noted, the recent changes in the collective management of research and research doctoral education within the OECD nations and EU universities also appear to be making positive improvements. Finally, substantial reforms in the processes for providing and managing university public services, including technology transfer, are under way in most nations. Understanding the impacts of these processes and how they can be continually improved for the public good remains an important challenge.

Given the critical importance of higher education to individuals and society, collective actions to improve the effectiveness of university governance would genuinely be in the public interest. Consistent with the traditional values of academic research, the best means for assuring and continually improving the core academic processes of university instruction, research, and public service is through systematic, evidence-based analysis. As suggested, an economic perspective on organizational behaviour in higher education can make a valuable contribution to this effort.

Notes

1 I am grateful for the valuable comments on an earlier draft of this paper by Ron Barnett, Steven Hemelt, Paul Temple, and Boone Turchi, but I remain solely responsible for the arguments presented.

2 One of the classic models of organizational behaviour traditionally applied to universities is Weick's (1976) concept of 'loose-coupling'. In his original article Weick used educational organizations to illustrate his conception of decentralized or loosely coordinated units within organizations. However, in a subsequent reconceptualization (Orton and Weick, 1990) Weick expressed concern that the concept was being interpreted in the unidimensional sense of 'decoupled', when his original meaning was a dialectic, that is, autonomous units that are still connected and coordinated, but loosely so. The recent research on governance in high-ranking universities (Paradeise and Thoenig, 2013) echoes the importance of the organizational integrating processes of communication, social interaction, and reaffirmation of shared values, which Weick also emphasized in his reconceptualization.

[3] For an insightful analysis of the collegial university processes in the USA that contribute to producing high-quality academic work, see Thoenig and Paradeise (2014).

[4] See for example the ICT-related university courses available from the Open Learning Initiative at Carnegie Mellon University that were rigorously designed and developed utilizing research on student learning: http://oli.cmu.edu/.

References

Aghion, P., Dewatripont, M., Hoxby, C., Mas-Colell, A., and Sapir, A. (2010) 'The governance and performance of universities: Evidence from Europe and the US'. *Economic Policy*, 25, 7–59.

Baldridge, J. (1971) *Power and Conflict in the University: Research in the sociology of complex organizations*. New York: John Wiley.

Baumol, W. and Bowen, W. (1966) *Performing Arts, the Economic Dilemma: A study of problems common to theater, opera, music, and dance*. Cambridge, MA: MIT Press.

Becker, G. (1994) *Human Capital: A theoretical and empirical analysis with special reference to education*. Chicago: University of Chicago Press.

Bendor, J., Moe, T., and Shotts, K. (2001) 'Recycling the garbage can: An assessment of the research program'. *The American Political Science Review*, 95 (1), 169–90.

Bowen, W. (2013) *Higher Education in the Digital Age*. Princeton, NJ: Princeton University Press.

Bowen, W., Chingos, M., Lack, K., and Nygren, T. (2014) 'Interactive learning online at public universities: Evidence from a six-campus randomized trial'. *Journal of Policy Analysis and Management*, 33 (1), 94–111.

Byrne, J., Jørgensen, T., and Loukkola, T. (2013) *Quality Assurance in Doctoral Education: Results of the ARDE project*. Brussels: European University Association.

Carroll, K., Dickson, L., and Ruseski, J. (2012) *Do Faculty Matter? Effects of faculty participation in university decisions*. Department of Economics, University of Maryland, Baltimore County (UMBC). Online. http://economics. umbc.edu/files/2014/09/wp_13_06.pdf (accessed 11 April 2016).

Clark, B. (1987) *The Academic Life: Small worlds, different worlds*. Princeton, NJ: The Carnegie Foundation for the Advancement of Teaching.

Cohen, M. and March, J. (1986) *Leadership and Ambiguity: The American college president*. Cambridge, MA: Harvard Business Press.

Cohen, M., March, J., and Olsen, J. (1972) 'A garbage can model of organizational choice'. *Administrative Science Quarterly*, 17 (1), 1–25.

— (2012) 'A "garbage can model" at forty: A solution that still attracts problems'. In Lomi, A. and Harrison, J. (eds) *The Garbage Can Model of Organizational Choice: Looking forward at forty*. Bingley, UK: Emerald Group.

Colombo, M. and Delmastro, M. (2008) *The Economics of Organizational Design: Theory and empirical insights*. Basingstoke: Palgrave Macmillan.

Dill, D. (2014) 'Academic governance in the US: Implications of a "commons" perspective'. In Shattock, M. (ed.) *International Trends in University Governance: Autonomy, self-government and the distribution of authority*. Abingdon: Routledge.

— (2015) 'Assuring the public good in higher education: Essential framework conditions and academic values'. In Filippakou, O. and Williams, G. (eds) *Higher Education as a Public Good: Critical perspectives on theory, policy and practice*. Oxford: Peter Lang.

Dill, D. and van Vught, F. (2010) *National Innovation and the Academic Research Enterprise: Public policy in global perspective*. Baltimore, MD: Johns Hopkins University Press.

Garvin, D. (1980) *The Economics of University Behavior*. New York: Academic Press.

Geiger, R. (1993) *Research and Relevant Knowledge: American research universities since World War II*. Oxford: Oxford University Press.

Gibbons, R. and Roberts, J. (eds) (2013) *The Handbook of Organizational Economics*. Princeton, NJ: Princeton University Press.

Hage, J. (1974) *Communication and Organizational Control: Cybernetics in health and welfare settings*. New York: John Wiley.

Hood, C. (1991) 'A public management for all seasons'. *Public Administration*, 69 (1), 3–19.

Huisman, J., de Boer, H., Dill, D., and Souto-Otero, M. (eds) (2015) *The Palgrave International Handbook of Higher Education Policy and Governance*. Basingstoke: Palgrave Macmillan.

Kaplan, G. (2004) 'How academic ships actually navigate'. In Ehrenberg, R. (ed.) *Governing Academia*. Ithaca, NY: Cornell University Press.

— (2006) 'Institutions of academic governance and institutional theory: A framework for further research'. In Smart, J. (ed.) *Higher Education Handbook of Theory and Research*. Vol. XXI. Dordrecht: Springer.

Kezar, A. and Eckel, P. (2004) 'Meeting today's governance challenges: A synthesis of the literature and examination of a future agenda for scholarship'. *The Journal of Higher Education*, 75 (4), 371–99.

Kogan, M. (1984) 'The political view'. In Clark, B. (ed.) *Perspectives on Higher Education: Eight disciplinary and comparative views*. Los Angeles, CA: University of California Press.

Lazega, E. (2001) *The Collegial Phenomenon: The social mechanisms of cooperation among peers in a corporate law partnership*. Oxford: Oxford University Press.

Lomi, A. and Harrison, J. (eds) (2012) *The Garbage Can Model of Organizational Choice: Looking forward at forty*. Bingley, UK: Emerald Group.

McPherson, M. and Schapiro, M. (1999) 'Tenure issues in higher education'. *The Journal of Economic Perspectives*, 13, 85–98.

Mintzberg, H. (1979) *The Structuring of Organizations*. Englewood Cliffs, NJ: Prentice Hall.

Olsen, J. (2001) 'Garbage cans, new institutionalism, and the study of politics'. *The American Political Science Review*, 95 (1), 191–8.

Orton, J. and Weick, K. (1990) 'Loosely coupled systems: A reconceptualization'. *The Academy of Management Review*, 15 (2), 203–23.

Ostrom, E. (2005) *Understanding Institutional Diversity*. Princeton, NJ: Princeton University Press.

— (2010) 'Beyond markets and states: Polycentric governance of complex economic systems'. *American Economic Review*, 100 (3), 641–72.

Ostrom, E. and Hess, C. (2007) 'A framework for analyzing the knowledge commons'. In Hess, C. and Ostrom, E. (eds) *Understanding Knowledge as a Commons: From theory to practice*. Cambridge, MA: MIT Press.

Paradeise, C. and Thoenig, J.-C. (2013) 'Academic institutions in search of quality: Local orders and global standards'. *Organization Studies*, 34 (2), 189–218.

Shattock, M. (2010) 'Managerialism and collegialism in higher education institutions'. In Peterson, P., Baker, E., and McGaw, B. (eds) *International Encyclopedia of Education*. Third edition. Oxford: Elsevier.

Tapper, T. and Palfreyman, D. (2010) *The Collegial Tradition in the Age of Mass Higher Education*. Dordrecht: Springer.

Thoenig, J.-C. and Paradeise, C. (2014) 'Organizational governance and the production of academic quality: Lessons from two top U.S. research universities'. *Minerva*, 52, 381–417.

Weick, K. (1976) 'Educational organizations as loosely coupled systems'. *Administrative Science Quarterly*, 21, 1–19.

Weimer, D. and Vining, A. (1996) 'Economics'. In Kettl, D. and Milward, H. (eds) *The State of Public Management*. Baltimore, MD: Johns Hopkins University Press.

Williams, G. (1984) 'The economic approach'. In Clark, B. (ed.) *Perspectives on Higher Education: Eight disciplinary and comparative views*. Los Angeles, CA: University of California Press.

— (1995) 'The "marketization" of higher education: Reform and potential reforms in higher education finance'. In Dill, D. and Sporn, B. (eds) *Emerging Patterns of Social Demand and University Reform: Through a glass darkly*. Oxford: IAU Press/Pergamon.

— (1997) 'The market route to mass higher education: British experience 1979–1996'. *Higher Education Policy*, 10 (3/4), 275–89.

— (2004) 'The higher education market in the United Kingdom'. In Teixeira, P., Jongbloed, B., Dill, D., and Amaral, A. (eds) *Markets in Higher Education: Rhetoric or reality?* Dordrecht: Kluwer Academic Publishers.

— (2013) 'A bridge too far: An economic critique of marketization of higher education'. In Callender, C. and Scott, P. (eds) *Browne and Beyond: Modernizing English higher education*. London: IOE Press.

Chapter 6

Massification, austerity, and the academic profession

D. Bruce Johnstone

It was an honour to be asked to contribute to this much-deserved Festschrift for Gareth Williams and to be recognized as a scholarly peer not only of Gareth, but of the other eminent contributors to this volume. Our paths first crossed when I began to study higher education finance and student loans in international comparative perspective in the 1970s. I maintained this interest, albeit at a much reduced scholarly output, through successive higher education administrative posts, culminating in chief executive officer of the State University of New York system, which I left in 1994 to assume a professorship in higher and comparative education at the University at Buffalo. There I began the International Comparative Higher Education Finance and Accessibility Project through which I became even more aware of the significance of Gareth's work. It helped me to understand better not only my developing theory of higher educational *cost-sharing*, but also the great diversity of political, ideological, and cultural forms the financing of higher education takes in its worldwide context. Gareth has been keenly interested in the phenomena of massification and financial austerity. This chapter will examine both of these forces, with particular attention to their effect on the academic profession – to which all contributors to this Festschrift in some way belong.

Introduction

Higher education throughout the world has come under great and accelerating stress from two phenomena, separate but highly related. The first is 'massification', or increasing enrolments, which have a profound impact on the very nature of higher educational institutions (colleges and universities); on the way they are organized and governed; on their curricula and the degrees, diplomas, and certificates awarded; on the nature of the students enrolled (e.g. their academic preparedness, aspirations, and programmatic interests); and on the academic profession.

The second phenomenon profoundly affecting higher education in almost all countries is increasing financial austerity, or the diverging trajectories between surging costs of instruction and research, and the increasingly limited revenues in most countries to meet these needs. Some degree of financial austerity, at least to those of us within the industry, as it were, has been part of most universities (public and private alike) in most countries at most times. However, financial austerity seems to be growing, driven in part by a seemingly natural tendency of college and university instructional costs – and thus their revenue needs – to rise at annual rates generally exceeding the rates of increase of costs and prices in the larger economies. Thus, increasing enrolments, or massification, which was posited as the first of the two phenomena to be examined, compound these naturally increasing costs and revenue needs, further straining public budgets and greatly contributing to financial stress in higher educational systems.

This chapter will first elaborate on these two phenomena – massification and financial austerity – and then address their effects on the academic profession worldwide. In each case, special attention will be placed on the *margins* of growth (or decline). For increases in enrolment, for example, we will look for a difference (on average) between the additional students – that is, those who in the recent past were not seeking entry to higher education, but now are – compared with those traditionally accommodated. For increasing fiscal stress, we look to the impact on the nature and quality of instruction between having to increase average class size from 20 to 30, as may have had to have been done in the past, compared with an increase from 50 to 60, which may be today's marginal impact – or of adding one course to a teaching load compared with adding two courses, or of having to cut a university budget by 5 per cent during the first year of cutbacks compared with having to do it for the fourth and then a fifth year in a row. Similarly, the effect on the academic profession can also be viewed *on the margin*: that is, the average qualifications of the newly added professors compared with the degree levels, teaching experience, or scholarly contributions of the professoriate prior to, or at an earlier stage of, massification.

Massification

The numbers of students and of institutions have been surging worldwide for decades. Increasing enrolments – which of course exacerbate the underlying increase in per student costs, and thus exacerbate the financial austerity of institutions and especially of national systems of higher education – are a function of three primary forces that vary greatly among countries. The first of these is *demographics*: specifically the change (generally the growth) over time in the number of youth within the conventional college or university age cohort (ages 18 to about 24). Some countries – most notably Japan and Russia, but also including Germany, Italy, and other countries in southern Europe – are experiencing demographic declines. Most countries, however, and nearly all middle- and low-income countries, are experiencing increases in the traditional university-age cohort.

The second force affecting enrolments is the *participation rate* of this (generally increasing) university-age cohort. Increasing participation, in turn, is a function of: (a) increases in enrolments and completions at academic secondary levels; (b) changing employment opportunities, especially the loss of unskilled jobs in manufacturing and agriculture, and a belief that one's chances for the remaining good jobs require – or will at least be enhanced by – higher or further education; and (c) an increasing political and civic regard for social and economic mobility and more equal opportunities, leading to policies designed to increase higher educational participation, particularly among those traditionally less represented, such as ethnic and linguistic minorities, girls (in some cultures), or students from poor secondary schools or otherwise thought to be educationally disadvantaged.

Sub-Saharan Africa illustrates the effect of an increasing population compounded by increasing participation, as measured by a country's gross enrolment ratio (GER), and the massive enrolment increases that lie ahead for that generally impoverished part of the world. The UNESCO Institute of Statistics reports that tertiary enrolments grew from fewer than 200,000 in 1970 to more than 4.5 million in 2008, or an increase of more than 20 times. In spite of this surge, fuelled in part by increases in most countries of their higher educational participation rates, the GERs in 2009, with few exceptions such as Mauritius and Namibia, remained extremely low: under 4 per cent in countries such as Burkina Faso, Burundi, Central African Republic, Chad, Eritrea, Ethiopia, Madagascar, Malawi, Niger, and Uganda. In other words, in spite of the remarkable surge in tertiary enrolments, these (and many other African countries) are still at what Martin Trow (1974) termed an 'elite stage' – with massification and the millions of additional students and billions of annual revenue needs so implied – still lying ahead (UNESCO, 2010).

A final factor affecting enrolments in some countries is the increasing amount, or final level, of higher education per entering student. This, too, is an *accelerating* factor, as many first degree graduates perceive a need for even higher levels of education to be competitive (e.g. the growth of MBAs and other professional master's degrees) and as professions (especially licensed professions such as teachers, and the non-physician health professions) endeavour to raise the required higher educational credentials for professional licensure to master's or beyond in order to limit the numbers allowed to practise and thus enhance their status and remuneration.[1]

The effect of massification, or enrolment expansion, can be viewed in three dimensions, which vary in significance among countries and which markedly affect a country's vulnerability or resilience to massification. The first is the size or scale of enrolments that the system, including both public and private sectors and the academic profession, must accommodate – generally at some substantial cost to taxpayers. For analytic purposes, total country or system enrolments need to be viewed relative to the size of the traditional university-age population, to the number of secondary school graduates, and to such other country-specific metrics as per capita income, overall public spending, and the nature of the economy and its present and future manpower needs.

The second is the rate of increase of these enrolments: a function of the rate of increase of the university-age population and the current rate at which this population surge is completing the academic secondary level and going on to a tertiary institution. The significance of the rate of enrolment growth lies in the commensurately necessary rate of growth of capital and infrastructure needs, as well as the time and investment required to produce the annually increasing numbers of faculty with appropriate qualifications to serve the additional students.

The third dimension of massification is the stage of the enrolment expansion: that is, whether the expansion is just emerging from Trow's *elite* stage – suggesting that the students on the edge of the expansion could be relatively well prepared and academically motivated – or whether the expansion is towards the upper edge of *universal*, in which case the newer students may be statistically more likely to be seeking a shorter cycle, more vocationally oriented institution and be more likely to need special attention in order to persevere and complete.

Teichler and Bürger reported more than 51 million tertiary education students worldwide in 1980, which number nearly tripled to more than 139 million by 2006 (2009: 155). The official background paper for the UNESCO World Conference on Higher Education (Altbach *et al.*, 2009) reported an estimate of some 150 million students worldwide. While the rate of enrolment increase will surely slow in the wealthy countries of the OECD, due both to a slowdown (and in a few countries to a reversal) of demographic increases, and also to what may be a near-saturation in participation, the rapid increase in the numbers of university-age youth and the still-low participation rates in most of the rest of the world portend a continuation of these surging enrolments for decades to come.

Financial austerity

The other dominant phenomenon impacting higher education and the academic profession in recent decades is financial austerity. As stated in the introduction, austerity is partly a function of the massification that imposes on higher education the costs of – or at least the needs for – additional faculty, classrooms, laboratories, and lecture theatres as well as entirely new institutions and campuses. However, even without increasing enrolments, higher education faces a natural upwards trajectory of increasing unit, or per student, costs – and therefore of increasing revenue needs – that tend to exceed a country's prevailing rate of inflation generally, as well as, in some nations, the rate of increase of average household income. Most seriously, when this underlying rate of increase in per student costs is combined with the rate of increase in enrolments in most countries – and especially in middle- and low-income countries – the result is a trajectory of increasing costs and revenue needs that almost inevitably exceeds the rate of increase of available revenues, whether from the state or families or students.

The basis for this supposedly natural rate of increase in per student costs is the assumption that this rate tends to track the rate of increase of wages and salaries in the academic profession, which in turn tends to track wage and salary increases in the general economy – which, if there is any real growth in the economy, tend to rise at a rate of increase slightly in excess of the prevailing rate of inflation. This is the so-called *cost disease*, or the phenomenon of the *rising relative unit costs* in the labour-intensive, productivity-resistant, sectors of the economy, including symphony orchestras, schools, and universities, which have few opportunities for the substitution of capital for labour – the main engine of growth in the goods-producing sectors of the economy (Baumol and Bowen, 1966; Johnstone and Marcucci, 2010).

In fact, the only way for unit costs in higher education (within the productivity-resistant sectors of an economy) not to increase faster than those in manufacturing (within the productivity-receptive sector of the economy) would be either for wages in higher education to lag below wages generally, or for a form of productivity increase to be forced upon colleges and universities – as when budgets are cut, student:faculty ratios forced upwards, and the costs per student thus held below unit costs in the general economy – both of which have been occurring in higher education in many countries, effectively reversing the historic tendency of per student costs to rise at rates greater than the prevailing rate of inflation. At the same time, while the per student costs of instruction can indeed be lowered by increasing class size and teaching loads and by employing low-paid, part-time faculty, such steps almost certainly diminish the quality of both instruction and scholarship: *cheaper instruction* is not necessarily more productive higher education.

Accelerating the rate of unit (or per student) cost increases in higher education is the great infusion of technology. Admittedly, technology has had a profound and mainly beneficial impact, enhancing both instruction and research. Its contributions include, for example: the Internet, which allows students to access readings, lectures, and even entire courses; word processing, which allows students, faculty, and staff to write faster and more cleanly and with far less (if any) secretarial assistance; student information systems, which allow students and advisers to track and advise on academic progress better; the ubiquitous digitization of books, journals, and other information and their low-cost accessibility to students and scholars; high-speed computing and advanced statistical packages, which allow faster and vastly more complex calculating and modelling. These and other examples surely enhance the amount and quality of research, the effectiveness of management, the potential quality of instruction – and greater all-round convenience.

However, public budgets and tuition dollars are still associated with an output not of learning, or of the quality of scholarship, or of convenience, but with credit hours accumulated, or full-time equivalent students served. These so-called outputs are only marginally, if at all, increased by these otherwise costly increments of technology. And thus the productivity-enhancing effects of technology in higher education are typically not recognized, while the increased costs of the equipment and the labour associated with technology – and hence the increased per student costs – are.

Other features of higher education that tend to increase per student costs include:

- academic drift: away from a concentration on teaching towards costlier research and scholarship, as well as the smaller classes and lighter teaching loads associated with graduate instruction;
- constant change as new programmes are added, almost always faster than old ones – and their faculty and staff – can be shed;
- the already high and rapidly increasing costs of research, especially in the physical and biomedical sciences with their high technology expenses, and especially where faculty and administrative ambition are content not simply with a constant share of prestige or of the enrolment market, but where the elite and the *would be* elite universities seek

greater scholarly recognition, better and more academically qualified students, and higher rankings on such international league tables as the *Times Higher Education*'s 'World's Top 200 Universities' or Shanghai Jiao Tong University's 'Academic Ranking of World Universities'.

Higher education finance, then, is burdened with a natural unit cost trajectory that in normal years it will exceed the average rate of increase of consumer prices generally: that is, it will naturally exceed the rate of inflation. When the accelerating factor of enrolment expansion is added – which of course differs dramatically among countries, but is greatest in the low- and middle-income countries – the upwards trajectory of higher education's costs and revenue needs is dramatic. At the same time, the sources of revenue to meet these rapidly increasing needs are in very many countries limited. Governments everywhere struggle under escalating burdens of pensions and the rising costs of elementary and secondary education, health care, public infrastructure, security, and other social welfare costs. Electorates in many highly industrialized countries have been getting more conservative, particularly in their distaste for taxation and what they perceive to be wasteful government spending. Many European countries, with their high social welfare costs, and typically spending from a third to more than half of national gross domestic product in the public sector, are trying to shift productive resources to the private sector and to reduce public deficits to comply with the requirements of the European Community and the Euro Zone.[2]

Russia and the other countries that emerged from the former Soviet Union, as well as the transitional countries of Central and Eastern Europe, continue to labour under the costs of building an internationally competitive economy and weaning a labour force away from its former dependence on state enterprises and governmental employment. The USA struggles with an over-consuming, under-saving population that is unwilling to tax itself for the public benefits it demands. Japan faces labour shortages even in its still-stagnant economy. Even China faces an ageing population, an insufficient number of new high knowledge content jobs to absorb its soaring annual numbers of new college and university graduates, and a declining growth rate.

Taxation in the developing countries, where production and incomes often tend to be low anyway, is technically difficult. The financial challenge to governments is how to get a share of purchasing power when relatively little wealth comes from large, stable enterprises that can be taxed and that can also be counted upon to withhold taxes from their employees. Former communist countries, once dependent on easy and extensive turnover taxes on state-owned enterprises, now need to tax personal or corporate incomes, retail or commercial transactions, and/or property – all of which are difficult to calculate, expensive to collect, and relatively easy to evade. Businesses and individuals in many countries seem increasingly able to hide incomes and the value of their taxable assets. And even in the wealthy, highly industrialized countries with efficient tax systems, the increasing globalization of the world economy encourages productive enterprises and wealthy individuals to move to countries with lower taxes.

Aside from the limitations on taxation, governments everywhere are contending with politically and socially compelling competing needs for these increasingly scarce tax revenues. In much of the developing world and in many transitional countries, the competitors for public revenue include the replacement of decrepit public infrastructure, unfunded pension obligations, the need for a more adequate social safety net, and the cost of reversing generations of environmental degradation. Finally, although the government (or taxpayer) in most developing countries as throughout the world will continue to be the principal revenue source for public higher education, most or even all of whatever limited additional revenue can be squeezed out of the public treasuries for higher education will be absorbed by the need to accommodate the inevitably expanding enrolments, leaving little or nothing to accommodate what ought to be the rising unit, or per student, costs (much less allowing investment in new programmes and pedagogies or in academic research).

Adding to the financial austerity affecting higher education – particularly in the USA, Europe, and most other advanced industrialized countries – was the serious economic downturn that began with the collapse of the US financial markets in 2008, but then quickly spread, revealing such problems as high levels of public debt and possibly unsustainable future pension and health-care obligations. Unemployment in many OECD countries in the middle of the second decade of the twenty-first century remains high, and economic growth in many countries remains tepid. The response in most governments has been to curtail public spending wherever possible; and public colleges and universities in many countries have been especially vulnerable to such budget cuts. In the USA, for example, Mitchell *et al.* for the Center on Budget and Policy Priorities wrote:

> Most states have begun in the past year to restore some of the cuts they made to higher education funding after the recession [of 2008–10]. Eight states, though, are still cutting, and in almost all

states – including those that have boosted their support – higher education funding remains well below pre-recession levels. The large funding cuts have led to both steep tuition [fee] increases and spending cuts that may diminish the quality of education available to students at a time when a highly educated workforce is more crucial than ever to the nation's economic future.

(Mitchell *et al.*, 2014: 1)

The State Higher Education Executive Officers (SHEEO) Association, which monitors the finances of public higher education in the 50 US states, reported that appropriations as a percentage of total public higher education revenue fell from a high of 68 per cent in 2008 (the first year of the financial collapse) to a low of 50.4 per cent in 2013 before rising only slightly to 51.1 per cent in 2014 – vividly documenting the shift in the higher educational cost burden in the USA from government to parents and students (SHEEO, 2014: 9).

As in the USA, public institutions in Canada, Australia, Chile, Japan, and in no country more so than England, have supplemented declining governmental tax revenues with steeply rising tuition fees, paid either by parents or by students through loans, or through so-called deferred fees (Johnstone and Marcucci, 2010; ICHEFA website). However, even this source of revenue seems to have limits – reflected in the mounting debt loads and rising defaults, which simply place the burden back on governments and taxpayers. Public colleges and universities in most US states, for example, while subsidized, pass 40 to 60 per cent or more of undergraduate instruction costs on to parents and students in the form of tuition fees. At my own State University of New York at Buffalo, which remains slightly lower in cost to students than many US research universities, in-state students in 2015/16 will pay $9,334 in tuition and other fees, another $12,762 for university-provided lodging and meals, and an estimated average of $3,624 in other expenses, or a total cost to the student and family for one year of more than $27,000.

Expansion at the margins

Clearly, the expansion of enrolments – assuming some increase in resources to meet at least some of the additional costs – means some concomitant increase in the number of institutions and academic programmes as well as in the number of faculty and other members of the higher educational profession. However, as the numbers of students, institutions, programmes, and faculty continue to increase, those additions – at the margin – will probably be unlike the typical or even the average students, institutions, and faculty of the past, even of the very recent past. In other words, the marginal student – that is, the student who is entering higher education now, but would probably not have been entering a decade ago – is likely to be statistically different from the average and the marginal student of the past, when far fewer completed academic secondary school, both aspiring and financially able to go on to a university. Similarly, the new institutions at the margin of institutional expansion are likely to look less like the country's more venerable universities and feature academic standards and programmes that are thought to be more appropriate for the new students. And the new faculty that are hired to teach at these new institutions will, at least on average, be less likely to hold the highest degree in their field and be less oriented to research than the faculty of the existing universities.

Thus, the concept of *marginal* as is being used here does not mean *inferior*, but merely statistically likely to be different from the typical past or current average. As applied to the nature of students at the margin of expanded enrolments, the likelihood of going on to higher education in all countries has always been to some degree *socio-economically constructed*: that is, drawing both on the quality of secondary schools (and in some cultures tutors), the cultural capital of parents and peers, the typically more ambitious academic expectations of upper-middle and upper-class families, and their financial ability to afford both the fees and the student living expenses associated with higher education. The marginal student, then, as we are using this term, is statistically less likely to draw on these advantages.

At early stages of massification, such as moving from elite to mass higher education, which is still the case in many low-income and some middle-income countries, the principal barriers to the expansion of higher educational participation are likely to be all of the following:

- cultural (i.e. little expectation of higher – or sometimes even of secondary – education, especially for girls);
- financial (i.e. the inability to afford fees or the expenses of living away from home);
- ethnic or linguistic discrimination;
- poor secondary schools (especially in rural areas); or
- insufficient higher educational capacity (most often restricting the growth of colleges and vocationally oriented, short-cycle institutions).

These early stage barriers are theoretically remediable by economic growth, modernization, and the right governmental policies. However, the improvement of elementary and secondary schools, the expansion of higher educational capacity, and overcoming the financial barriers to higher educational participation take time and a great deal of money – which, especially in low- and middle-income countries, must overcome the sheer difficulties of collecting taxes and then having to compete with all other claims on public revenue (including waste and corruption). Moreover, the essence of massification is not simply increasing enrolments, but increasing enrolment rates, or participation. A rapidly growing population can consume much additional public revenue and added higher educational capacity and still do little to move the participation rate.

In later stages of massification, as the quality of secondary education is improved throughout a country, as higher educational capacity is increased (sometimes, as in Latin America and much of East Asia, by the growth of private higher education), and as the academic ability for, and interest in, education beyond the secondary level becomes closer to universal, the barriers to even greater participation remain and may seem even more difficult to surmount. Culture still matters, but the barriers become more narrowly associated with extreme poverty, family breakdown, and ethnic or linguistic marginalization. The quest for increased participation may focus less on access and more on persistence and successful completion. Academic resources beyond faculty, laboratories, and lecture theatres may become more significant: professional advisers, counsellors, financial aid experts, remedial education specialists, and on-the-job training programmes.

The goal in most countries is for the young person at the margin of higher educational participation to be defined less by the socio-economic status of his or her parents or by gender, ethnicity, region, or home language than by academic interest or native intellectual capacity. There will always – even in affluent countries well into the stage of universal higher education – be those students on the participation marginal who are statistically likely to be:

- less well prepared, as they will increasingly come from more rural locations and from less well-resourced and less academically intensive secondary schools;
- less financially secure, and thus more subject to the need to borrow and/or to have to work concurrently at a part-time (or even a full-time) job, and thus to be more likely to drop out;
- less academically motivated and more ambivalent about the sacrifices and personal discipline that higher educational success requires, and thus less inclined to persist on to degree completion;

- less inclined, as well as less financially able, to matriculate full time in a college or university far away from home, and thus commensurately more inclined to attend a local, less academically selective, and less prestigious institution;
- for all of the above reasons, more attracted to the shorter-cycle, more vocationally oriented programmes and to attend part-time.

Following on from the above conjectures, as enrolments expand and new institutions are created to accommodate this increased demand, the newer institutions – that is, at the institutional margin of enrolment expansion, whether new public institutions or the new institutions of an expanding private sector – are more likely to feature less costly programmes (thus favouring the social sciences and humanities over the sciences or engineering), shorter-cycle programmes (favouring bachelor's and sub-bachelor's over master's and doctoral programmes), and institutions of less selectivity and academic prestige. The older, more venerable higher educational institutions in almost all countries tend to conform to the classic research university model, which features academically selective students, an academic staff that has gained their posts through a lengthy period of graduate study and apprenticeship and who are oriented primarily to research and to their (increasingly globalized) disciplines, an orientation to graduate (master's and doctoral) programmes in the traditional arts and sciences and the advanced professional fields, and a university governance model that vests substantial authority and influence to the senior faculty (as opposed to authority and influence vested more in management and governing boards).[3] In contrast, the newer institutions that have been added to national systems to accommodate increased demand for places – whether public, private non-profit, or private for-profit – are more likely to be less academically selective, to feature more applied programmes at the bachelor and sub-bachelor levels, and to incorporate a largely teaching academic staff that are more part-time and less apt to possess the highest degree in their fields. Furthermore, as the fastest growing enrolments – driven by rapidly increasing youth cohorts and rapidly increasing participation rates – are occurring mainly in the low- and middle-income countries, which also tend to have the most constrained state treasuries as well as the most socially and politically compelling competition for the available public revenue, these newer public institutions will tend to be less well-resourced than the existing institutions.

In combination with a student body that tends, as we noted above, to be somewhat less affluent and less academically prepared, and more inclined towards the shorter-cycle practical programmes, the newer, or *marginal*, institutions are likely to focus on teaching rather than research, on bachelor and sub-bachelor programmes, and on less expensive part-time rather than full-time faculty. In fact, in many low- and middle-income countries, the surging revenue needs implied by the rapidly increasing student enrolment demands simply cannot be met by public institutions, even by short-cycle bachelor and sub-bachelor colleges with lower per student costs than the older universities. Throughout Latin America, much of Asia, Africa, and the former Communist, or transitional, countries, the inability of the public sector to meet the expansion of student numbers has led to very rapid increases in the numbers of institutions that are private (either non-profit or for-profit) or to private (or self-funded) tracks within public universities – or in the case of China to essentially separate, self-funded colleges owned by public universities. For the most part (although with significant exceptions), the more prestigious, selective institutions continue to be the older public universities; the newer private institutions – those on the institutional margin – are sometimes termed *demand absorbing*.

Massification and financial austerity impacting the academic profession

Finally, the perspective of the marginal being statistically different from the typical or the average in the face of rapid and lasting expansion applies as well to the academic profession. In keeping with the likelihood that the marginal student is likely to be less academically prepared and committed, and the marginal institution less scholarly and less well-resourced, the faculty on the margin of expansion are less likely to be full-time, to hold the highest degree in their fields, and to be oriented to research. Again, this assertion should not be construed as suggesting a newer or younger academic profession that is necessarily less able or less committed to their profession. But the veritable explosion of enrolments in so many countries – nowhere more than in China – has required a yearly numerical increase in the academic profession that would have been impossible to accommodate by the annual numbers completing the highest degrees in their fields and desiring to join the academic profession. Altbach *et al.*, in their report prepared for UNESCO's 2009 World Conference on Higher Education, stated that the academic profession is 'under stress as never before [and that] responding to the demands of massification with the fast deployment of greater numbers of teachers has resulted in a decline of the average qualification for academics in many countries' (Altbach *et al.*, 2009: 5).

In summary, the academic profession at the margin of higher education's great expansion can be expected to be:

- less likely to be full-time and more likely to hold several part-time teaching jobs;
- if full-time, less likely to be permanent or tenured;
- less likely to hold a PhD (or other terminal degree); and
- less likely to be oriented to research and one's scholarly reputation.

But changes in the academic profession that are linked to financial austerity (as well as political demands for greater accountability) will not be limited to the institutions we have identified as short-cycle, teaching-oriented, or otherwise on the margin of institutional expansion. Even in research universities that are generally well-resourced and able to retain the classical Humboldtian configuration, the academic staff are being increasingly differentiated, with fewer of the professors able to count on the low teaching loads and specialization that permitted a lifetime orientation to research. Martin Finkelstein, in his essay *The Morphing of the American Academic Profession* (2003), wrote of:

> ... attempts to functionally re-specialize the full-time faculty role: that is, create full-time positions that do not require the integrated (and costly) Humboldtian model wherein full-time faculty are now hired as teaching-only or even lower division / introductory courses teaching-only; or in the natural sciences and the professions, research- or clinical-only or even primarily administrative roles in program development and management.
>
> (Finkelstein, 2003: 6)

With respect to the wealthy industrialized countries, the Centre for Educational Research and Innovation of the OECD conducted a study, published in two volumes in 2009, on the likely effects of demography and globalization on tertiary education within the 30 member countries of the OECD.[4] The Executive Summary of the Demography volume concluded with three summary points on the impact of expansion and other forces upon the professoriate in these countries, concluding that:

- the academic profession will be more internationally oriented and mobile, but still structured in accordance with national circumstances;
- the activities of the profession will be more diversified and specialized, and subject to varied payment contracts; and

- the profession will move away from the traditional conception of a self-regulated community of professionals and towards a model and consensus to be based on fresh principles.

(OECD, 2009: 14)

The financial downturn that began with the 2008–10 so-called Great Recession and the related European debt crisis are still, as of 2015, affecting mainly the wealthier countries of the OECD, although low- and middle-income countries such as China, whose prosperity depends on exports, have also been affected. However, the countries that have been least affected by the downturn include most of the countries that are low-income to begin with and that have felt the greatest financial pressure from the sheer expansion of enrolment demand. In short, whether from unrelenting massification, from prolonged economic weakness, or from governments and electorates forcing budget cuts and so-called *efficiencies* on to their public colleges and universities, higher education has been contending with a worsening financial austerity almost throughout the world in the decades around the turn of the twenty-first century. And as expansion and state financial distress have much the same effect on the academic profession, these two forces complement and aggravate one another.

Thus, just as surging enrolments alone can outrun the supply of PhD holders seeking full-time college and university posts in a particular country, leading to the need to employ more part-time and less credentialled faculty, fiscal distress and collapsing college and university budgets have the same effect. Just as the natural marginal growth of enrolments and institutions tends to shift in the direction of bachelor's and sub-bachelor's colleges and away from costlier research universities, so does governmental fiscal stress, whether stemming from recession, other public priorities, or the need to reduce a long-term public deficit. And both fiscal stress and expansion seem here in the world to stay, at least for several more decades.

The salient question, then, for the academic profession is whether the changes of the past decade or two will turn around – as they might with the return of good economic times to the countries of the OECD – or whether they are here to stay, and perhaps to portend changes in the profession that are even more profound. Might instructional technology, for example, bring great changes to institutions, to instruction as we have known it, and thus to the academic profession – quite apart from the need to accommodate far more students or to adjust to a permanent financial downsizing? Might more and more students receive instruction from the Internet, changing the instructional role of professors from lecturers to guides and assessors?

Might the conduct of research return from the universities to private and public institutes and laboratories?

Richard Lewis, for the OECD's forecast of higher education through the year 2030 (Lewis, 2009: 348–9), considers what he called 'a possibly more fundamental change: the end of, or the redefinition of, higher education' with likely future changes including:

- greatly increased participation rates in higher education, already around 80 per cent in some developed countries;
- the growing gap between the content of the bachelor's and (in some cases) master's degree and the 'frontiers of knowledge'; and
- the perhaps inevitable consequence of the first two points that a very much smaller percentage of those engaged in teaching undergraduates will be engaged in research or even advanced scholarship or consultancy.

Conclusions

Clearly, the academic profession is changing throughout the world. At least for the senior professoriate at reasonably well-resourced research universities (such as the contributors to this volume), the academic profession has accorded prestige, job security, and a level of autonomy (including control over one's time and an absence of supervision) that is virtually unknown to other professions or occupations. Massification is diminishing these features, particularly (but not exclusively) for those engaged on the margin of institutional expansion, which is increasingly more teaching-oriented, less scholarly, less prestigious, more regimented, and less secure.

Financial austerity, which leads to similar changes, is partly a function of massification, particularly in countries in which the expansion of youth seeking admittance to higher education is surging, propelled by increasing numbers of youth and low current enrolment ratios – both features associated with low- and middle-income countries that are also facing the greatest public revenue constraints and the most formidable queues of competing public needs. But financial austerity is a function of far more than massification. It derives as well from inefficiency and corruption, from an inability to tax fairly and cost-effectively, from the perception of an academic profession viewed as insufficiently productive and insufficiently committed to teaching, and in some advanced industrialized countries from a political ideological impatience with governments and governmental agencies generally. And it is the combination of massification and financial austerity that is so profoundly changing the nature of the academic profession.

The question posed here, but not answered, is whether these changes – particularly those diminishing the professionalism, job satisfaction, and job security once associated with the professoriate – will be ameliorated by economic and fiscal recovery and by the inevitable slowing of massification, thus restoring much of the lustre of the profession, or whether other forces, like technology, are already at work in altering the nature of colleges and universities as we have come to know them, and thus the nature of our profession.

Notes

[1] This may be countered in the European Bologna region with a shortened (bachelor's) first degree on the Continent. But early indications are that most bachelor's degree recipients in continental Europe prefer to go on, either for the master's in the same field or, as in the USA, to pursue a professional master's degree.

[2] Economic problems in Europe have been exacerbated by the debt crisis, especially, continuing in 2015, in Greece, but have also been worrisome in Ireland, Italy, Spain, and Portugal.

[3] Many observers note a shift in the direction of managerial authority in all institutions of higher education. However, this trend is most pronounced in the newer institutions at the margin of institutional expansion: that is, the public universities of applied science and technology on the European continent, the so-called *deemed* universities of India, the new provincial universities in China, the university colleges of East Africa, and virtually all of the newer private colleges and universities throughout the world.

[4] These 34 countries (as of 2015) include most of the highly industrialized countries of the world, including Europe (including the Central/East and European countries of the Czech Republic, Slovakia, Poland, Hungary, and Slovenia, as well as Turkey and Israel); the USA, Canada, Mexico, and Chile in the Americas; Japan and Korea in East Asia; and Australia and New Zealand in Oceania.

References

Altbach, P., Reisberg, L., and Rumbley, L. (2009) *Trends in Global Higher Education: Tracking an academic revolution.* Paris: UNESCO.

Baumol, W. and Bowen, W. (1966) *Performing Arts, the Economic Dilemma: A study of problems common to theater, opera, music, and dance.* Cambridge, MA: MIT Press.

Finkelstein, M. (2003) 'The morphing of the American academic profession'. *Liberal Education*, 89 (4), 1–12. Online. www.aacu.org/publications-research/periodicals/morphing-american-academic-profession (accessed 12 April 2016).

International Comparative Higher Education Finance and Accessibility Project (ICHEFA). Online. www.gse.buffalo.edu/org/IntHigherEdFinance (accessed 12 April 2016).

Johnstone, B. and Marcucci, P. (2010) *Financing Higher Education Worldwide: Who pays? Who should pay?* Baltimore, MD: Johns Hopkins University Press.

Lewis, R. (2009) 'Quality assurance in higher education: Its global future'. In OECD (ed.) *Higher Education to 2030, Volume 2: Globalisation.* Paris: Centre for Educational Research and Innovation, 323–55.

Mitchell, M., Palacios, V., and Leachman, M. (2014) *States Are Still Funding Higher Education Below Pre-Recession Levels*. Center for Budget and Policy Priorities. Online. www.cbpp.org/sites/default/files/atoms/files/5-1-14sfp.pdf (accessed 21 April 2016).

OECD (ed.) (2009) *Higher Education to 2030, Volume 1: Demography*. Paris: Centre for Educational Research and Innovation.

SHEEO (2014) *State Higher Education Finance 2014*. Online. http://tinyurl.com/gw8plwn (accessed 21 April 2016).

Teichler, U. and Bürger, S. (2009) 'Student enrollments and graduation trends in the OECD area: What can we learn from international statistics?' In OECD (ed.) *Higher Education to 2030, Volume 1: Demography*. Paris: Centre for Educational Research and Innovation.

Trow, M. (1974) 'Problems in the transition from elite to mass higher education'. In *General Report on Future Structures of Post-Secondary Education*. Paris: OECD.

UNESCO Institute for Statistics (UIS) (2010) *Trends in Tertiary Education: Sub-Saharan Africa*. UIS Fact Sheet, December, No. 10. Online. www.uis.unesco.org/FactSheets/Documents/fs10-2010-en.pdf (accessed 12 April 2016).

Chapter 7

Financing creativity in the global research economy: Performance management or knowledge construction?

Louise Morley

Introduction

As an eminent economist of higher education, Gareth Williams has been posing questions over the decades about the economic nature and dimensions, value, values, growth mechanisms, and future directions of the global academy. This chapter engages with one of Gareth Williams's concerns in relation to marketization. In this case, the focus will be the global research economy. I examine how the neoliberal policy cultures of financialization and market values are now entangled in research processes and management, and how the neoliberal gaze on research quality is installed and maintained. Performance indicators now relate overtly to income generation, research impact, and the number and grading of publications. Knowledge, it seems, is a significant form of capital. As such, it has the potential to produce and reinforce exclusions and maldistributions. Research is increasingly being instrumentalized as a vehicle for performance management, and is a major relay of power in the construction and destruction of academic identities, with symbolic, material, and affective consequences. In the context of economics imperialism, there are questions about what the future holds for critical scholarship.

The neoliberal research economy

Roger Brown (2008) attributed the early use of the term 'marketization' to Gareth Williams (1992). In his original usage, Williams applied it to student choice, and the construction of students as consumers in an expanding and competitive global market. Now, it appears to relate to the corporatization of the entire higher education sector. The economic doctrine has resulted in new forms of control that have been extended to employment regimes and research management. In this chapter, a goal is to interrogate the alignment of academic research with the political economy of neoliberalism. I do this by discussing how neoliberalism has been installed, via the discursive-material effects of the financialization and marketization of research, and consider its effects on academic identities. I examine how research financialization is in danger of producing an exclusionary and highly commodified research economy.

Neoliberalism is characterized by four central processes of change in the political economy of capitalism: privatization, deregulation, financialization, and globalization (Morley, 2015; Radice, 2013). These four processes privilege market relations and the knowledge economy, with its emphasis on cognitive capitalism (Moulier-Boutang, 2012). However, it would be erroneous to suggest that there is consensus about what constitutes neoliberalism or how its processes operate (Brown, 2015). Ball (2015) argues that it is incoherent, complex, unstable, and contradictory. The quixotic and somewhat abstract nature makes it hard to contest and contradict. A key goal of the neoliberal agenda is to reduce producer capture and disrupt monopolies. A common belief is that higher education benefits from being organized according to the market principles of privatization and competition (Teixeira and Dill, 2011). Neoliberalism's policy agenda in higher education is based on economic and social transformation under the sign of the free market, with institutional arrangements installed to implement this project (Connell, 2013). One aim of the neoliberal agenda is to reduce public investment in higher education. A further aim is to ensure more accountability for any investment that does come from the public purse (Morley, 2003). The introduction of new managerialism into the public services in the 1980s and 1990s made much of the bad old days where the public services were represented as self-serving, user-unfriendly, and impenetrable (Pollitt, 1993). Universities, argued Williams, 'provided fertile soil for the growth of market forms of organization and entrepreneurial behaviour' (2004: 242). Williams and Kitaev argued that the drivers of entrepreneurialism were ideology, expansion, the knowledge society, globalization, and financial stringency (2005: 129). Neoliberalism can be constructed as the force of modernization on archaic institutions. It is also heavily linked to austerity cultures that use financial stringency as a means of regulating values and priorities. However, neoliberalism can be experienced as a form of domination and injury, as it massively transforms employment regimes (Gill, 2010). Wherever it is conceptually located, neoliberalism represents a major values shift in the governance and purpose of higher education (Cribb and Gewirtz, 2013). One such value shift is the recasting of research in terms of an economic doctrine. In a moment of futurology, Williams suggested that: 'Research is likely to continue to be seen as one of the most powerful drivers of long-term improvements in economic and social welfare' (2011: 10).

It is pertinent to ask whether the socially driven values are being eroded by the focus on economics. Knowledge is now represented as a valuable form of capital and as a global commodity (OECD, 2013). Capitalism is increasingly about services, or higher-order production, rather than production of goods (Deleuze, 1992). In the neoliberal theory of knowledge production, the value of research is being financialized and technologized, producing effects that can be metricized, audited, and used for performance management (Holmwood, 2014; Power, 2014). New spaces of calculation and new visibilities are emerging (Ball, 2012). In other words, academics and their work are graded and classified in relation to how well they meet performance indicators and targets for income generation – often in a very public way. Financialization attempts to reduce all value that is exchanged into either a financial instrument or a derivative of a financial instrument (Peters *et al.*, 2014). It places higher education within a system of accounts (McGettigan, 2013). Altbach (2014) suggests that research productivity more readily lends itself to measurement than other kinds of academic work. Measurement takes the form of income from research grants, for example, as an indicator of excellence, as well as publications, knowledge mobilization, and research impact (Watermeyer, 2014).

Knowledge production, through academic research, is now part of the neoliberal project that values income generation, commercialization, mobilization, and performance management over creativity, criticality, discovery, or scholarly independence (Barnett, 2014; Evans, 2005). Ball and Olmedo observe: 'Results are prioritized over processes, numbers over experiences, procedures over ideas, productivity over creativity' (2012: 91). Market-rational behaviour or 'economics imperialism' (Allais, 2012) is privileged, suggesting that knowledge needs to demonstrate its quantifiable use and applied value.

Research impact: Re-visiting cause and effect?

The UK's impact agenda is an example of the financialization of research. The impact agenda is producing new norms that require research to produce demonstrable social, economic, or cultural impact and benefit beyond academia (HEFCE, 2011). Research impact in the UK has been financialized and is now firmly linked to institutional funding via the Research Excellence Framework (REF), with Research Impact Case Studies graded and contributing to 20 per cent of the overall score for research excellence. It is predicted that this will rise to 25 per cent in 2020 (Watermeyer, 2014). The value indicator of research impact involves an accounting form with effects that can be audited, including solicited and causal testimonies from users or 'impactees' (Power, 2014), and rectilinear accounts of cause and effect, suggesting that it is possible to draw a straight line between particular pieces of research and their effect on policy, society, or the economy. The policy understanding of change is caught up in the notion of continuity, causality, and easily identifiable attribution. For example, it assumes that policymakers can specifically locate and name the precise pieces of research that have influenced their policy formation.

Impact is conceptually confusing, as it combines market rationality with social and economic responsibility (Colley, 2013; D'Aoust, 2014). Knowledge exchange, mobilization, and transfer suggest that research is thought to have had impact when auditable occasions of influence are recorded from university research to another agent or organization. Scrutiny of public monies means that UK research councils now require impact plans to be submitted with research proposals and impact reports one year after research projects are completed. This has been a controversial development, with critics berating the fact that knowledge is no longer seen as legitimate in its own right, but only in its application, and that a *mechanics* of knowing has emerged with simplistic notions of cause and effect (Colley, 2013). Additionally, the impact agenda casts macro-level policy and social change in the language of personal (researcher) responsibility. A further question is what we appeal to when we appeal to impact. The requirement for auditable effects and accountable knowledge transferred into diverse contexts raises questions about attribution and the rational–purposive understanding of change (Saunders, 2011). How do we know if changes that take place are a result of research findings or the consequences of other more abstract or contingent social and policy processes? Holmwood (2014) argues that the impact agenda is an attempt to turn research into a contract model, as stakeholders' views now shape research purposes, value, design, and evaluation of quality. The emphasis is on the technicization of knowledge – research that can be applied to policies and practices, with a major emphasis on what works. This expository tactic is an attempt at social transparency, that is, reassuring, explaining, and describing to taxpayers that they are getting a return on their investment in publicly funded social research. Collini (2012) suggests that these are attitudes to which politicians find it expedient to appeal – especially in a policy context of austerity.

Impact is creating new academic identities that contribute to elite formation and privilege in the global academy. It is becoming an increasingly important metric in the evaluation of research quality. Metrics imply norms. Butler (2006) observed that the multiplicity and continual changes in academic norms require us to ask which norms are evoked in judging any piece of work, and how they are interpreted. The installation of the neoliberal gaze on research quality requires a series of re-significations and endless repetitions – often through the regulatory mode of audit (Morley, 2003). Academics, it seems, are increasingly governed by numbers (Cooke, 2013; Lynch, 2014; Ozga, 2008). Research management in the neoliberalized global academy produces a range of truth telling, including the governance of self and the confessional and aspirational mode of academics' individual research plans and appraisal. It also involves what purports to be disinterested truth telling about others via peer review and technologies of audit in which every organizational member is made calculable (Ball, 2014). The researcher is produced through multiple metrics that have a market value, for example in the prestige economy of global tables (Amsler and Bolsmann, 2012; Lynch, 2014).

The global prestige economy, enacted through rankings such as league tables, privileges research as an indicator of quality and the proxy measure of organizational success (Blackmore, 2015; Collyer, 2013; Holmwood, 2014). League tables brand and stratify institutions and are a major influence in the definition of the field of higher education, offering positional advantage, esteem, and material rewards in the form of student recruitment and research funding. As an aspirational framework, they seem to drive a global knowledge race and meet a collective desire for hierarchy (Marginson, 2014). They also represent index values for investment and are mechanisms by which neoliberal principles are inserted into organizations (W. Brown, 2014; Gane, 2014). As an installation of power and an aspirational framework, league tables co-create academic entrepreneurs, and reinforce the move from exchange to competition in the global academy. League tables and the diverse performance indicators that contribute to them are facilitating the growth of a stratified higher education sector, in which elite organizations and privileged social groups capture the bulk of the resources (Husu, 2014).

Elite formation in the research economy: Winning, losing, and quitting

One of Williams's many interests has been the part that higher education plays in elite formation (Williams and Filippakou, 2010). His discussions on symbolic capital can be applied to the research economy as well as entry to the elite social groups via studying at the top universities. There are questions about who controls research and whether research policy favours a concentration agenda, i.e. awarding funding to those institutions and individuals that already possess material and symbolic research capital. The concentration of research power in the hands of the elite (Russell Group, 2010), and the linkage of research with particular policy priorities, could result in some services, service providers, and individuals becoming eliminated from the field. This raises questions about what research does to and for academic identities. For example, which values, themes, and methodologies are rewarded and anointed, and which are excluded. Research makes the world intelligible in specific ways and contributes to the foreclosure of other patterns of intelligibility (Rouse, 2004). Opaqueness in decision making, unsympathetic classifying gazes, cognitive errors in assessing merit, lack of transparency, and unsupportive and discriminatory institutional practices have all been cited as mechanisms of exclusion in the evaluation of research excellence (Morley, 2013). It is questionable whether non-economics, counter-hegemonic, or critical scholarship is becoming unfundable or unknowable, and hence socially illegitimate (Butler, 2006). Conversely, there is an assemblage of rewards for those servile to the priorities of the market and exclusions for refusers and resisters to dominant ideologies. In the neoliberal economy, research is frequently initiated in response to funding flows and by responses to policy concerns that are determined outside epistemic communities. Epistemic exclusions of a range of social groups, topics, methods, and methodologies could imply the possibility of normative reproduction and intellectual closure in a global knowledge economy that purports to be opening up new possibilities and networks.

The neoliberal research economy is producing a powerful binary of winners (elite) and losers (disqualified). On occasions, these binaries are disrupted, exposing the instability of the truth telling of audit and peer review. For example, Peter Higgs, who won the 2013 Nobel Prize for science, suggested that by today's standards of research excellence, he would not be considered 'productive' enough. He published fewer than ten papers after his groundbreaking work, which identified the mechanism by which subatomic material acquires mass, was published in 1964. He reported doubts that a similar breakthrough could be achieved in today's academic culture, because of the expectations on academics to collaborate and keep churning out papers and research grant applications. Higgs said that he became 'an embarrassment to the department when they did research assessment exercises'. A message would go round the department saying:

'Please give a list of your recent publications', Higgs said: 'I would send back a statement: 'None' (Aitkenhead, 2013).

The neoliberal project is not just about injury or subjectification, but also about how the academic profession is complicit in promoting the indices and indicators that regulate the profession (Gill, 2010; Leathwood and Read, 2013; Lucas, 2006). It is a relationship of entanglement, with many academics and managers internalizing the goals, priorities, and classifications of the neoliberal research economy. Income generation, as an indicator of research success, has been absorbed into academic identities to reconfigure professional goals in performance management. Neoliberalism has extended the economic form of the market to the wider social body (Lazzarato, 2009). In her high-profile resignation from academia, Marina Warner compared UK higher education to Chinese communist corporatism:

> ... where enforcers rush to carry out the latest orders from their chiefs in an ecstasy of obedience to ideological principles which they do not seem to have examined, let alone discussed with the people they order to follow them, whom they cashier when they won't knuckle under ...
>
> (J. Brown, 2014).

Warner was inundated with responses to her resignation from across the globe. In 2015, she summarized some of the injuries that colleagues reported in their correspondence:

> Others wrote to say that once they had contributed significantly to the REF (Research Excellence Framework), their posts were terminated: their usefulness was over. Some had obtained large grants, and found themselves pushed out when the funding ended. Some have agreed to contracts that require them to obtain x amount of grant money if they are to keep their jobs or look forward to any kind of promotion. Some had been told to change their research topic to something that lay outside their expertise entirely ...
>
> (Warner, 2015: 8)

A body of 'quit lit' is emerging (Flaherty, 2015). These are testimonies from academics who have decided to leave the academy and who have applied their critical skills to an analysis of the neoliberal employment and research regimes that they could no longer tolerate or that could not tolerate them. These affect-laden narratives have been compared to 'end of relationship' rancour – full of the vocabulary of disappointment, loss, and resentment.

Many academics experience a passionate attachment to their disciplines and to their professions, and feel impeded, contaminated, and frustrated by the shifting values. The 'quit lit' accounts suggest neoliberal reforms can be experienced as intolerable amounts of surveillance and performance management, creating increasingly toxic and unhealthy workplace cultures (Thornton, 2014). Zabrodska *et al.* (2011) argue that the twin rhetorics of economic responsibility and fear of non-survival are mobilized to make academics more governable. This can lead to bullying, exit, and, in extreme cases, self-destruction (Lutgen-Sandvik, 2006). The neoliberal academy, while not essentially male, can reinforce particular masculinities, producing a virility culture which values people in relation to how much money they make – the *homo oeconomicus* (Brown, 2015). Accounts of the suicide of Professor Stefan Grimm, who worked at Imperial College, reveal the pressure that he was under to meet financialized research targets (Parr, 2014). Shame was mobilized, via a calculus of his research grant capture success or management by numbers (Cooke, 2013). There is a powerful relationship between shame and indebtedness (Probyn, 2005; Mantyla, 2000). Shame is both individualizing – the failure to win grants or publish – and collective, such as institutions falling down the global league tables (Adams, 2013). The failed academic entrepreneur is treated with the same contempt as recipients of welfare benefits. That is, as a retainer and burden on more 'productive' colleagues. An email to Stefan Grimm from his head of department six months before his death suggested that his failed attempts at academic capitalism in the enterprise culture meant that he was no longer the ideal citizen: 'Despite submitting many grants, you have been unsuccessful in persuading peer-review panels that you have a competitive application' (cited in Parr, 2014).

The financialization of research becomes a truth about its quality. The granting of competitive awards is one of the favoured mechanisms for recognizing individuals who have excelled, or performed in excess of the norm (Davies *et al.*, 2013). Rewards also confirm compliance with norms, and are regulatory forms of recognition. Targets for achieving research income are now a part of performance management, or indeed tenure in diverse national locations. Professor's Grimm's 'failure' to achieve the required annual research income co-constructed a negative academic (loser) identity sufficient to threaten expulsion from his profession. In the precarity of research funding, this is akin to blaming someone for not winning the lottery. His agency, or ability to act, had no value outside the outcomes of his research bids. The knowledge economy, while presented as an economic conceit, is deeply embodied (Hey, 2013). Examples of how the corporate research-supported business model abuses employees and strips them of their dignity are not unique to the UK. In 2014, Carole Vance and Kim Hopper, long-time professors at Columbia University, learned that they were losing their jobs because they had failed to generate enough research grant money (Goldberg, 2014). If neoliberal resisters or 'failures' quit, or are dispatched, then what or who remains, and does this signal the end of critical scholarship in academia (Eagleton, 2015)?

As the above examples illustrate, academic identities and indeed survival increasingly depend on success in gaining research funding in a highly marketized research economy. However, the logic of research funding as institutional income has been interrogated by Newfield's studies (2014) that have demonstrated how universities, in fact, lose millions on research costs from grants. Newfield is particularly critical of how humanities and social sciences are represented as loser fields in research. For example, Dingwall (2013) argues that social science research in the UK is failing to inform the public accurately about key social policy issues including crime and the demographics of immigration, with the consequence that the public massively overestimates social challenges. There have also been several attempts to defend the value of the humanities in the face of threatened disinvestment (e.g. Small, 2013). Newfield (2014), however, argues that it is the STEM (science, technology, engineering, and mathematics) fields that lose the most money and traditionally need to be supported by fee incomes from humanities and social sciences. Hence, the financialization of research is itself ideological and about symbolic production rather than an actual material value in today's global academy – used largely to render individuals and institutions more governmentable. Governmentality means that power is exercised through people being responsibilized to govern themselves. In this analysis, government extends from political government to forms of self-regulation, or technologies of the self (Lemke, 2001). Neoliberalism, as a dominant political rationality, moves between state policy and the interior worlds of the subject, normatively constructing and demanding that individuals are entrepreneurial actors, or units of resource (Brown, 2005: 40). Financial goals for research become embodied and internalized as academics refashion their desires, resources, and priorities to align with dominant performance indicators. Neoliberalism is a discourse that works on and through desire, making individuals want to win on its terms (Zabrodska *et al.*, 2011). The interplay between policy, desire, and 'success' or 'failure' materializes academic identities. Those people who might offer different accounts of the world are in danger of being illegible and inaudible to the quality apparatus of the global academy.

In conclusion

Research capital is a key performance indicator and co-constitutes reputation, power, status, rewards, and continued employment in the global academy. Individual academic identities materialize through the interplay between research policy discourses, performance, and productivity within the confines of dominant performance indicators. Insecurity, inequality, and individualization are fostered as part of ensuring the conditions for power to exercise a hold over conduct (Lazzarato, 2009). In the neoliberalized research economy risk is redistributed, as academics are made to feel indebted to their organizations and responsibilized for generating income in financial systems over which they have little or no control. What is valued in research and scholarship is increasingly being shaped by market demands, often outside epistemic communities. Income generation, enterprise, impact, innovation for the market, and the exchange value in the global prestige economy are dominant indicators of the value of research. Productivity and quality are connected and classified according to financial returns and the predictability of research utility. The knowledge economy is invested, situated, exclusionary, and embodied, and as such, infused with power and control. The empty signifiers of excellence, talent, and merit are frequently invoked, yet value indicators can be unstable, transitory, contingent, and contextualized. The knowledge economy is driven by the materialities of financialization, but also by a powerful affective economy of shame, pride, humiliation, and disappointment. As Ball (2015) observes, neoliberalism is about money and minds.

The logic of relationality suggests that for every winner there are many losers. It is argued that 'conceptual, theoretical and critical "thorn-in-the-side" research' could be 'marginalised or disappear' (Parker and van Teijlingen, 2012: 50), and that social research has become colonized by the 'cultural circuits' of capitalism (Mills and Ratcliffe, 2012). The dominant value in the enterprise culture is the size of the research grant, rather than its intellectual contribution. As Peters argues, 'value displaces values' (2001: 17). Stefan Collini suggests that rate-of-return education reduces academics to 'door-to-door salesmen (*sic*) for vulgarized versions of their market-oriented product' (cited in Jenkins, 2013). There are questions about what the future holds for critical scholarship and whether there is an alternative to the neoliberal corporate logic (Leathwood and Read, 2013).

A role of research – especially in the social sciences – is to render the world problematic by formulating and elaborating questions. One task for social research could be to resist co-option by narrow research policy agendas. There is a need to imagine and research desired futures. Academic creativity needs to incorporate transgression and re-signification, and not just compliance and mechanistic, industrialized productivity. This necessitates a troubling of the neoliberal realisms and a re-invigoration of knowledge production as a site of transformation and change. All of these are activities in which Gareth Williams has been engaged throughout his long career.

References

Adams, R. (2013) 'Sussex tumbles down Guardian league table of universities'. *The Guardian,* 3 June. Online. www.theguardian.com/education/2013/jun/03/sussex-tumbles-down-guardian-league-table-of-unis (accessed 11 April 2016).

Aitkenhead, D. (2013) 'Peter Higgs: I wouldn't be productive enough for today's academic system'. *The Guardian,* 6 December. Online. www.theguardian.com/science/2013/dec/06/peter-higgs-boson-academic-system (accessed 11 April 2016).

Allais, S. (2012) 'Economics imperialism, education policy and educational theory'. *Journal of Education Policy*, 27 (2), 253–74.

Altbach, P. (2014) 'What counts for academic productivity in research universities?' *University World News,* July, 329. Online. www.universityworldnews.com/article.php?story=20140715105656393 (accessed 11 April 2016).

Amsler, S. and Bolsmann, C. (2012) 'University ranking as social exclusion'. *British Journal of Sociology of Education*, 33 (2), 283–301.

Ball, S. (2012) 'Performativity, commodification and commitment: An I–spy guide to the neoliberal university'. *British Journal of Educational Studies*, 60 (1), 17–28.

— (2014) 'Universities and "the Economy of Truth"'. Paper presented at the Governing Academic Life Conference, 25–26 June, London School of Economics.

— (2015) 'Neoliberalism – how it travels, and how it can be resisted'. Online. http://guerillawire.org/education/neoliberalism-how-it-travels-and-how-it-can-be-resisted (accessed 11 April 2016).

Ball, S. and Olmedo, A. (2012) 'Global social capitalism: Using enterprise to solve the problems of the world'. *Citizenship, Social and Economics Education*, 10 (2), 83–90.

Barnett, R. (2014) *Thinking and Rethinking the University: The selected works of Ronald Barnett*. London: Routledge.

Blackmore, P. (2015) *Prestige in Academic Life: Excellence and exclusion*. London: Routledge.

Brown, J. (2014) 'Marina Warner compares UK university managers to "Chinese communist enforcers"'. *The Independent,* 3 September. www.independent.co.uk/news/people/novelist-marina-warner-compares-uk-university-managers-to-chinese-communist-enforcers-9709731.html (accessed 11 April 2016).

Brown, R. (2008) 'Higher education and the market'. *Perspectives: Policy and Practice in Higher Education*, 12 (3), 78–83.

Brown, W. (2005) 'Neo-liberalism and the end of liberal democracy'. *Theory and Event*, 7 (1), 37–59.

— (2014) 'Between shareholders and stakeholders: University purposes adrift'. Paper presented at the Governing Academic Life Conference, 25–26 June, London School of Economics.

— (2015) *Undoing the Demos: Neoliberalism's stealth revolution*. New York: Zone Books.

Butler, J. (2006) 'Academic norms, contemporary challenges: A reply to Robert Post on academic freedom'. In Doumani, B. (ed.) *Academic Freedom after September 11*. New York: Zone Books.

Colley, H. (2013) 'What (a) to do about "Impact": A Bourdieusian critique'. *British Educational Research Journal*, 40 (4), 660–81.

Collini, S. (2012) *What are Universities For?* London: Penguin.

Collyer, F. (2013) 'The production of scholarly knowledge in the global market arena: University ranking systems, prestige and power.' *Critical Studies in Education*, 54 (3), 245–59.

Connell, R. (2013) 'The neoliberal cascade and education: An essay on the market agenda and its consequences'. *Critical Studies in Education*, 54 (2), 99–111.

Cooke, W. (2013) 'Kill the REF in complex circumstances'. Online. http://tinyurl.com/z9th4rl (accessed 12 April 2016).

Cribb, A. and Gewirtz, S. (2013) 'The hollowed-out university? A critical analysis of changing institutional and academic norms in UK higher education'. *Discourse: Studies in the Cultural Politics of Education*, 34 (3), 338–50.

D'Aoust, A.-M. (2014) 'Ties that bind? Engaging emotions, governmentality and neoliberalism'. *Global Society*, 28 (3), 267–76.

Davies, B., De Schauwer, E., Claes, L., De Munck, K., van De Putte, I., and Verstichele, M. (2013) 'Recognition and difference: A collective biography'. *International Journal of Qualitative Studies in Education*, 26 (6), 680–91.

Deleuze, G. (1992) 'Postscript on the societies of control'. *October*, 59 (Winter), 3–7.

Dingwall, R. (2013) 'Why social science education is as important as STEM'. Online. www.socialsciencespace.com/2013/07/why-social-science-education-is-as-important-as-stem (accessed 12 April 2016).

Eagleton, T. (2015) 'The slow death of the university'. Online. http://chronicle.com/article/The-Slow-Death-of-the/228991 (accessed 9 May 2016).

Evans, M. (2005) *Killing Thinking: The death of the universities*. London: Continuum.

Flaherty, C. (2015) 'Public good-byes'. *Inside Higher Ed*. 9 September. Online. www.insidehighered.com/news/2015/09/09/essays-academics-fed-higher-ed-mark-resurgence-quit-lit (accessed 12 April 2016).

Gane, N. (2014) 'Neoliberalism: How should the social sciences respond?' Paper presented at the Governing Academic Life Conference, 25–26 June, London School of Economics.

Gill, R. (2010) 'Breaking the silence: The hidden injuries of the neo-liberal university'. In Ryan-Flood, R. and Gill, R. (eds) *Secrecy and Silence in the Research Process*. London: Routledge.

Goldberg, M. (2014) 'Columbia University fired two eminent public intellectuals. Here's why it matters'. *The Nation*, 12 March. Online. www.thenation.com/article/178821/columbia-university-fired-two-eminent-public-intellectuals-heres-why-it-matters (accessed 12 April 2016).

HEFCE (2011) *Decisions on Assessing Research Impact*. Bristol: Higher Education Funding Council for England. Online. www.ref.ac.uk/media/ref/content/pub/decisionsonassessingresearchimpact/01_11.pdf (accessed 12 April 2016).

Hey, V. (2013) 'Privilege, agency and affect in the academy: Who do you think you are?' In Maxwell, C. and Aggleton, P. (eds) *Privilege, Agency and Affect: Understanding the production and effects of action*. Basingstoke: Palgrave Macmillan.

Holmwood, J. (2014) 'Neo-liberalism as a theory of knowledge and its implications for the social sciences and critical thought'. Paper presented at the Governing Academic Life Conference, 25–26 June, London School of Economics.

Husu, L. (2014) 'Research funding gap: Her excellence dwarfed by his excellence'. Online. http://tinyurl.com/jzmwuzz (accessed 12 April 2016).

Jenkins, S. (2013) 'Universities should ditch the talk of investing in the future'. Online. www.theguardian.com/commentisfree/2013/oct/23/universities-ditch-talk-investing-future (accessed 12 April 2016).

Lazzarato, M. (2009) 'Neoliberalism in action: Inequality, insecurity and the reconstitution of the social'. *Theory, Culture and Society*, 26 (6), 109–33.

Leathwood, C. and Read, B. (2013) 'Research policy and academic performativity: Compliance, contestation and complicity'. *Studies in Higher Education*, 38 (8), 1162–74.

Lemke, T. (2001) '"The birth of bio-politics": Michel Foucault's lecture at the Collège de France on neo-liberal governmentality'. *Economy and Society*, 30 (2), 190–207.

Lucas, L. (2006) *The Research Game in Academic Life*. Buckingham: SRHE/Open University Press.

Lutgen-Sandvik, P. (2006) '"Take this job and . . .": Quitting and other forms of resistance to workplace bullying'. *Communication Monographs*, 73, 406–33.

Lynch, K. (2014) 'Control by numbers: New managerialism and ranking in higher education'. *Critical Studies in Education*, 56 (2), 190–207.

McGettigan, A. (2013) *The Great University Gamble: Money, markets and the future of higher education*. London: Pluto Press.

Mantyla, H. (2000) 'Dealing with shame at academic work: A literary introspection'. *Psychiatria Fennica*, 31, 148–69.

Marginson, S. (2014) *International Higher Education*. Online. www.international.ac.uk/media-centre/blogs/prof-simon-marginson,-ioe,-international-he.aspx (accessed 12 April 2016).

Mills, D. and Ratcliffe, R. (2012) 'After method: Anthropology, education and the knowledge economy'. *Qualitative Research*, 12 (2), 147–64.

Morley, L. (2003) *Quality and Power in Higher Education*. Buckingham: Open University Press.

— (2013) *Women and Higher Education Leadership: Absences and aspirations*. Stimulus Paper. London: Leadership Foundation for Higher Education.

— (2015) 'Troubling intra-actions: Gender, neo-liberalism and research in the global academy'. *Journal of Education Policy*. Online. http://dx.doi.org/10.1080/02680939.2015.1062919 (accessed 9 May 2016).

Moulier-Boutang, Y. (2012) *Cognitive Capitalism*. Cambridge: Polity Press.

Newfield, C. (2014) 'The price of privatization'. Paper presented at the Governing Academic Life Conference, 25–26 June, London School of Economics.

OECD (2013) *Supporting Investment in Knowledge Capital, Growth and Innovation*. Online. www.oecd-ilibrary.org/industry-and-services/supporting-investment-in-knowledge-capital-growth-and-innovation_9789264193307-en (accessed 9 May 2016).

Ozga, J. (2008) 'Governing knowledge: Research steering and research quality'. *European Educational Research Journal*, 7 (3), 261–72.

Parker, J. and van Teijlingen, E. (2012) 'The Research Excellence Framework (REF): Assessing the impact of social work research on society'. *Practice: Social Work in Action*, 24 (1), 41–52.

Parr, C. (2014) 'Imperial College Professor Stefan Grimm "was given grant income target"', 3 December. Online. www.timeshighereducation.com/news/imperial-college-professor-stefan-grimm-was-given-grant-income-target/2017369.article (accessed 12 April 2016).

Peters, M. (2001) 'Education, enterprise culture and the entrepreneurial self: A Foucauldian perspective'. *Journal of Educational Enquiry*, 2, 58–71.

Peters, M., Paraskeva, J., and Besley, T. (eds) (2014) *The Global Financial Crisis and Educational Restructuring*. New York: Peter Lang.

Pollitt, C. (1993) *Managerialism and the Public Services: Cuts or cultural change in the 1990s*. Oxford: Blackwell.

Power, M. (2014) 'Accounting for the impact of research'. Paper presented at the Governing Academic Life Conference, 25–26 June, London School of Economics.

Probyn, E. (2005) *Blush: Faces of shame*. Sydney: UNSW Press.

Radice, H. (2013) 'How we got here: UK higher education under neoliberalism'. *ACME: An International E-Journal for Critical Geographies*, 12 (3), 407–18. Online. http://ojs.unbc.ca/index.php/acme/article/view/983 (accessed 9 May 2016).

Rouse, J. (2004) 'Barad's feminist naturalism'. *Hypatia*, 19 (1), 142–61.

Russell Group of Universities (2010) *The Concentration of Research Funding in the UK: Driving excellence and competing globally*. http://russellgroup.ac.uk/media/5046/7concentration-of-research-funding.pdf (accessed 27 April 2016).

Saunders, M. (2011) 'Setting the scene: The four domains of evaluative practice in higher education'. In Saunders, M., Trowler, P., and Bamber, V. (eds) *Reconceptualising Evaluation in Higher Education: The practice turn*. Maidenhead: McGraw-Hill/Open University Press.

Small, H. (2013) *The Value of the Humanities*. Oxford: Oxford University Press.

Teixeira, P. and Dill, D. (2011) (eds) *Public Vices, Private Virtues? Assessing the effects of marketization in higher education*. Rotterdam: Sense Publishers.

Thornton, M. (ed.) (2014) *Through a Glass Darkly: The social sciences look at the neoliberal university*. Canberra: ANU Press.

Warner, M. (2015) 'Learning my lesson'. *London Review of Books*, 19 March, 37 (6), 8–14. Online. www.lrb.co.uk/v37/n06/marina-warner/learning-my-lesson (accessed 12 April 2016).

Watermeyer, R. (2014) 'Impact in the REF: Issues and obstacles'. *Studies in Higher Education*, 41 (2), 199–214. Online. www.tandfonline.com/doi/abs/10.1080/03075079.2014.915303 (accessed 9 May 2016).

Williams, G. (1992) *Changing Patterns of Finance in Higher Education*. Buckingham: SRHE/Open University Press.

— (2004) 'The higher education market in the United Kingdom'. In Teixeira, P., Jongbloed, B., Dill, D., and Amaral, A. (eds) *Markets in Higher Education: Rhetoric or reality?* Dordrecht: Kluwer Academic Publishers.

— (2011) 'Will higher education be the next bubble to burst?' In *The Europa World of Learning 2011*. Online. www.educationarena.com/pdf/sample/sample-essay-williams.pdf (accessed 15 April 2016).

Williams, G. and Filippakou, O. (2010) 'Higher education and UK elite formation in the twentieth century'. *Higher Education*, 59 (1), 1–20.

Williams, G. and Kitaev, I. (2005) 'Overview of national policy contexts for entrepreneurialism in higher education institutions'. *Higher Education Management and Policy*, 17 (3), 125–41.

Zabrodska, K., Linnell, S., Laws, C., and Davies, B. (2011) 'Bullying as intra-active process in neoliberal universities'. *Qualitative Inquiry*, 17 (8), 709–19.

Chapter 8

Branding and the commodification of academic labour

James Pringle and Rajani Naidoo

Introduction

A series of structural and ideological transformations since the 1980s linked to globalization and the ascendance of neoliberal political frameworks have resulted in the destabilization of traditional mechanisms governing higher education institutions (Parker and Jary, 1995). Gareth Williams's corpus of work has encompassed the changing relations between the state, the market, and society across different time periods with important and insightful analyses of how this has impacted on the policies and practices of universities. We would like to follow in his footsteps by reflecting on how intense forms of competition for domestic and international students in the face of major reductions in public funding (Currie and Vidovich, 2000) have combined to transform universities into organizational actors responsible for the strategic management of reputation. This has, in turn, led to the perception of the university brand as a valuable asset.

While branding as a marketing concept has become increasingly common in higher education over the last decade as universities search for new ways to position themselves in a competitive marketplace (Hemsley-Brown and Goonawarddana, 2007), research into branding in higher education is at an early stage (Hemsley-Brown and Oplatka, 2006). A small number of studies have been published that analyse branding in higher education in generic terms (Temple, 2006), or focus on the problematic relationship between branding as practised in the for-profit corporate sector and its application to public systems of higher education (Jevons, 2006; Maringe, 2005). In general, such studies focus on how various brand attributes are perceived by students (Ali-Choudhury *et al.*, 2009; Bennett and Ali-Choudhury, 2009; Chapleo, 2010). The branding literature, however, also identifies employee behaviour as vitally important and strongly influential in shaping consumer perceptions of their most and least preferred service brands (De Chernatony and Segal-Horn, 2003; Elliot and

Percy, 2007; Judson *et al.*, 2009). Therefore, it can be argued that the same attention to branding as directed to students should be directed internally to academic faculty, since it is at the intersection of service providers and customers that brand meaning is realized. With some exceptions (Naidoo and Pringle, 2014; Waeraas and Solbakk, 2009), there has been relatively little research on the responses and interactions of academics with branding. In addition, the studies in existence in general focus on single institutions or disciplines. Our paper addresses this gap by undertaking an in-depth analysis of the responses of academic faculty to branding across disciplines at three universities in Ontario, Canada characterized by diverse heritage and locations.

We begin by presenting an overview of relevant branding literature that offers important definitions and concepts as well as insights into corporate branding strategies. We then develop a conceptual analysis of branding in higher education. This is followed by our empirical study of how brands are constructed, adopted, and resisted intra-organizationally. We conclude by offering key insights from our research and implications for practice.

Conceptualizing branding in higher education

Early research conceptualizing brands as delivering on promises to passive consumers has been replaced by conceptualizations of brands as an interface that enables a set of relations between products and services through time and a two-way exchange between producers and consumers (Lury, 2004). Hearn (2008) has also demonstrated how brands have become the sign of different types of social identity, which summon consumers into a relationship with them. Thus, brands do not just create products but also act as specific cultural resources for the construction of social identities, relationships, lifestyles, and particular types of communities (Arvidsson, 2005; Holt, 2002).

While external stakeholders are important in brand management, the importance of internal stakeholders, particularly in relation to service brands, has been highlighted. As indicated by many authors (Burmann and Zeplin, 2005; De Chernatony and Segal-Horn, 2003; Elliot and Percy, 2007; Judson *et al.*, 2009; Karreman and Rylander, 2008), employee behaviour has been identified as strongly influential in shaping consumer perceptions of their most and least preferred service brands. Employees' engagement with and enactment of the values and vision of the brand thus becomes a key element in the differentiation strategies and thus provides competitive advantage for the company. Knowledge-intensive companies in particular encourage employees to 'live the brand', which requires an alignment and an investment of the personal self with the brand.

Some authors, however, suggest that this relationship is complex and fraught with challenges. Smith and Buchanan-Oliver (2011: 66) argue this relationship is multifaceted, where there is 'accommodation with the brand (conforming but not believing too much), but ... also resistance to the brand (separateness), and there is also dissonance (different vision, connected but separate)'. The problems with dissonant brand meaning gaps is also highlighted by Wilson *et al.* (2014). Russell speaks to employee branding through a more sinister lens of regulation and control, where employees are prevented from expressing critical thought and where '[i]t regulates employees' identities by encouraging them to present themselves in a way that is valuable for the organization and supports its core beliefs, norms and mindsets' (2011: 101).

All of these point to the centrality of employee adoption of organizational values and the challenges this can present when this relationship goes awry. Within the branding literature, the work of Hatch and Schultz and their Vision, Culture, Image (VCI) model are regarded as seminal (2002, 2008). These authors note that the greater the coherence of vision, culture, and image, the stronger the brand. When culture aligns with vision, employees personalize top management's aspirations for the organization and they will then have the motivation to pursue strategic vision and cement a powerful corporate brand identity (Hatch and Schultz, 2008: 129). In other words, branding is conceptualized and authenticated through a management of relationships where values are shared, reflected, and reinforced internally within the organization as well as externally with the broader stakeholder community.

Before applying these insights directly to higher education, it is important to consider the note of caution from Hemsley-Brown and Oplatka (2006) who indicate that the literature on higher education marketing is:

> ... incoherent, even inchoate and lacks theoretical models that reflect upon the particular context of HE and the nature of their service ... Further we argue that the research on HE marketing draws its conceptualizations and empirical frameworks from services marketing, despite the differences in context between HE institutions and other service organisations.
>
> (Hemsley-Brown and Oplatka, 2006: 318)

It is therefore extremely important to analyse the specific context of higher education in relation to branding. In order to do this we draw on the wider higher education studies literature that captures the culture, values, and organization of higher education as a historically inscribed and culturally specific sector.

In many respects, branding marks a form of continuity as well as a sharp break with earlier struggles in higher education. Reputation struggles were always part of the university. These reputation-enhancing strategies, however, drew on criteria, practices, and representations that were based on academic criteria, which were relatively autonomous from the economic context. Reputation was gained through institutional processes controlled by academic peers. The hierarchical ordering of universities and faculties was thus internally judged and then projected outwards and accepted as legitimate by external stakeholders (Naidoo *et al.*, 2014).

In contemporary times, higher education reform has ushered in new systems of external accountability (Naidoo, 2008). In addition, changes in state regulation and funding, pressures for massification, the requirement for performative excellence, the construction of national and global quasi-markets, and the positioning of students as consumers (see Naidoo *et al.*, 2011) have combined to propel universities to engage with forms of marketing practices that are more closely aligned to the corporate world. Indeed this commodification of higher education has led to the provision of a 'range of services that can, in effect, be purchased from a brochure rather than a transaction of trust between student and teacher' (Williams, 2004: 88). Contemporary branding practices therefore attract the concentration of financial and administrative resources and introduce an outer-directed process of conscious organizational projection, packaged and distributed according to external performance measures and market criteria. In other words, higher education institutions must now strive to embody the values and images required by the external world within the confines of corporate imagery and popular culture, while at the same time maintaining close identification with traditional norms and values.

Given the above context, it is unlikely that the grafting of marketing practices derived from the commercial sector onto a sector with a deeply embedded professional and public culture will translate easily into the outcomes intended by managers. While marketing managers are largely in agreement on the power of branding, it has been argued that faculty members have a distinctly different perception of branding where 'the most common academic stance is simply to ignore brands as too crass and too popular to deserve serious inquiry' (Holt, 2006: 300). Similarly, others have commented on the nature of faculty as a service provider and hypothesize that it is natural that faculty will resist and feel conflicted with the concept of identifying with a single organizational identity, since they identify more with their academic discipline (Waeraas and Solbakk, 2009: 459).

While organizational members are increasingly understood as prime opportunities to express the brand (Kornberger, 2010: 115), Waeraas and Solbakk (2009) felt faculty clearly identified more with their discipline and academic units rather than the university as a whole, and were therefore resistant to a single university identity.

Enders and Kaulisch explain that the 'commitment of the individual [academic] to the organization is low, while their commitment to the discipline and a sense for individual accomplishment is considered the key to their professional identity' (2006: 88). In distinguishing the traditional separation between the roles and responsibilities of academics and their institution, Henkel states that for most of the twentieth century academics were considered members of interconnected communities, notably disciplines and higher education institutions, which afforded them stable and legitimizing identities. She argues that marketization has led to challenges 'first, to the power and importance of the discipline in academic beliefs and working practices and second, to academic autonomy, individual and collective, in the setting of agendas and the production of knowledge' (2005: 156). Adopting like reasoning to Enders and Kaulisch (2006) she suggests '[t]he department is now only one, and not necessarily the most secure or important, focus of academic activity and identification' (Henkel, 2005: 164). She argues, however, that academics still appear to value most strongly the importance of the discipline and their academic freedom (ibid: 169–70).

In the Canadian context, in order to understand the rise of branding practices in higher education institutions in Ontario, it is worthwhile appreciating some key policy initiatives. In February of 2005 the Honourable Bob Rae released his report 'Ontario, a leader in learning' (Rae, 2005). The report was commissioned by Ontario premier Dalton McGuinty to review the design and funding of post-secondary education in the province of Ontario in five key areas: accessibility, quality, system design, funding, and accountability. Since then, periods of economic contraction have led to increasing pressure on universities to control costs, become more efficient, and to compete for additional funding opportunities (Usher and Dunn, 2009).

Metcalfe argues that 'nationally and in particular provinces, Canada has moved from a system of block public subsidy that was described by Slaughter and Leslie to a system where public funds are used to strategically position Canadian institutions (particularly research universities) on the path toward increased revenue generation' (2010: 509). As highlighted by Metcalfe (2010), these developments have been met with resistance by some Canadian faculty concerned with academic autonomy (Polster, 2003), but also embraced by some who see technology transfer and commercialization as a core value and responsibility of universities (Pries and Guild, 2007). Metcalfe goes on to recommend future research should be undertaken to explore the tensions between faculty on either side of the commercialization debate to better understand the effect of academic capitalism on the Canadian academic profession (2010: 510).

The following excerpt from *Academic Callings* illustrates the ideological shift seen at Canadian academic institutions due to these recent federal and provincial policy adjustments:

> That is not to say that university administrations haven't shifted their approaches to fit with the ways governments allocate funds. They have adopted more competitive styles in going after grant money, for example and they direct a lot of their resources towards promoting their own institution as the best bet for government and corporate investments. Universities are involved more in competing with each other to get funding and less involved in collaboration with each other to preserve the ideals of the university. They believe they have to do this in order to survive, This is the corporate approach and I don't think it's good.
>
> (Bakan and Newson, 2010: 199)

Branding at three universities in Ontario

A multi-site case study approach was designed consisting of three institutions in Ontario, Canada. As demonstrated above, like many industrialized countries, Canada and the Province of Ontario are experiencing pressures that have resulted in the increasing marketization of higher education. Metcalfe, for example, has indicated that Canada has 'increased reliance upon private sources of income, namely through tuition, the sales of goods and services, and industrial partnerships' (2010: 509). This is supported by Fisher *et al.*, who demonstrate the increasing marketization of the system (2009: 560). With this rising competitive landscape, the need to distinguish one higher education institution from its peers through powerful brand messaging becomes increasingly vital to institutional survival and future growth. As a result, there has been growing attention directed to a university's raison d'être and communicating that message through a powerful brand identity has never been more important.

The central research question was to explore how faculty members perceive branding in the context of their university and the role they play in branding their university. We were also interested in discovering whether age (used as a proxy for status) and location (urban/rural) had an influence on how faculty members respond to branding activities.

The research utilized a case study approach because it provided a detailed description of the environment in which faculty members live and work, and provided a richness that other approaches were less likely to generate (Eisenhardt and Graebner, 2007: 25). A multi-case approach was taken because it allowed the study to explore differences within and between cases further, thus strengthening findings which facilitate theoretical development (Yin, 2009).

The case study universities were selected for differences based on the age of the university and the location of the university, as these features have been deemed important by previous research. Melewar and Akel (2005), for example, have noted the importance of heritage as a key factor, while Ali-Choudhury *et al.* (2009) have noted that urban universities are more attractive to young people than rural universities.

As Figure 8.1 below indicates, University A was selected for its older heritage and urban location. In contrast, University B was selected for its older heritage and rural location, while University C was selected for its young/new heritage and urban location.

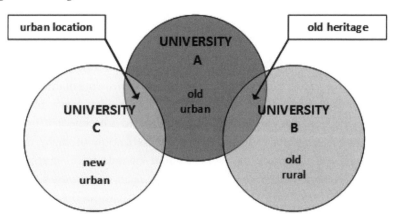

In addition to documentary analyses, a total of 42 semi-structured interviews were conducted with faculty members from the three institutions matched by academic discipline and rank. Interview questions were designed to probe a wide range of factors suggested by the literature review while leaving room for respondents to raise issues they thought were important. Prior to the faculty interviews, three management interviews were conducted with administrators with direct responsibility for branding at each institution to provide context for the faculty interviews. Written consent was provided by each interviewee and the interviews were taped, transcribed, and coded following the approach outlined by Creswell (2009: 186–7). All interviewees were given an identifying number to ensure confidentiality and these numbers are used in this paper.

In the next sections we discuss our findings and draw out cross-case comparisons, reflecting on both similarities as well as differences across the cases.

Faculty responses to branding

While there were many unique differences between the case-study universities, there were also many similarities. Faculty members at all institutions expressed a general recognition of the economic factors that have led to the rise in branding and pointed to their own inability to resist these trends. However, in relation to general responses to branding, there were interesting differences when institutions were contrasted by age and location.

While faculty members of the more established institutions with greater prestige responded negatively to branding activities, at the same time they expressed pride at belonging to a prestigious institution. They perceived the focus of branding to be related to the recruitment of specific types of students or faculty members with the goal of furthering a research agenda or supporting a particular diversity agenda. Faculty members from established institutions most commonly described their brand identity as 'prestigious', 'research intensive', and 'innovative'. This was reflected in interviews as well as in marketing materials, which commonly reflected similar language like 'cutting edge', 'best', 'brightest', and 'world class'.

At the newer institution branding elicited a more defensive reaction. Instead of embracing their historical context as a polytechnic, they hoped to obscure this link, as they felt this had an unfair and negative impact on the recognition of their achievements and relative status. As a result, many faculty members of the new institution were less concerned about the adoption of marketing and branding strategies, as they saw branding as an opportunity to elevate the image to the relatively new status as a university. Faculty members focused more on the connection of being 'new', 'entrepreneurial', and 'urban' and on the practical 'career-focused' education that would position students well for employment upon graduation.

Another institutional factor of importance was the location of that institution. Faculty members in the urban institutions reflected on the importance of location as a desirable brand element. While both urban institutions highlighted the descriptor 'urban' as a brand identifier, the rural institution drew on different descriptors such as the beauty of the lakeside campus and the recreational activities such as sailing, kayaking, and canoeing. In addition, faculty members of the rural institution felt a much stronger sense of brand identity related to institutional spirit and community. This may also be reflective of the relatively smaller size of this institution. Faculty members at University B reported that this symbolic bonding was embedded in a culture that was reinforced and authenticated through common rituals, such as the singing of university chants and songs and the wearing of distinctively emblematic and traditional garments. Many also commented on how this provides a sense of connectedness so students and faculty feel 'happier', and in their opinions this helps to facilitate 'better work'.

However, as well as collaboration, branding also caused contestations, fears, and conflict, which we will now turn to.

The commodification of higher education

Faculty members in all institutions expressed concerns about branding representing the commodification of higher education. They linked branding to a creeping infiltration of business ideology. The strongest criticisms came from faculty members from the social sciences and humanities disciplines, who spoke of the erosion of criticality and the role of higher education in protecting the interest of the public good.

Faculty members also expressed concerns that branding represented the growing influence of outside commercial forces in reshaping the internal activities in higher education. They feared that large donations were linked implicitly or explicitly to pressures for change in general university values or to curriculum changes. For many, branding initiatives also appeared to be linked to external foci such as employability, generating economic gain, and conforming to political agendas. For example, one respondent stated:

> When the Premier, Mike Harris, went on and on about how universities waste so much money, the example is used, because they produce too many geographers, it just sent a chill down our spine because ... it's a kind of command economy attitude towards universities saying that in this five year plan, we're going to need 46 engineers, so we produce 46 engineers.
>
> (Faculty 13)

Faculty members in all institutions expressed grave concern over the erosion of liberal arts in higher education. Several faculty members reported that private funders tended to gravitate to the professional schools, providing them with additional resources and flexibility in comparison to the traditional higher education disciplines found within the social sciences and humanities. Furthermore, they noted that branding activities were directed towards highlighting the quality and relevance of one programme over another, and this often relied on metrics that were simply inappropriate:

> ... Arts is being judged against standards that have nothing to do with arts. And that's a problem because those standards are being used to determine which programmes are important and which programmes should receive funding.
>
> (Faculty 42)

There were also major concerns that business strategies such as branding were linked to new policies driven by economic constraints, which led to greater competition for research funding from commercial sources. Many faculty members questioned the impact of adopting closer ties with the corporate world on research. They were concerned that if research was driven by commercial need, universities would be sacrificing ground-breaking research and other types of research that would be in the best interests of the research community and society at large. They also noted the brand implications for research universities and stated that they did not wish to become branded as 'think tanks' or 'consulting companies'.

Competition versus collaboration

While, in general, faculty members in our study continued to speak to a culture of collegiality that valued academic freedom and critical thought, their discussions on branding led to them expressing fears that this was changing. Most faculty members in this study saw an academic culture that is undergoing a metamorphosis, where collegiality is being replaced by a culture of accountability and efficiency and where advancing technology has made direct and informal interaction with colleagues unnecessary. Regardless of rank, it would appear that the traditional culture of collegiality is being tested with a tension brought on by new competitive pressures to perform in an environment with reduced fiscal resources and increasing administrative demands for performance and accountability measures. However, there was also complexity and diversity of opinion depending on the historical context and location of the university and the level of academic seniority and professional discipline.

Much of the marketing and promotional materials at University A, for example, spoke of a culture embedded with the 'best' and 'brightest', implying a highly competitive culture. However, some faculty members commented on the problems of being identified as the best and how this level of competiveness has negative as well as positive associations, particularly when talking about one of the stronger and desired brand qualities like excellence in research:

> Faculty are very competitive with each other as well as with other institutions ... I'm still grappling with whether you have to let people be rapacious, you know, attention-seeking ... whether you have to encourage that in order to see excellence in research.
>
> (Faculty 7)

It was also noteworthy that faculty members from the rurally located university seemed to speak more strongly of a collegial atmosphere when compared with their downtown counterparts. Faculty members at University B would speak of walking around campus and getting to know all their colleagues and often seeing these same colleagues in the pubs and restaurants around town:

> ... a professor might know you by your name as opposed to some of the larger factory institutions where you're a number.
>
> (Faculty 17)

This cultural divide between competitiveness and collaboration was also reflected by faculty rank and seniority. The perception was that junior faculty express their competitiveness in seeking promotion and obtaining tenure while more senior faculty express their competitiveness through access to research funding, resources (including graduate students), and securing the limited and prized senior academic positions:

> The worst ones actually are the Assistant Professors who are on tenure track.
>
> (Faculty 1)

> ... Director of Graduate programmes or Director of Research; those are plum jobs ... And there's a lot of competition amongst senior faculty for those roles.
>
> (Faculty 5)

While there were not many instructors or teaching fellows interviewed for this study, those interviewed often described a culture fractured from the rest of the university, and from which they felt their worth was considered less than other faculty members:

> I don't necessarily feel that it's perceived that you have any value with respect to the direction of the department or the university … So I think there's a very distinct demarcation.
>
> (Faculty 36)

Lastly, our findings find some support for the argument that the professional disciplines align more naturally with corporate ideology and branding practices and therefore have disproportionate value and negotiating power at academic institutions:

> … in terms of wanting the departments to market themselves, yes, the pressure is on … So, we're supposed to be working with the community, you know, to get kids out doing philosophy or philosophical points of interest or … that was very difficult.
>
> (Faculty 31)

> … So in other words it is a kind of complex set of negotiations in which this concept of branding, self-identification and the almost negotiating of perspective and position is a continuous occupation. And some departments are not strong in research so they will say, okay we're not strong in research. What we'll do is we'll have small classes and we train our undergraduates well. Others say, look we have very large classes because we're heavy in research and it means we cannot allow our faculty members to teach more than two full courses a year because it will take them out of the lab so we can't do that. So it's a balance.
>
> (Faculty 13)

Leadership: Tensions and communication issues

The role of leadership in communicating brand messages to faculty members that balances the corporate vision but still reflects the unique values and beliefs of academic life was found to be a challenging balancing act, and one which was full of ambiguities.

Faculty members expressed mixed feelings about senior management and their role in branding. However, they agreed that senior management should communicate their vision of the brand and acknowledge and listen to feedback from faculty members. They further contended that leadership needed to be mindful of the historical place of the university and to reflect that in their messaging so it resonates as authentic to the faculty members they are asking to deliver the brand.

As reflected in the statements below, there are major challenges in achieving faculty engagement when there is a perceived lack of communication or where the communication is one way and does not recognize the significant role faculty members play in transmitting and living the brand. Some faculty members reflected that some leaders in pursuit of the 'brand' manage the performance and priorities of their colleagues in ways that are precisely contrary to what is required to engender increased commitment amongst key academic staff:

> ... no, I can tell them honestly, that I think they are missing the point about their brand, I really do. I think that what the brand is according to the students and according to the faculty and according to alumni for some reason is being abandoned by the management in favour of a very different model ... they are missing the point about what makes [University B] interesting and special [and] attracts students – and in a way they are being pressured into abandoning their brand as it is perceived by those who participate in it.
>
> (Faculty 23)

> I have mixed feelings about this [faculty engagement with brand]. I think it has a tendency to make it look more like a grocery store than a deli ... I just will not get into the entertaining business.
>
> (Faculty 31)

Another faculty member from University A expanded on the general statements above, highlighting the consequences of trying to steer the university brand:

> ... universities have been directing themselves towards this market by trying to find vocabulary and the instruments in order to attract the best of them to internationalize, because of course, that's one of the buzz-words in contemporary education ... And how do you do it? Do you simply take students who can afford to go and are willing to pay or are you trying to attract the best students who will then make a particular contribution, both to the University and then subsequently to either Canada or their own nation? ... They are in fact clearly targeted markets ... in order to achieve what the university has defined as the ideal student mix; national, international, out-of-province, Ontario students, direct-entry, older students, trying to get more women in Engineering and more men in Humanities. Trying to get more

non-Asians in Pharmacy and trying to get recent immigrants out of the instrumental professional faculties into more broadly based subjects. So this is what I think is going on – this is my perception.

(Faculty 13)

Building on the importance of senior leadership, our findings revealed that faculty's relationship with management was often reflective of their relationship during contract negotiations, which often led to feelings of distrust and betrayal. At University B in particular, faculty at higher levels of seniority felt their relationship with administration had been strained by past years of contract negotiations. They described these negotiations as adversarial and further described their relationship with administration as a culture of distrust that impacted on all initiatives including branding:

> ... so it became a real administration–faculty divide – And so people have a lot of distrust of the administration.

(Faculty 22)

Faculty in this study also expressed tension when they were required to assume dual administrative roles that demanded a more direct acknowledgement for the fiscal constraints and challenges universities are facing. Further layers of complexity to the academic culture were revealed, particularly when academics adopt managerial responsibilities and have to set their academic values against competing corporate ideologies, in effect requiring them to balance different and sometimes polarizing perspectives. This complexity is supported in the literature, as Henkel reminds us that the university is more than a community of scholars, it is also a public service and often explicitly a business (2005: 169–70). Whitchurch and Gordon add that:

> Movements in academic and/or professional identities are, therefore, complex, varied and contested, raising a key question for managers and leaders as to how the university can become a place where all roles and identities are valued in adding to the achievement of the reputation and success.

(2010: 138)

In exploring how faculty interpret and react to branding activities, it was interesting to explore how they responded to the iconography at their university. Most faculty members were aware of the university seal and prescriptive style guidelines and emblems, but chose to engage and adopt them minimally, and some did so with a focus directed more towards developing and updating their individual school/department logo with the goal of being easily recognizable, visible, and translatable:

> ... in the school of nursing we developed our own logo. Four years ago, we developed a design for our own uniform so that all of our students are immediately recognized as [a University C] student, which is really important in a clinical setting ... It has got the school logo on it along with their identification ... I think for us that was really successful ... we were seeing so much inappropriate dress – which didn't make the school look good – didn't make the profession look good – so by that [developing a standard uniform] when I walk in I immediately picked out who were the [University C] students. It also gave the students a sense of pride that they were representing [University C] so I think that is also very important.
>
> (Faculty 29)

Drori *et al.* (2013) support these observations, arguing that university branding has shifted the iconography of institutions, which were traditionally represented by academic seals, to images more represented by logos. They argue that the purpose is to create differentiation among otherwise similar products. In this context it is interesting to consider the Marketing Director's comments about the challenges he had to create a sub brand logo which was 'hip' and 'cool'. He described it as 'cutting edge', 'innovative', and 'assertive' and as a 'metamorphosis' from the older, more generic brand iconography:

> ... like kids with a chip on our shoulder ... we are trying to say we're just as good ... We're innovative, we're cutting edge, we're on the grow.
>
> (Manager C, University C)

Brand authenticity questioned: Promises made versus promises delivered

Further, our findings revealed a certain degree of cynicism for branding, as the messaging was essentially the same at all institutions, with all institutions striving for the same key brand elements including research excellence, teaching excellence, excellence in student experience, and an international and global presence. This homogenization is not a new concept and has been highlighted by several authors (Jones, 2009; Naidoo, 2008; Shanahan, 2009). Their argument is that higher education policy is being driven by private sector ideologies and a desire for increasing accountability and comparability between institutions. Oddly enough, while these policies have been designed to drive competiveness and differentiation in the higher education sector, this desire for accountability has driven policy and incentives (e.g. research grants) in the opposite direction, and led to more standardization of curriculum and an organizational structure that promote homogenization rather than differentiation.

While institutions are driven to make similar brand claims, the authenticity of these claims is often at odds with the reality, as institutional history in many ways restricts faculty in supporting an authentic brand message. University C comes from a history embedded with values consistent with a polytechnic education and an academic identity more associated with career-based education and training, and therefore making claims more aligned with a history embedded in research creates a tension for some faculty members where they have expressed conflicting views on this brand message. Similarly, University A has a historical reputation as a large competitive research-based university, which is likewise difficult to reconcile with brand elements such as excellence in student experience, particularly when faculty have pointed out that many of them are teaching classes of 500 plus students, with little personal contact or student engagement.

As indicated earlier, several faculty members spoke of dual managerial roles that required them to adopt certain business ideologies more consistent with a sales pitch, and which is often not consistent with reality. As one faculty member (Faculty 33) expressed, '[i]t's just an empty signifier for one-on-one interaction' and is not representative of the kind of interaction students receive, effectively suggesting it is in fact a lie.

Building on this reasoning, some faculty spoke of the falsehoods around advertising and marketing materials, with one faculty member commenting on a photo used to promote the engineering department that featured three female students, suggesting the engineering department had a healthy gender balance. This faculty member argued this represented almost all the females currently enrolled in engineering and described the advertisement as a 'lie', and 'offensive' because it was so 'disingenuous'.

The question raised by the above is whether or not these branding activities through marketing and advertising are not only inauthentic but are designed with intent and the goal of misleading students, funders, and other external stakeholders. This was particularly challenging, as faculty members stated that they associate their role with the kinds of activities that are consistent with seeking truth, exposing lies, and protecting the social and public good. Our findings highlight the tension faculty members feel when they are asked to support and participate in branding activities, where they see themselves as perpetuating false statements that may also be inconsistent with their own values and beliefs.

In summary, the above sections shed further light on the complex role faculty members play in branding universities and the unique tensions that arise as a result of the distinctive values, beliefs, and basic assumptions that characterize the academic environment. Just as previous studies on corporate identity reveal, it is an amalgamation of several elements. In the same way the possibility of successful branding in higher education will need to take on board the multiplicity of competing attributes encompassed in branding higher education institutions.

Conclusions

The significance of this research is that it illustrates how branding practices are influenced and mediated by the organizational dynamics and internal culture of higher education institutions. Further, it shows how organizational cultures of public-sector higher education institutions that were previously insulated from market forces and business sector ideologies are adapting to, resisting, and responding to forces that represent a challenge to the traditional practices of the university. We have also shown how such responses are somewhat mediated by institution heritage and status as well as location.

This research also offers insights and implications for practice. For university administrators, managers, and leaders, this study reveals the complex relationships that faculty members have with branding and branding activities at their university. If administrators wish to engage faculty in branding activities, they must first acknowledge and respect academic traditions and culture, and understand the specific culture of higher education and the normative concern with the public good. Further, to ensure faculty do not feel the process is meaningless, administrators must work with faculty to avoid brand homogenization by seeking distinctive brand elements that distinguish them from other institutions. In doing so, senior leadership must be mindful of the historical place of the university and understand faculty responsibility to uphold the truth and ensure authenticity in their brand claims. Lastly, all the above will require both university administrators and faculty to work together to nurture and build a culture of trust through respectful and transparent communication processes.

References

Ali-Choudhury, R., Bennett, R., and Savani, S. (2009) 'University marketing directors' views on the components of a university brand'. *International Review on Public and Nonprofit Marketing*, 6 (1), 11–33.

Arvidsson, A. (2005) 'Brands – A critical perspective'. *Journal of Consumer Culture*, 5 (2), 235–58.

Bakan, J. and Newson, J. (2010) 'The university and its political economy: An academic callings interview'. In Newson, J. and Polster, C. (eds) *Academic Callings: The university we have had, now have, and could have*. Toronto: Canadian Scholars Press Inc.

Bennett, R. and Ali-Choudhury, R. (2009) 'Prospective students' perceptions of university brands: An empirical study'. *Journal of Marketing for Higher Education*, 19 (1), 85–107.

Burmann, C. and Zeplin, S. (2005) 'Building brand commitment: A behavioural approach to internal brand management'. *Journal of Brand Management*, 12 (4), 279–300.

Chapleo, C. (2010) 'What defines "successful" university brands?' *International Journal of Public Sector Management*, 23 (2), 169–83.

Creswell, J. (2009) *Research Design: Qualitative, quantitative and mixed methods approaches*. Third edition. Thousand Oaks, CA: SAGE.

Currie, J. and Vidovich, L. (2000) 'Privatization and competition policies for Australian universities'. *International Journal of Educational Development*, 20 (2), 135–51.

De Chernatony, L. and Segal-Horn, S. (2003) 'The criteria for successful services brands'. *European Journal of Marketing*, 37 (7/8), 1095–118.

Drori, G., Delmestri, G., and Oberg, A. (2013) *Branding the University: Relational strategy of identity construction in a competitive field*. Online. www. portlandpress.com/pp/books/online/wg86/086/0137/0860137.pdf (accessed 12 April 2016).

Eisenhardt, K. and Graebner, M. (2007) 'Theory building from cases: Opportunities and challenges'. *Academy of Management Journal*, 50 (1), 25–32.

Elliot, R. and Percy, L. (2007) *Strategic Brand Management*. New York: Oxford University Press.

Enders, J. and Kaulisch, M. (2006) 'The binding and unbinding of academic careers'. In Teichler, U. (ed.) *The Formative Years of Scholars*. London: Portland Press.

Fisher, D., Rubenson, K., Jones, G., and Shanahan, T. (2009) 'The political economy of post-secondary education: A comparison of British Columbia, Ontario and Québec'. *Higher Education*, 57 (5), 549–66.

Hatch, M. and Schultz, M. (2002) 'The dynamics of organizational identity'. *Human Relations*, 55 (8), 989–1018.

— (2008) *Taking Brand Initiative: How companies can align strategy, culture, and identity through corporate branding*. San Francisco, CA: Jossey-Bass.

Hearn, C. (2008) 'Meat, mask, burden: Probing the contours of the branded self'. *Journal of Consumer Culture*, 8, 197–217.

Hemsley-Brown, J. and Goonawarddana, S. (2007) 'Brand harmonization in the international higher education market'. *Journal of Business Research*, 60, 942–8.

Hemsley-Brown, J. and Oplatka, I. (2006) 'Universities in a competitive global marketplace: A systematic review of the literature on higher education marketing'. *International Journal of Public Sector Management*, 19 (4), 316–38.

Henkel, M. (2005) 'Academic identity and autonomy in a changing policy environment'. *Higher Education*, 49 (1–2), 155–76.

Holt, D. (2002) 'Why do brands cause trouble? A dialectical theory of consumer culture and branding'. *Journal of Consumer Research*, 29 (1), 70–90.

— (2006) 'Toward a sociology of branding'. *Journal of Consumer Culture*, 6 (3), 299–302.

Jevons, C. (2006) 'Universities: A prime example of branding gone wrong'. *Journal of Product and Brand Management*, 15 (7), 466–7.

Jones, G. (2009) 'Sectors, institutional types and the challenges of shifting categories: A Canadian commentary'. *Higher Education Quarterly*, 63 (4), 371–83.

Judson, K., Aurand, T., Gorchels, L., and Gordon, G. (2009) 'Building a university brand from within: University administrators' perspectives of internal branding'. *Services Marketing Quarterly*, 30 (1), 54–68.

Karreman, D. and Rylander, A. (2008) 'Managing meaning through branding: The case of a consulting firm'. *Organization Studies*, 29 (1), 103–25.

Kornberger, M. (2010) *Brand Society: How brands transform management and lifestyle*. Cambridge: Cambridge University Press.

Lury, C. (2004) *Brands: The logos of the global cultural economy*. London and New York: Routledge.

Maringe, F. (2005) 'Interrogating the crisis in higher education marketing: The CORD model'. *International Journal of Educational Management*, 19 (7), 564–78.

Melewar, T. and Akel, S. (2005) 'The role of corporate identity in the higher education sector: A case study'. *Corporate Communications: An International Journal*, 10 (1), 41–57.

Metcalfe, A. (2010) 'Revisiting academic capitalism in Canada: No longer the exception'. *The Journal of Higher Education*, 81 (4), 490–514.

Naidoo, R. (2008) 'Building or eroding intellectual capital? Student consumerism as a cultural force in the context of knowledge economy'. In Valimmaa, J. and Ylijoki, O.-H. (eds) *Cultural Perspectives on Higher Education*. Dordrecht: Springer.

Naidoo, R. and Pringle, J. (2014) 'Branding business schools: Academic struggles with the management of reputation'. In Pettigrew, A., Cornuel, E., and Hommel, U. (eds) *The Institutional Development of Business Schools*. Oxford: Oxford University Press.

Naidoo, R., Gosling, J., Bolden, R., O'Brien, A., and Hawkins, B. (2014) 'Leadership and branding in business schools: A Bourdieusian analysis'. *Higher Education Research and Development*, 33 (1), 144–56.

Naidoo, R., Shankar, A., and Veer, E. (2011) 'The consumerist turn in higher education: Policy aspirations and outcomes'. *Journal of Marketing Management*, 27 (11–12), 1142–62.

Parker, M. and Jary, D. (1995) 'The McUniversity: Organization, management and academic subjectivity'. *Organization*, 2 (2), 319–38.

Polster, C. (2003) 'Canadian university research policy at the turn of the century: Continuity and change in the social relations of academic research'. *Studies in Political Economy*, 71/72, 177–99.

Pries, F. and Guild, P. (2007) 'Commercial exploitation of new technologies arising from university research: Start-ups and markets for technology'. *R&D Management*, 37 (4), 319–28.

Rae, B. (2005) *Ontario a Leader in Learning: Report and recommendations, February 2005*. Toronto: Queen's Printers for Ontario. Online. www.tcu.gov. on.ca/eng/document/reports/postsec.pdf (accessed 12 April 2016).

Russell, S. (2011) 'Internalizing the brand? Identity regulation and resistance at Aqua-Tilt'. In Brannan, M., Parsons, E., and Priola, V. (eds) *Branded Lives*. Cheltenham: Edward Elgar.

Shanahan, T. (2009) 'Accountability initiatives in higher education: An overview of the impetus to accountability, its expressions and implications'. Accounting or Accountability in Higher Education Conference, 8 January, Toronto.

Smith, S. and Buchanan-Oliver, M. (2011) 'The branded self as paradox: Polysemic readings of employee–brand identification'. In Brannan, M., Parsons, E., and Priola, V. (eds) *Branded Lives*. Cheltenham: Edward Elgar.

Temple, P. (2006) 'Branding higher education: Illusion or reality?' *Perspectives*, 10 (1), 15–19.

Usher, A. and Dunn, R. (2009) *On the Brink: How the recession of 2009 will affect post-secondary education*. Toronto: Education Policy Institute.

Waeraas, A. and Solbakk, M. (2009) 'Defining the essence of a university: Lessons from higher education branding'. *Higher Education*, 57, 449–62.

Whitchurch, C. and Gordon, G. (2010) 'Diversifying academic and professional identities in higher education: Some management challenges'. *Tertiary Education and Management*, 16 (2), 129–44.

Williams, G. (2004) 'The changing political economy of higher education'. In Shattock, M. (ed.) *Entrepreneurialism and the Transformation of Russian Universities*. Paris: International Institute for Educational Planning.

Wilson, E., Bengtsson, A., and Curran, C. (2014) 'Brand meaning gaps and dynamics: Theory, research, and practice'. *Qualitative Market Research: An International Journal*, 17 (2), 128–50.

Yin, R. (2009) *Case Study Research: Design and methods*. Fourth edition. Thousand Oaks, CA: SAGE.

Part Three

The uses of higher education

Chapter 9

Too many or too few?
The perennial debates on higher education and the world of work

Ulrich Teichler

Introduction

For more than five decades, the relationships between higher education and the world of work have been among the key themes both of higher education policy and higher education research. Throughout these years, it has been a controversial discourse. Thereby, the discourse of scholars – in the disciplinary domains of economics and sociology, and in the thematic domains of educational research, labour market research, professional research, and related areas – has been closely linked to the political discourse.

The most popular theme can be summarized by the question: do we have too few or too many students, and eventually graduates? In the political arena of economically advanced countries, we note upward and downward mood swings, but the suspicion that we have too many is often evident. Clearly, the growth of higher education – from about one-tenth on average in economically advanced countries in the late 1950s to about half of the corresponding age group about five decades later – was not smoothly linked to developments in the employment system. This question was the pet issue among economists, and some of them were very vocal in spreading their conviction that the highly educated continue to be the winners, and that higher education expansion promises more economic growth.

The second most popular theme is that of the socio-biographic composition of those who succeed in education and in subsequent careers: how equal or unequal is education? Do we have too many of the same? This second question is linked to the first one, because higher education had to be 'open' in providing access for many young people whose parents had not been through it themselves – otherwise such an expansion could not have occurred. For various reasons, however, the relatively high openness of higher education in terms of overall quantity of students did not turn out to be linked with a regular erosion of inequality according to socio-biographic characteristics. The political debate was more complicated than that regarding shortage or oversupply of graduates. This theme was the pet issue of sociologists, and the most vocal sociologists in this debate claimed that inequality tends to persist as regards parental background (see the discussion in Shavit and Blossfeld, 1993; Brennan and Naidoo, 2008).

The persistence of these discourses both in the political arena and among scholars certainly suggests that the phenomena are ambivalent and that no easy answers can be provided. The aim of this contribution to the Festschrift in honour of Gareth Williams, however, is not to discuss the dilemmas of trends and policies, but rather those of the scholars addressing these thematic areas. Both in observing policy and research trends (Teichler *et al.*, 1980; Teichler, 1999, 2009), the author of this contribution came to the conclusion that the academic debates had a specific fault: the usual arguments were repeated by scholars with limited scopes, i.e. remaining in their respective disciplinary cage (either of economics or sociology) and concentrating their observations solely on quantitative–structural aspects of the relationships between higher education and the world of work.

I had the opportunity of getting to know both Gareth Williams in person and his writings in the 1970s, but two memories of the 1980s dominate. First, Gareth Williams wrote a review of a book written by me and my colleagues on the state of research on higher education and the world of work (Teichler *et al.*, 1980); he argued that our interpretations as sociologists were more similar to those presented by economists than we seemed to perceive. The second memory was impressive. In 1982, Burton Clark invited eight prominent scholars to Los Angeles to summarize the state of higher education research (Clark, 1984). Gareth Williams was invited to explain 'the economic approach' (Williams, 1984), and I was invited to add a 'non-economist's comment'. Gareth Williams made clear that he was not the purist economist and that our understanding of the world would be widened if we transgressed disciplinary borders. He also underscored that we do not understand the dynamics of higher education properly if we concentrate solely on quantitative–structural features. So, he made a plea for cross-disciplinary higher education research interested in understanding the complexity of the thematic area, and, thus, any chance of concentrating my response on the usual allegations economists make about sociologists, and sociologists about economists, was removed. This was the start of easy mutual understanding, even though we only met a dozen times or so at conferences, project meetings, and so on.

The following analysis will not therefore pay much attention to the isolated literature of pure economists and sociologists (e.g. as predominantly summarized in Marginson, 2015), but rather will draw primarily from analyses transgressing disciplinary barriers. It also aims to show how beneficial it is not to be confined only to quantitative–structural features. Rather, two other discourses will be addressed. First, the functional discourse: what role should future graduate employment play in the educational objectives and activities of higher education? Second, the substantive and procedural discourse about learning and future job tasks: what aspects of knowledge and competences are crucial for job tasks and job performance, and which of them should and could higher education strive for?

The following analysis will focus on the first question named above: do we have too few or too many students, and eventually graduates? This choice was made because, after all, the pet themes of the economists are the most familiar ones for Gareth Williams, even though he did not remain in their cages.

Education and employment: The quantitative–structural issues

Concepts of economics of education (*cf.* Psacharopoulos, 1987) experienced a breakthrough in popularity in the 1960s, according to which high investment in education and a high level of educational attainment of the workforce of a country are likely to lead to economic growth. This was the time of the Cold War, when such a message could lead to fights for superiority in education and research. It was also the time of the foundation of the OECD, which became a major advocate for educational investment (see Papadopoulos, 1994). In West Germany, for example, we noted controversial reactions initially ranging from a forecast of an 'educational catastrophe' unless substantial educational expansion was not strived for, to a warning of an 'academic proletariat' as the consequence of expansion.

Entry rates to higher education increased from about 5 per cent on average for the economically advanced countries in the early 1950s to 20 per cent around 1970. But scepticism spread as regards the desirability of expansion, and the oil crisis of 1973 is often named as a turning point from a dominant advocacy of higher education expansion towards a dominance of more cautious views. The development of entry rates was quite varied from the early 1970s to about the mid-1980s. Thereafter, growth picked up again in many countries and continued up to the present. The rate of persons with at least a bachelor's degree among the 25 to 64 year olds across the OECD countries was on average 7 per cent in 1960, 10 per cent in 1970, and eventually 16 per cent in 1980. It increased to 28 per cent in 2000 and reached 39 per cent in 2010 (OECD, 2012). And we continue to note concurrently optimistic voices (e.g. Hanushek and Woessmann, 2011), but also signs of adjustments (e.g. OECD, 1998), with warnings about the dangers of higher education expansion (e.g. Büchel *et al.*, 2003).

According to what could be called the 'shortage and need for expansion narrative', substantial expansion would contribute to higher economic growth and societal well-being in many respects, e.g. reduced inequality of opportunity and greater social justice, a more comfortable life, and a society shaped by knowledge in general. In contrast, according to the 'over-education and mismatch narrative', the oversupply of graduates would lead to increasing graduate unemployment, employment based on 'credentialism', 'diploma disease' or 'screening', with frequent employment in positions not adequate to the level of educational attainment, declining income rewards for education, and 'under-utilization' of competences.

Altogether, quantitative planning of higher education according to presumed needs of the employment system did not play a strong role in most market-oriented economically advanced countries (see Fulton *et al.*, 1982; Hüfner, 1983). Rather, the belief was widespread that the employment system has unpredictable dynamics that make futile eventual forecasts of future demands and corresponding planning of supply. Also, the conviction was widespread that higher education should serve the expectations of the learners and the actual 'social demand'.

The discourse about whether we have too few or too many graduates was fairly similar at every moment in time across market-oriented economically advanced countries. This holds true, even though the level of expansion differed strikingly: when the entry rate was about 10 per cent in some countries, it had already surpassed 30 per cent in others. In 2010, graduation rates from higher education ranged from 23 to 60 per cent among OECD member states (OECD, 2012). Some experts concluded that the discourse was more strongly influenced by the rampant influence of international organizations than by actual conditions in the individual countries.

The quantitative debate was mostly linked to the structural debate: what elements of institutional type or programme type diversity within higher education are meaningful in this respect? Of course, there has been a long tradition of analysing the links between fields of study and occupational areas. In the wake of expansion, however, increasing attention was paid to the vertical diversity. Martin Trow (1974) coined the terms that became most popular: 'elite higher education' prevails as long as not more than 15 per cent of an age group enrol; 'mass higher education' emerges as a second sector alongside serving the increased variety of students' talents, motives, and job prospects, and the term 'universal higher education' is used when more than half enrol. The question remained: what features of higher education (institutional types, levels of study programmes, qualitative and reputation ranks of institutions) or of specific programmatic thrusts of institutions and programmes are important for graduates' careers (see Neave, 2011)?

The process of expansion was accompanied by a changing understanding of the borderlines of this educational sector. In the 1960s, we note a shift from 'university education' to 'higher education', thus also including shorter programmes as well as programmes taught at institutions without any substantial research function. In the 1980s, international organizations coined the term 'tertiary education', thereby also including short and strongly vocationally oriented programmes without a 'higher' intellectual emphasis. This term, however, did not become popular in all countries.

Actually, the controversy about shortage versus over-education referred primarily to education and labour market statistics. As regards the latter, one tended to look at the employment status (employed, unemployed, and other activities), possibly income, and certainly the occupational category, whereby managers and professionals were commonly viewed to be the typical occupational outcomes for university graduates. Views differed on whether semi-professional jobs, such as technicians, could be considered appropriate for graduates, while those employed in clerical and sales positions, or as skilled or unskilled workers, were viewed as over-educated.

Critique spread in the 1970s that measuring relationships between higher education and employment with the help of occupational categories helped support the over-education and mismatch narratives in an artificial way, because higher education might also enrich work in the less-privileged occupational sectors. Graduate surveys turned out to be useful in identifying the impact of higher education beyond the dichotomies of 'too many/too few' or 'match/mismatch'. Surveys were addressed to individual institutions, individual occupational areas, or graduates of a whole country (see Paul *et al.*, 2000), and they were often viewed as useful feedback for possible improvements in higher education.

The first major comparative study of this kind – undertaken about three to four years after graduation in various European countries and Japan in 1999 – suggested that graduates more often noted a link between study and employment than a glance at the occupational categories suggested. On average across the European countries referred to, 28 per cent of those employed had no managerial or professional positions. Only 19 per cent stated that they made little use of their knowledge acquired in the course of study, only 14 per cent each noted that their field of study was wrong or irrelevant and that their position was hardly appropriate to their level of educational attainment, and only 11 per cent were dissatisfied with their professional situation.

The survey showed that a close link between a person's field of study and subsequent occupational category is by no means a norm. On average across countries, only 39 per cent agreed with the statement 'my field is the only possible/by far the best field', 40 per cent agreed that 'some other fields could prepare for the area of work as well', thus indicating a relatively high degree of flexibility, while only 9 per cent agreed that 'another field would have been more useful' (Schomburg and Teichler, 2006).

In sum, statistics and research on graduate employment showed that the number of typical graduate jobs spread, but less than the number of graduates. The majority of additional graduates took over jobs immediately below the traditional strata of graduate jobs and considered their education to be somewhat related to their study.

Altogether, a look at the quantitative–structural developments allows us to conclude that the overall distribution of levels of educational attainment became flatter. As the occupational hierarchy did not change to the same extent, fine informal differences between institutions of higher education became more important in the selection among graduates. What has already been common in some countries for many decades, for example in Japan (see Dore, 1976; Teichler, 1977), has since spread all over the world: an interest in 'rankings', i.e. considering tiny distinctions between the 'quality' of research or teaching as sufficiently important to embark on a 'rat race' with the hope that tiny differences 'matter' enormously (see Shin *et al.*, 2011; Hazelkorn, 2011).

In contrast, graduate surveys were a step forward in looking beyond the quantitative–structural relationships phenomena. One has to consider as well the various functions higher education might be expected to serve. As well as the substance and processes of learning and their relationship to the work of graduates, it is necessary to understand the changed role of higher education on the way towards a 'highly educated society' (Teichler, 1991).

What purpose is higher education expected to serve? The functional issues

Higher education is generally assumed to have a broad range of functions as regards teaching and learning, notably:

(1) to stimulate students intellectually in the academic domain and help them understand and master the academic theories, methods, and knowledge domains;
(2) to contribute to cultural enhancement and personal development;
(3) to prepare students for subsequent work and other life spheres through laying the foundation of relevant knowledge and helping them to understand and utilize the typical 'rules and tools' of their professional life;
(4) to foster the ability to challenge established practice: to be sceptical and critical, to be able to challenge conventional wisdom, to cope with indeterminate work tasks, and to contribute to innovation.

As regards professional preparation, higher education is often called on not to be closely geared to professional 'demands' – certainly to a lower extent than vocational training on lower levels of educational attainment, because such a close link is less efficient if job tasks are highly complex and highly dynamic and if the job holders are often expected to make independent decisions. Moreover, modern societies have accepted the principle of academic freedom of the academic profession with a primary emphasis on seeking 'truth' (Shils, 1991), as well as socializing students according to the virtues of critical and unbounded inquiry and problem-solving.

Research on the relationships between higher education and graduate employment has also highlighted various practical reasons why higher education is unlikely to prepare graduates as closely for their job tasks as advocates of a strong 'match' are inclined to favour. There are endemic imperfections in the matching – by employers and others – of job requirements with jobseekers' abilities. There is also a planning gap, because much time is needed from the identification of new requirements to the actual 'production' of new graduates. Finally, the dynamics in the quantitative development of occupations force many graduates to change major professional activities, occupations, or employers during their lifespans. Proposals have been made to counteract these phenomena by providing relatively general pre-career study programmes and leaving specialization to initial training and lifelong learning, but available continuing education thus far has not fundamentally changed the character of pre-career study.

Notions vary across disciplines as regards the expected professional emphasis: they are not identical for dentistry and philosophy. In the USA, a distinction is common between 'academic' and 'professional' fields. In countries such as the UK and France, some professional associations are involved in the accreditation of study programmes and in the professional 'licensing' of graduates. In Germany, 'state examinations' traditionally prevailed in some fields. By contrast, in some countries the award of a university degree implies an *effectus civilis*, i.e. both an academic degree and a typical professional entry qualification (see Jablonska-Skinder and Teichler, 1992).

From the 1960s to the 1980s, the view spread in economically advanced countries that some kind of professional emphasis should play a stronger role in higher education, because an increasing number of graduates would take over positions where a direct professional preparation had been customary in the past. But the notions of such professional emphasis varied enormously (see Teichler, 2009). Some preferred laying the foundation for professional work, while others wanted higher education to prepare students for academic work. Some advocated an 'applied' emphasis in terms of directing the transfer of knowledge to practical problem-solving. Others advocated an 'orientation towards practice' in terms of learning to understand the tensions between theory and practice during the course of study. Others emphasized innovation in terms of coping with indeterminate work tasks and innovation. There were divergent views as regards the extent to which general versus specific knowledge helped to master job tasks. Finally, while some suggested that graduates needed a sound knowledge base, others called for an emphasis to be placed on competences acquired by the end of study.

Actually, a certain degree of professional emphasis in all higher education institutions and study programmes was called for in the higher education legislation enacted in West Germany and Sweden in the 1970s. And many countries opted for a model of inter-institutional diversification of the higher education system, whereby universities were expected to strive for a creative mix of academic learning and laying the foundation for professional work, while other institutions of higher education had a more applied emphasis. This divide survived in most countries despite the decision in the UK to upgrade the 'polytechnics' to universities and thus to blur that distinction. The term 'universities of applied sciences' spread across Europe for the latter types of institutions, even though their character varies substantially across countries (Taylor *et al.*, 2008).

In the 1990s and more strongly in the first decade of the twenty-first century, a new movement emerged in Europe that emphasized a closer functional link between higher education and the presumed demands of the employment system. 'Employability' became a popular catchword (Yorke, 2007; Vukasovic, 2007), which is in line with the new slogans of the 'knowledge society' and 'knowledge economy' often employed to call for directly visible 'outcomes' of higher education.

Actually, the meanings of 'employability' are varied: so the institutions of higher education should do whatever they can in order to enhance their graduates' career success; the students should choose an institution, a field, or a programme most likely to lead to reward in the employment system; the substance of study programmes should be geared to the expected substance of work tasks; students should be trained for problem-solving; students should be trained in areas outside their major field, e.g. to acquire socio-communicative skills; and finally, institutions of higher education ought to help students with job seeking and the transfer to employment.

The term 'employability' is certainly misleading, because it was initially employed in labour market research and policy for 'youth at risk'. Moreover, higher education can directly care for knowledge, competences, and work, but not for salaries and social benefits. Therefore, terms such as 'professional relevance' would be more suitable (see Teichler, 2009). I noted in analysing the headlines and abstracts in journal articles collected in *Research into Higher Education Abstracts* that British authors talk about 'employability' more than five times as often as authors from other European countries when they address the relationships between higher education and the world of work. Is this a response to a strong general emphasis in the past, or to the upgrading of the polytechnics, or an indication of exceptionally strong calls for utilitarian approaches in higher education?

Finally, the functional discourse on higher education does not only call attention to what employers, politicians, or academics call for. It also asks how close students are to, or how far away they are from, the vision of a *homo oeconomicus*, i.e. a person strongly motivated by the highest possible income and status. This 'ideal' of – in economic terms – a *homo oeconomicus* or – in sociological terms – of a 'status seeker' is by no means self-evident. It certainly was not the driving force for the student protests in the 1960s, and the concept of a possible spread of 'post-industrial' values (Inglehart, 1977) gained popularity in the 1970s.

In Schomburg and Teichler's international comparative survey (2006), six types of graduates' work orientations were identified, each comprising between 12 and 21 per cent: (1) 'traditional professionals', emphasizing demanding work tasks and expecting a high status as a matter of procedure; (2) 'new professionals', expecting less status attributes for demanding work and more of a work–life balance; (3) 'career-oriented graduates' being primarily interested in economic rewards; (4) 'socially oriented graduates'; (5) 'self-development-oriented graduates'; and finally, (6) those who could be called non-professionals, i.e. those who did not emphasize strongly any of the dimensions named above (Schomburg, 2007).

How does higher education prepare for a career? The substantive and procedural issues

As pointed out above, efforts at understanding the relationships between higher education and the world of work and possibly finding better solutions cannot merely rely on statistical data and surveys on the quantitative–structural relationships between higher education and employment. Also, a discourse on the functions of higher education vis-à-vis graduate employment and work does not disclose concrete options. Therefore, a third question has featured constantly in this framework over the years: what is the impact of the substance of study programmes and of the modes of teaching and learning on graduate work?

In considering recent debates in this domain, we tend to believe that study programmes in higher education have traditionally had certain features or ranges of options irrespective of variations by country, disciplines, type of higher education institutions, and levels of degree programmes (Teichler, 1985). While the public discourse often addresses differences by discipline and occupational areas, many scholars underscored variations across countries that reflect both curricular traditions in higher education (e.g. Rothblatt, 2011) and different general links between education and work, such as a strong 'professional' emphasis in, for example, France and Germany, and a looser 'market' linkage notably in Anglo-Saxon countries and Japan (Müller and Shavit, 1998).

Analyses of curricular variations, first, point out that the learning thrusts in higher education are clearly in the cognitive domain. We note, however, the varying attention paid – according to the terms coined by Benjamin Bloom – to the 'affective' domain, and that 'sensu-motoric' abilities could play a role in some fields, e.g. dentistry or sport. Second, the understanding of research-based reasoning seems to be a common goal, but views vary as to whether this should be the exclusive emphasis. Third, curricula differ in various respects according to academic or professional emphasis: whether fields were shaped according to disciplines or prospective professional areas, training of the knowledge base versus training of the professional application of knowledge. Fourth, curricula vary as regards the coverage of academic knowledge: whether breadth or in-depth knowledge in a specialized area is emphasized; whether the programme focuses on a single discipline, also covers other disciplines, or has an interdisciplinary approach; whether emphasis is placed on the settled foundations of a field or the most up-to-date knowledge, etc. Finally, there is a rich discourse on the modes of teaching and learning: whether transmission of knowledge by experts in the content but amateurs in the teaching and learning processes is the norm, or whether academics have to build up professional expertise in teaching and learning and if so, what the most effective modes of teaching, learning, and assessment are.

As already pointed out, efforts have been made since about the 1970s to change curricular approaches in favour of a more articulate relationship between study and work, and we have witnessed a recent additional wave in this respect. Altogether, six directions of change might be named (see Teichler, 2015).

First, the relationship between academic knowledge and its professional utilization has become a salient issue. Terms such as 'orientation towards practice', 'applied study programmes', or even 'vocationalisation' (Williams, 1985) have been coined in this framework. Links between academic knowledge and professional problem-solving might be addressed directly in lectures and seminars. The distinction between basic and applied research might be stretched in study programmes.

Second, learning in classroom settings is supplemented by phases of practical experiences. In the USA, terms such as 'experiential learning' and 'co-operative education' are used. In various European countries, 'internships' are widespread, and 'learning in projects' and 'problem-based learning' have gained momentum, and research has shown that practice-oriented methods and practical experiences in the course of study were likely to contribute to graduates' professional success (Van der Velden and Allen, 2011).

Third, a stronger emphasis is placed on explicit teaching and learning in domains either not part of individual disciplines or professional programmes, or cutting across them. Terms refer to education and knowledge, e.g. general education and interdisciplinary learning, or to the results of learning, e.g. 'generic skills' or 'key competences'. This might imply general knowledge, understanding the logic of science, analytical thinking, written communication skills, learning to learn, or skills in supplementary areas, e.g. ICT, foreign languages, and management.

Fourth, study programmes are expected to be arranged in a way that learning processes contribute to personality development: concentration ability, team work, socio-communicative skills, working under pressure, time management, initiative, persistence, accuracy, leadership, and negotiation abilities.

Fifth, institutions of higher education are increasingly expected to define the results of study not in terms of the acquisition of knowledge, but rather of the abilities to be reached. Terms such as 'skills', 'qualifications' (in some countries), 'competences', or 'learning outcomes' are used to explain this shift (see Weinert, 2001; Bennet *et al.*, 2000). This is also reflected in the 'qualifications frameworks' that have spread across European countries since 2005 under the influence of the 'Bologna Process'.

Sixth, students are encouraged to acquire international experiences, and institutions of higher education are expected to provide respective opportunities for learning and mobility. For example, the ministers in charge of higher education in the European countries collaborating in the Bologna Process agreed in 2009 to the target that by 2020, 20 per cent of graduates should have experienced a period of at least three months of study or study-related activities in another country during the course of their studies. As surveys of employers, teachers, students, and graduates indicate, graduates who have had international experience in the course of study are somewhat superior to non-mobile persons in general cognitive competences, specific academic competences, and key skills – possibly due to having had contrasting experiences in those domains abroad compared with at home. And they are viewed to be clearly superior on average in terms of foreign language proficiency, knowledge of other countries, and intercultural understanding (see the overviews in Teichler, 2007; Wächter, 2008).

Most of these envisaged or realized changes want to overcome the traditionally dominant approach, according to which students are helped by higher education to acquire the competences, but have to find ways of transferring this knowledge to job-related competences and actual work themselves. Rather, this transfer should be an integral element of pre-career learning – in classroom settings or outside.

This reflects the graduates' notions that they consider themselves to be well prepared as far as knowledge is concerned, but not with respect to other competences. According to Schomburg and Teichler's study (2006), graduates across Europe consider themselves relatively well prepared regarding 'knowledge' and not badly prepared regarding 'methodical skills' and 'intelligence'. They note shortages primarily regarding 'socio-communicative skills' and 'organizational skills' (Kivinen and Nurmi, 2007).

Links between study and career in a highly educated society

The number of graduates from higher education institutions in European countries is nowadays about ten times as high as it was about six decades ago. Statistics and research focusing on quantitative–structural issues indicate by and large that about two-thirds of graduates experience a 'match' in vertical terms, i.e. get a position that is considered typical for graduates, and that four-tenths experience a 'match' in horizontal terms, i.e. report work tasks for which their field of study is clearly essential. A substantial number of graduates do not observe such clear links, but at most only a tenth of them believe that they have ended up 'in misery'. The interesting question on the way towards a 'highly educated society' or to a 'knowledge society' is obviously how the competences and the work tasks of those for whom neither a clear 'match' nor 'mismatch' applies develop. Beyond that, it is important to understand the consequences of the discrepancy between a flattening of competences, i.e. a smaller vertical dispersion, in the wake of higher education on the one hand, and on the other, the relative stability of professional inequity and in many countries an even bigger vertical dispersion of income. The most important issue of the future might not, as one could believe in analysing current discourses, be the race to the top of higher education, but possibly that of a 'mass knowledge society': how does work in the middle of the occupational hierarchy and the division of labour change, when eventually more than half of the population have experienced higher education?

The popular controversy over whether we have 'too many' or 'too few' graduates is driven by the notion that there are clear yardsticks, and that the graduates can clearly be segmented into those who experience a 'match' between study and employment/work and those who experience a 'mismatch'. In reality, however, there is no consensus as regards the yardstick, and there are intermediate zones according to any measure, which can be viewed as characteristic of neither a 'match' nor a 'mismatch'.

In order to analyse the variations of criteria and the zones between the extremes, the isolated disciplinary approaches of economists and sociologists are insufficient. Both concentrate their analyses on quantitative–structural features, and infer from that about job requirements and tasks, learning and competences, etc. Rather, interdisciplinary approaches are needed and research designs that link quantitative–structural, functional, and substantive–procedural education, and work perspectives. Gareth Williams is by background one of the economists who started at a relatively early stage of his career to advocate such shifts. Some decades ago, research on higher education was altogether scarce and was undertaken predominantly by scholars addressing issues of higher education only occasionally and from their disciplinary perspective alone. Philip G. Altbach (2014) recently estimated that there are more than 6,000 academically based higher education researchers all over the world. If, for example, half of them could be viewed as having the identity of higher education researcher, i.e. wanting to address this thematic area comprehensively while taking care of its complexity, opportunities might improve in the future for an in-depth understanding of the major issues involved in phenomena such as those that were simply circumscribed in the past by the question: do we have too many or too few graduates from institutions of higher education?

References

Altbach, P. (2014) 'Knowledge for the contemporary university: Higher education as a field of study and training'. In Rumbley, L., Altbach, P., Stanfield, D., Shimmi, Y., Gayardon, A., and Chan, R. (eds) *Higher Education: A worldwide inventory of research centers, academic programs, and journals and publications*. 3rd edition. Bonn: Lemmens.

Bennet, D., Dunne, E., and Carré, C. (2000) *Skills Development in Higher Education and Employment*. Buckingham: SRHE/Open University Press.

Brennan, J. and Naidoo, R. (2008) 'Higher education and the achievement (and/or prevention) of equity and social justice'. *Higher Education*, 65 (3), 287–302.

Büchel, F., de Griep, A., and Martens, A. (eds) (2003) *Overeducation in Europe: Current issues in theory and policy*. Cheltenham: Edward Elgar.

Clark, B. (ed.) (1984) *Perspectives on Higher Education: Eight disciplinary and comparative views*. Los Angeles, CA: University of California Press.

Dore, R. (1976) *The Diploma Disease*. London: George Allen and Unwin.

Fulton, O., Gordon, A., and Williams, G. (1982) *Higher Education and Manpower Planning: A comparative study of planned and market economies*. Geneva: International Labour Office.

Hanushek, E. and Woessmann, L. (eds) (2011) *Handbook of Economics of Education*. Amsterdam: North Holland.

Hazelkorn, E. (2011) *Rankings and the Reshaping of Higher Education: The battle for world class excellence*. Basingstoke: Palgrave Macmillan.

Hüfner, K. (1983) 'Educational policy, planning and educational success'. In OECD, *Educational Planning: A reappraisal*. Paris: OECD.

Inglehart, R. (1977) *The Silent Revolution: Changing values and political styles among Western publics*. Princeton, NJ: Princeton University Press.

Jablonska-Skinder, H. and Teichler, U. (1992) *Handbook of Higher Education Diplomas in Europe*. Munich: Saur.

Kivinen, O. and Nurmi, J. (2007) 'Job requirements and competences: Do qualifications matter?' In Teichler, U. (ed.) *Careers of University Graduates: Views and experiences in comparative perspectives*. Dordrecht: Springer.

Marginson, S. (2015) *Equality of Opportunity: The first fifty years*. Presentation at the SRHE 50th Anniversary Colloquium, London, 26 June.

Müller, W. and Shavit, Y. (eds) (1998) *From School to Work: A comparative study of educational qualifications and occupational destinations*. Oxford: Clarendon Press.

Neave, G. (2011) 'Patterns'. In Rüegg, W. (ed.) *A History of the University in Europe. Volume IV: Universities since 1945*. Cambridge: Cambridge University Press.

OECD (1998) *Redefining Tertiary Education*. Paris: OECD.

— (2012) *Education at a Glance 2012: OECD indicators*. Paris: OECD.

Papadopoulos, G. (1994) *Education 1960–1990: The OECD perspective*. Paris: OECD.

Paul, J.-J., Teichler, U., and van der Velden, R. (eds) (2000) 'Higher education and graduate employment'. *European Journal of Education*, 35 (2). Special issue.

Psacharopoulos, G. (ed.) (1987) *Economics of Education: Research and studies*. Oxford: Pergamon.

Rothblatt, S. (2011) 'Curriculum, students, education: Graduation and careers'. In Rüegg, W. (ed.) *A History of the University in Europe. Volume IV: Universities since 1945*. Cambridge: Cambridge University Press.

Schomburg, H. (2007) 'Work orientation and job satisfaction'. In Teichler, U. (ed.) *Careers of University Graduates*. Dordrecht: Springer.

Schomburg, H. and Teichler, U. (2006) *Higher Education and Graduate Employment in Europe: Results of graduate surveys from 12 countries*. Dordrecht: Springer.

Shavit, Y. and Blossfeld, L. (eds) (1993) *Persistent Inequality: Changing educational attainment in thirteen countries*. Boulder, CO: Westview Press.

Shils, E. (1991) 'Academic freedom'. In Altbach, P. (ed.) *International Higher Education: An encyclopedia*. New York and London: Garland.

Shin, J., Toutkoushian, R., and Teichler, U. (eds) (2011) *University Rankings: Theoretical basis, methodology and impacts on global higher education*. Dordrecht: Springer.

Taylor, J., Brites Ferreira, J., de Lourdes Machado, M., and Santiago, R. (eds) (2008) *Non-University Higher Education in Europe*. Dordrecht: Springer.

Teichler, U. (1977) 'Kogakureki shakai: The modern education society from the comparative point of view'. *Asian Profile*, 5 (5), 487–506.

— (1985) 'Higher education: Curriculum'. In Husén, T. and Postlethwaite, T. (eds) *The International Encyclopedia of Education*. Oxford: Pergamon, 2196–208.

— (1991) 'Towards a highly educated society'. *Higher Education Policy*, 4 (4), 11–20.

— (1999) 'Higher education policy and the world of work: Changing conditions and challenges'. *Higher Education Policy*, 12 (4), 285–312.

— (2007) 'Higher education and the European labour market'. In Fromment, E., Kohler, J., Purser, L., and Wilson, L. (eds) *EUA Bologna Handbook: Making Bologna work*. Berlin: Raabe, part 3.2–1.

— (2009) *Higher Education and the World of Work*. Rotterdam: Sense Publishers.

— (2015) 'Higher education and the world of work: The perennial controversial debate'. In Shin, J., Postiglione, G., and Huang, F. (eds) *Mass Higher Education Development in East Asia*. Cham, Zug: Springer.

Teichler, U., Hartung, D., and Nuthmann, R. (1980) *Higher Education and the Needs of Society*. Windsor: NFER.

Trow, M. (1974) 'Problems in the transition from elite to mass higher education'. In *Policies for Higher Education*. Paris: OECD.

Van der Velden, R. and Allen, J. (2011) 'The flexible professional in the knowledge society: Required competences and the role of higher education'. In Allen, J. and Van der Velden, R. (eds) *The Flexible Professional in the Knowledge Society: New challenges for higher education*. Dordrecht: Springer.

Vukasovic, M. (2007) 'Deconstructing and reconstructing employability'. In Fromment, E., Kohler, J., Purser, L., and Wilson, L. (eds) *EUA Bologna Handbook: Making Bologna work*. Berlin: Raabe, part 1.4–2.

Wächter, B. (2008) 'Mobility and internationalisation in the European higher education area'. In Kelo, M. (ed.) *Beyond 2010: Priorities and challenges for higher education in the next decade*. Bonn: Lemmens.

Weinert, F. (2001) 'Competencies and key competencies: Educational perspective'. In Smelser, N. and Baltes, P. (eds) *International Encyclopedia of the Social and Behavioral Sciences*. Amsterdam: Elsevier, 2433–6.

Williams, G. (1984) 'The economic approach'. In Clark, B. (ed.) *Perspectives on Higher Education: Eight disciplinary and comparative views*. Los Angeles, CA: University of California Press.

— (1985) 'Graduate employment and vocationalisation in higher education'. *European Journal of Education*, 20 (2–3), 181–92.

Yorke, M. (2007) 'Employability in higher education'. In Fromment, E., Kohler, J., Purser, L., and Wilson, L. (eds) *EUA Bologna Handbook: Making Bologna work*. Berlin: Raabe, part 1.4–1.

Chapter 10

Higher education and the knowledge economy

Peter Scott

Introduction

The consensus, in the UK and elsewhere, is that higher education has never been more in thrall to the needs of the economy. A battery of programmatic terms – *employability, entrepreneurialism, impact* – appears to confirm that consensus, as does a similar battery of critiques – *marketization, commodification, managerialism*. But that consensus is wrong. The links between higher education and the economy were almost certainly stronger in the nineteenth and early twentieth centuries and reached a climax in the age of mass higher education. Today, those links, for all the loud rhetoric pro- and contra-, have become perhaps looser and certainly more problematic. That is the counter-intuitive argument that will be presented in this chapter.

In part, the drumbeat of 'employability' and 'impact', the apparently incontestable consensus that ever greater emphasis must be placed on the economic role of higher education in the twenty-first century, can be explained by the very complexity of the articulations between contemporary higher education systems (and institutions) and the emergent global, market-oriented, and post-industrial economy. It is an attempt to impose order, to deny these complexities. But two additional factors are also at work.

'Knowledge society'

The first is intellectual, the pervasive discourse of the 'knowledge society', derived from theoretical formulations of how advanced economies are likely to evolve that date back to at least the 1970s. Daniel Bell originally offered a sober and largely empirical account of the new post-industrial society but later writers have offered more theoretical accounts, notably Nico Stehr (Bell, 1973; Stehr, 1994). Now the 'knowledge society' has become a powerful imaginary, often only loosely related to the real economy.

Teasingly, it tends to both highlight and marginalize the contribution that higher education can make to this 'knowledge economy' – highlighting that contribution because, after all, the generation and dissemination of 'knowledge' appear to be the core business of modern universities and expressed in a myriad of ways – the production of highly skilled graduates, the development of cutting-edge science and technology, and now even the direct application (and commercialization) of both through consultancy, patents, spin-out companies, and the rest; but also marginalizing that contribution by contrasting the rigid and inflexible structures of higher education (and also perhaps its supposedly idealistic, liberal, 'public', and anti-entrepreneurial values) with the increasing velocity and volatility (and potential amorality) of market-led innovation within advanced economies.

User payments

The second is policy-driven, the rise of 'user payments' for higher education, not simply in the form of tuition fees paid by students but also in the guise of commissioned research projects. Although universities in the more distant past relied on mixed economies of private and public money, this was before the age of mass expansion, which was largely funded by public expenditure.

To some degree this trend towards relying more on 'user payments' has been a measure of necessity, as well-funded post-war welfare states have declined with the result that public funding has been concentrated in core areas such as defence, welfare, and health (although the so-called 'enterprise state' has also taken on powerful new roles as 'customer', commissioner, and regulator). The gap that has opened up between higher education's needs and available publicly provided resources has had to be filled by alternative income streams, the most important of which have been various forms of 'user payment'.

To some degree this shift has deeper roots, both structural and ideological. The emphasis on performance and accountability, technologically enabled by new information management systems and ideologically legitimated by new 'market' moralities, has also tended to highlight higher education's responsibilities with a new and more exact precision – to enhance 'value for money' in general, but also 'rates of return' on investment by individual students and measured 'impacts' of research.

However, the significance of these new factors should not be allowed to overshadow two key facts – that the relationship between the modern university (and wider higher education system) and the dynamics of the modern economy, whether in industrial or post-industrial forms, has always been a central component of its development; and that, despite insistent political rhetoric, this relationship has become more complex and less easy to characterize, in terms both of theory and of practice, in the twenty-first century.

Mass higher education and industrial society

The relationship between elite higher education systems – or, more accurately, the fragmented post-secondary education systems of which elite universities formed the peak – and the labour market was comparatively straightforward. A small number of universities, of which Oxford and Cambridge were the most prominent, were engaged principally in reproducing social and political elites. This process of reproduction was largely based on inter-generational recycling through semi-closed networks within which public schools and more traditional grammar schools played a key role, although a limited amount of 'new blood' was introduced through the recruitment of so-called 'scholarship boys' from lesser grammar schools from the 1930s onwards. As has already been suggested, its primary mode was a general education rooted in the humanities.

The majority of the universities, more recently chartered or still 'university colleges', trained doctors and members of other liberal professions (although many of these professions, such as law and accountancy, still depended predominantly on independent examination and apprenticeship routes to accreditation) and (secondary) school teachers. A range of non-university institutions such as technical colleges and teacher training colleges prepared students for more expert occupations (not only technical but also business occupations) and professions with more limited social prestige, notably elementary / primary school teachers. Finally, not to be forgotten, adult education and evening colleges (and organizations such as the Workers' Educational Association) offered courses to students who sought to 'improve' themselves (in almost a high Victorian sense) or, less often, to gain the critical tools to enable them more effectively to oppose the established social, economic, and political order. This configuration of different types of institution and various professional and occupational roles, of course, was constantly evolving. But the broad pattern was clear – and, as far as was possible in a dynamic society subject to ceaseless modernization, comparatively stable.

Expansion of higher education

The mass higher education systems that gradually replaced them after 1945, with increasing force after 1960, retained much of this institutional division of labour. But the greater increased scale of the system produced by rapid increases in the participation rate (from 3.4 of the relevant age in 1950 to 8.4 per cent in 1970 and 19.3 per cent in 1990) produced a transformation of the relationship between higher education and the economy (in terms both of the highly skilled labour market and the demand for, and uses of, research). It has sometimes been argued that this relationship became looser, in the sense that the expansion of higher education was largely conceived of as a social project rather than an exercise in workforce planning. While it is certainly true that the major impetus for this expansion came 'from below', as governments responded to pressures created by the increasing number of qualified school leavers seeking places in higher education, it would be wrong to see this as a rejection of the vocational orientation of the system.

The Robbins Committee, the report of which has often been regarded as a ringing endorsement of liberal forms of higher education, focused on the aspirations of individuals and had not doubted that securing better jobs and more satisfying careers were important components of those aspirations (Committee on Higher Education, 1963). Its report quoted with approval the saying attributed to Confucius that no one sought education with no thought 'to pay'. It also recommended that the existing colleges of advanced technology (CATs) should be granted university status and that a new type of institution should be developed: special institutions for scientific and technological education and research (SISTERs). Indeed by expanding both the idea of 'higher education', and also promoting the idea of a higher education 'system', to embrace what was then described as 'advanced further education' as well as teacher training alongside the universities, Robbins emphasized, whether intentionally or not, its vocational orientation. Similar language was employed, and similar policy interventions were recommended, in contemporary reports and initiatives in other countries – even ones as apparently contrasting as the original California Master Plan or the reform of the French universities associated with Edgar Faure, the Minister of Education (Douglass, 2010; Patterson, 1972). Community colleges were woven into these new mass systems by the former, and *instituts universitaires de technologie* (IUTs) were established as a result of the latter.

The association of mass expansion with the promotion of 'liberal' forms of higher education focused on self-realization – rather than professional and vocational formation – was strong in the 1960s, and embodied in the pseudo-Arcadian landscapes of the new campus universities (themselves derived from American exemplars). Their visual landscapes were deliberately un-urban – and often deliberately Arcadian. But they were profoundly misleading. Instead of becoming looser, the links between mass higher education and the post-war economy perhaps became more pronounced. This can be observed in four main domains.

Regulated capitalism

First, in many post-war societies, both in Europe and North America, chastened by the experience of the Great Depression there was a trend towards more regulated forms of capitalism. This took the form not so much of the narrow precautionary rule-setting and rule-keeping regimes by which regulation is now understood, but in the much more proactive form of 'planning' and structured development (within a private sector now characterized by large-scale restructuring and the widespread adoption of the principles of so-called 'scientific management', but also in the form of joint initiatives between the state and the private sector). This trend embraced more systematic efforts at workforce planning, especially in industrial and commercial sectors dependent on the recruitment of professional and other highly skilled workers. This had important implications for the nature of the graduate labour market. Within this more ordered environment new semi-professional career pathways were opened up. Subsequently, these efforts at 'manpower planning' may have been discredited and these pathways eroded during the 1980s by de-industrialization, downsizing, and outsourcing within a new corporate landscape. But most mass higher education systems were first developed when 'planning' was widely accepted across the private sector. Indeed the shift towards these more integrated as well as expanded systems was an important element within these post-war 'planning' efforts.

Growth of the public sector

Second, the growth of mass higher education systems was closely aligned with the growth of the public sector. The number of graduates grew from 19,700 to 90,000 between 1950 and 1990, and to 513,600 in 2010, UK higher education only having become a truly mass system in the past 25 years (House of Commons Library, 2012). The number of public sector employees peaked at 7.4 million in 1979 before the Thatcherite reaction began to take its toll (Cribb *et al.*, 2014). Of course, the rapid expansion in the number of (publicly supported) students was inevitably accompanied by a similar expansion in the number of (publicly funded) higher education teachers and other employees, while the establishment of new universities required substantial public investment. In these direct senses mass higher education contributed to the growth of the public sector. But it contributed equally powerfully in less direct senses. The 'planning' mode, popular even in parts of the private sector, was, of course, an absolute requirement in the expanding public sector. Teachers, doctors, and later nurses and other health–care workers were not only trained by the state in colleges and universities but predominantly employed by the state in local education authorities and the National Health Service. There may also have been an ideological and cultural effect that is impossible to quantify, legitimating collectivism through an elevation of the 'public'. The growth of a university-educated public sector workforce perhaps highlighted, and strengthened, the ethos of 'public service' within the expanding welfare state. Such an ethos acquired a new solidity, legitimacy, and even respectability.

New professions

Third, the development of mass higher education was also closely aligned with a substantial extension of a long-standing process of professionalization – partly because of the upgrading of existing occupations where additional skills became necessary (and where also considerations of prestige were an important factor in an escalating competition for new entrants); partly because of the emergence of entirely new para-professions (particularly, of course, in the burgeoning welfare state and wider public sector); and partly because of the 'vocationalization' of hitherto academic disciplines (economics is perhaps a good example). Primary school teaching and nursing are examples of the first; social work, but also human resource management, of the second; and the transition of economics into business management of the third. These new requirements stimulated demand particularly for the more applied social sciences. But new forms of technology had a similar effect, notably computing and information technology. It is no accident that the most rapidly expanding, and emblematic, subjects in universities between the 1950s and 1990s were education, health, and management. These were the growth nodes of the post-war economy (and, to a substantial extent, remain so in the twenty-first century). The intellectual landscape of higher education was transformed, to some degree because of the perceived (and arguably more vocationally oriented) needs of much wider student constituencies, but mainly because of these structural changes in the pattern of graduate employment.

The uses of research

Finally, perceptions of the role of research underwent a radical shift in the post-war university. It would perhaps be a mistake to interpret this as a shift towards the applied, because much of the research undertaken in universities (and similar research organizations) since the nineteenth century had been focused on the needs of the emerging industrial economy. There has never been a golden age of blue-skies research and purely academic scholarship. Also the independence of university research continued to be respected, although as much perhaps for efficacious as normative reasons. The UK's dual-support system – core funding plus project research – was regarded as a model for a balanced constitution. However, the intensity of university-based research's engagement intensified in a number of fields – not only in military technology, pharmaceuticals, and health care, but also social policy to reflect the new importance of the welfare state – to such a degree that between the 1940s and 1970s its purposes could be said to have been fundamentally reinterpreted. This process was most advanced in the USA, not coincidentally also the first nation that developed a truly mass system of higher education. Vannevar Bush's book was the emblematic text associated with this shift (Bush, 1945). But its message has been reported so often, in almost every developed country, that it has now become almost a truism difficult to challenge.

In the twenty-first century there is sometimes assumed to be a tension between world-class research and mass access. But this assumption was almost unknown half a century ago. It was in the first age of massification that research first established the powerful and pervasive presence in the modern university now taken for granted as a key part of its fundamental mission. This has sometimes been explained, and denigrated, as the unintended consequence of the explosion in the number of academic staff that accompanied the rapid expansion of student numbers, influenced by an academic culture that rewarded research and in which academic identities were shaped by scholarly and research achievements. But a more plausible explanation is that the new prominence of research was one element within a much broader engagement between the post-war university, and mass higher education systems, and a dynamic post-war society with voracious skills needs, a belief in the benefits of 'planning', a burgeoning public sector, and high social ambitions.

The Cold War – and economic prosperity

A footnote – it is often emphasized that mass higher education systems developed in an age of intense ideological rivalry and military confrontation during the Cold War. Certainly this left its mark on the development of higher education in a number of important ways. The growth of the post-war welfare state, in which greatly expanded educational opportunities were embedded, was in part a defence against the possibility that the masses might be attracted by the (false) promises of communist utopianism. The shift towards 'managed' capitalism, more focused on wage growth and oriented to wider social responsibilities through 'planning', may have had similar origins. Certainly public funding flowed into the post-war university as a result of military and technological rivalry. However, even more significant than the Cold War background is the fact that the first three post-war decades were a time of almost unprecedented economic growth. It was not only France that enjoyed '30 glorious years'. This growth was accompanied by a remarkable social optimism, and also cultural exuberance. Higher education came to be embraced within the growth of a consumer society. No longer predominantly part of the supply side of the modern economy, it began to play a more important role in the generation, and definition, of demand. Although the oil shock of the mid-1970s and the turbulence created by the shift back to 'neoliberal' economic policies in many Western countries from the 1980s onwards dented that social optimism, as is demonstrated by growing indifference to increasing inequality, economic growth rates remained high. This double-embedding of higher education in the economy, on both supply and demand sides, first apparent in the age of mass higher education, intensified – with unpredictable consequences.

The entrepreneurial university and the 'knowledge society'

In the introduction to this chapter it was suggested that, despite the overwhelming rhetoric about the closer and necessary links between contemporary higher education systems and the global knowledge economy, these links may in fact have become looser, in the sense that they are more difficult to specify and even that they may have become more problematical. This is a large and counter-intuitive claim that demands supporting evidence. In outline, there are two kinds of evidence. The first, which has been laid out in the preceding section, is that the development of mass higher education, far from simply being a social project focused on self-realization by individual students (still less an emancipatory project in a quasi-revolutionary sense), led to a tightening of the links between the outputs of higher education and research, on the one hand, and, on the other, the skills required in an increasingly graduate labour market and the knowledge needs of the dynamic post-war economy. The second kind of evidence, which will be discussed in this section, is derived from an examination of the major developmental characteristics of the twenty-first-century university – in shorthand, the 'entrepreneurial university' – and the major changes that have taken place in the shape of the twenty-first-century economy – in shorthand, the 'knowledge economy'.

The entrepreneurial university

The label 'the entrepreneurial university' was first used by the American sociologist Burton Clark almost 20 years ago and initially had a more restricted meaning. He intended it to describe the small minority of universities that stood out from the majority because they had gone further down the 'enterprise' road (Clark, 1998). Here it is used in a more generic sense to indicate the features that many universities in the USA and the UK, and more widely (including much of continental Europe, Australasia, parts of Latin America, and, pre-eminently, East Asia), now have in common and also some dominant themes in higher education policymaking that transcend national frontiers.

1. 'COST-SHARING'

First is the trend towards 'cost-sharing', in other words the substitution of tuition fees paid by students (although often with the help of state-provided loans) for direct state funding of universities. This is not the place to consider the wider arguments for and against such a substitution, nor the adequacy of the 'markets' in higher education that have emerged (Johnstone, 2004). The concern here is merely with the effects of this substitution. Two deserve special emphasis:

- The first is that charging tuition encourages (and is designed to encourage) students to regard themselves as 'customers' who are 'consumers' of the 'products' of higher education, in contrast to earlier conceptions of their role that emphasized rather intellectual curiosity, self-fulfilment, or even social activism. It is difficult to escape the conclusion that this stronger focus on a university education as a consumption good reinforces an instrumental account of its purposes, perhaps crowding out other accounts.
- The second is that the key relationship with the labour market, and future careers, is now more likely to be expressed in terms of the rates-of-return on the investment of individual students rather than of any form of workforce 'planning', however broad-brush (but with important exceptions that are discussed below). In other words, the future shape of the graduate labour force is now primarily to be determined by an aggregation of individual choices (subject to ceaseless change) based on perceptions of future earnings (which, of course, may not be accurate). It is assumed that any corporate, let alone public, benefits will automatically accrue.

This is a radical reconceptualization of the links between higher education and the labour market. Whether it is more effective is a matter for debate; it is certainly less direct and so more volatile (and therefore problematical). However, it is far from complete.

2. Persistence of 'planning'

The second trend is for governments, even those of a free-market persuasion, not to abate but to increase their interventions, although this is often disguised by creating quasi-markets. Competition within the global knowledge-based economy is now regarded as the arena in which national success, or failure, is determined. It is widely believed that some subjects, principally in science, technology, engineering, and mathematics (STEM) but also some languages, cannot safely be left to the market in student choices – first, because of their high cost and lengthy investment cycles; second, because current student demand is often insufficient to maintain their viability; and third, because they make a crucial strategic contribution to realizing national goals (geopolitical or economic). So interventions (i.e. public subsidies) are required to sustain this essential capacity.

At the same time, older forms of workforce planning have persisted, whether mandated by the state itself in the case of doctors and other health-care workers and teachers, or exercised indirectly through various forms of professional regulation that restrict and ration access to key professions in order to preserve high standards of practice, for example in pharmacy or architecture. As a result, directive and collective modes of workforce planning coexist uneasily with newer modes that realize their effects indirectly through the exercise of 'consumer' choice as exercised by aspirant members of that workforce. This has produced acute dilemmas for universities, which are obliged to adopt full-on consumerist practices while retaining the ability to respond to political (and often highly politicized) agendas and initiatives, and also maintaining the corporatist skills to engage in direct dialogue with industry and employers.

3. Commercialization

The third trend within the twenty-first-century university is the development of explicitly entrepreneurial, quasi-commercial, and even commercial activities. The most obvious examples are commissioned applied research and consultancy, customized updating and continuing professional development programmes (CPD), patents, spin-out companies, and shared-equity partnerships with the private sector. These 'external' forms of commercialization have received most attention, although the evidence is that any profit they generate for universities is slight (with a few, high-profile, exceptions). Another form of 'external' commercialization has been the positive encouragement of for-profit higher education providers, most conspicuously in the USA and Central and Eastern Europe but visible in most higher education systems. However, it is still far from clear that a private for-profit sector will develop on a scale to challenge the heartland of 'public' higher education. For-profit institutions need to be clearly distinguished from more traditional forms of private provision, sometimes funded through accumulated endowments as well as student fees (as in the case of elite US and Japanese institutions) but often indicating a deficit in public provision (as in parts of Latin America).

More important perhaps are 'internal' forms of commercialization such as both the out-sourcing of what are regarded as non-core activities to private sector providers, for example catering and student residences, and the establishment of service units as separate budget centres or wholly owned subsidiary companies. It is by these means that a more commercial culture has penetrated higher education. An important effect has been to generate difficult, even existential, debates within the twenty-first-century university – about what is meant by the 'public' and the 'private', between 'core' and 'non-core' services (which has not been a straightforward task because at the same time, the need to provide seamless services and a holistic experience to students, embracing both academic and non-academic elements, has also been emphasized as best practice), but also between 'profitable' and 'non-profitable' activities in terms of the financial contribution they make (again, not an easy task because universities have had little experience of operating formal and explicit systems of cross-subsidy).

A different, but equally important, form of entrepreneurialism is the teaching of explicitly entrepreneurial skills, often now glossed as 'employability' skills, in the higher education curriculum. In one sense this may amount to little more than the rebadging of the problem-solving, transferable, critical, and research skills that have always been regarded as the core of a general (if not liberal) higher education. In another sense it has more radical implications. Students are themselves defined as entrepreneurs – for example, as authors of undergraduate projects on 'real' rather than simply 'academic' topics, or art and design students already at work in their university-provided ateliers. This entrepreneurialism in the university curriculum can then be linked with the 'external' forms of commercialization undertaken by institutions to weave a grander over-arching narrative such as the notion of 'clever cities', within which universities with their creative habits and practices are crucial components, popularized by Richard Florida (2005).

4. THE RISE OF MANAGEMENT

A fourth trend, already identified by Clark, is the strengthening of central management in universities. He saw this 'strengthened core' in terms of developing a strategic capacity at the centre to manage the entrepreneurial activities of operating units, whether academic or service departments, which should be free to pursue their – perhaps different – objectives. In other words, this trend was explicitly linked to the rise of entrepreneurialism. However, it has other sources such as the growing scale and complexity of universities, the more intrusive accountability regimes to which they are now subject, and, in many European countries, the devolution of administrative responsibilities from ministries to universities. This multi-causal trend has given rise to new debates and practices, such as the continuing relevance of traditional forms of university governance (in particular, the role of senates as guardians of academic self-government) and the nature of leadership in higher education (in particular, whether traditional models of academic–collegial leadership need to be supplemented, or even supplanted, by new corporate and executive models).

5. OPEN RESEARCH SYSTEMS

A fifth trend is the development of more open research systems, accompanied paradoxically perhaps by the imposition of more prescriptive and targeted research funding regimes. The latter may be an attempt to combat the potentially chaotic, and centrifugal, effects of the former. But the major policy driver has been to align the priorities of university-based research more closely to the perceived needs of the knowledge economy. In the third quarter of the twentieth century this attempt was one element within a wider effort to 'plan' the mixed economies that developed, initially with remarkable success, in the post-war period. But, as with the parallel attempt to align graduate output with the needs of the labour market, it produced mixed results. There was also perhaps in that period a more balanced approach, in which respect for the autonomy of the university, and belief in the benefits of curiosity-driven research, were still high. In the past two decades, although in the market state 'planning' as such has been disavowed, the pressures on higher education to demonstrate the 'impact' of its research, reinforced by the increase in earmarked funding for research projects that have a tendency to be over-specified within a wider policy environment in which performance measurement has acquired a privileged place, has increased the pressure to align research with the perceived needs of the economy (and society more broadly).

However, it may be misleading to regard this trend as entirely contrary to the first, and more important trend, development of more open research, or knowledge production, systems. This has been characterized in both narrow terms – for example, the notion of the 'triple helix' of academy, government, and industry (sometimes expanded to include other partners, in more recent literature) – and also more expansive terms – for example, the notion of 'Mode 2' knowledge generated in a context of application (and implication) and now very widely distributed in social terms with multiple actors, both expert and lay (Etzkowitz, 2008, 2014; Gibbons *et al.*, 1994; Nowotny *et al.*, 2003). More intrusive targeting of research priorities and funding by the state and the growth of (at times incestuous) dependency of universities on research funding provided by industry need to be seen in the wider context of much more intensive, and reflexive, relationships between researchers and multiple social actors. These more open knowledge systems, therefore, combine both *dirigiste* and democratic elements.

The implications for universities have been equally ambiguous. At a strategic level they have had to balance two contrary imperatives. The first has been to concentrate on their research strengths by attempting to create centres of excellence able to attract targeted funding. The second has been to develop more pervasive research cultures among all their academic staff and also many of their students that address the needs of a knowledge economy within which traditional forms of expert knowledge jostle with socially generated 'knowledge' and commercial 'knowledge' expressed through images and brands. At an operational level, among other things, universities have had to come to terms with new forms of scholarly and scientific publications, in the shape of open-source and open-access publishing and also of new media, and how these can be incorporated into traditional forms of evaluation and reward.

The knowledge economy

These far-reaching changes in the twenty-first-century universities reflect equally far-reaching changes in the twenty-first-century economy – or, better perhaps, society-cum-economy, because market ideologies (if not always true market practices) have now penetrated deeply into activities once the preserve of the state or of 'civil society'. There is only room in this chapter to sketch out these changes, highlighting the ones that appear to have had the greatest and most immediate impact on higher education.

1. THE POST-INDUSTRIAL ECONOMY

The first has been the shift from an industrial to a not so much *post-industrial* as a *services-led* economy – and from a production-oriented economy to a consumption-oriented one. Despite the – cross-party – celebration of 'hard-working families', which emphasizes their role as producers, it is as much in the guise of consumers that most people now engage with the economy. As far as employment patterns are concerned the workforce has now splintered

– into a super-elite, often globally mobile and concentrated in the higher reaches of the corporate sector (in particular, financial services), with salaries that enable it to aspire to levels of consumption last seen in the 'gilded age' and *belle époque* of the late nineteenth century; a squeezed middle of public and private sector workers who, but for the explosion of personal credit, might well have experienced real declines in their income; and a growing underclass of poorly paid workers often in outsourced service industries and on insecure employment contracts (and, of course, a reserve army of the under- and unemployed persisting at a level well above the full-employment figures that would have been acceptable in the age of the welfare state).

However, at all three levels, the notion of a semi-lifetime career has been sharply eroded – with serious implications for a higher education system organized around the reproduction of professional workers. Graduates also feature in all three, possibly four, levels of this splintered labour market – hence the growing concerns about issues of graduate unemployment, the fit between graduate production and 'graduate' jobs, and employability (Brown and Lauder, 2012; Brown, 2013).

2. THE RESURGENCE OF INEQUALITY

Closely linked to this first change has been a second, the rapid growth of inequality in terms of incomes and assets (and so, inevitably, of life-chances too) (Piketty, 2014). This has had two effects that challenge higher education. The first is an increasing dissociation of rewards from professional expertise, of which an example is the drift of the 'best and brightest' graduates into financial services at the expense of the traditional professions (including, of course, academic careers). This may have led to a devaluing of expert skills and knowledge, although it can be argued that the acceleration of technological change in any case requires a re-evaluation of the basic construction of expertise. The second effect is that the 'best and brightest' can no longer be defined in terms of an incomplete but nevertheless inexorably advancing meritocracy but are shaped by reasserted patterns of inherited social privilege. There are uncomfortable affinities between the recruitment to Russell Group universities and the increasing use of unpaid internships as gateways into elite jobs (Jerrim, 2013).

3. DECLINE OF THE PUBLIC SECTOR

The third change has been the shrinking of employment in the public sector, more so admittedly among poorer paid (and generally non-graduate) workers, whose jobs have been outsourced; 700,000 public sector jobs have been lost since 2010. Although many of these jobs have simply been transferred to outsourcing companies, in the process secure public sector jobs have tended to be replaced by insecure, and lower-wage, jobs. As a result, the creeping sub-professionalization of mid-range jobs, which was most advanced in the traditional public sector, may have been thrown into reverse. At a minimum the strong connections between the public sector and the traditional graduate labour market have become more problematical. There have also been curbs on more higher-level professional public sector jobs, which had been a major focus of graduate production when mass higher education systems were first developed. For example, the number of doctors for every 100,000 people in the UK is barely half the number in Germany, partly because of an inadequacy of supply but mainly because of the underfunding of the National Health Service. But perhaps the most severe challenge to higher education has not been the direct impact of the shrinking of the public sector, but the indirect impact of the erosion of the ethos of 'publicness', which has opened up new and occasionally alarming possibilities (most obviously for the funding of higher education because not only the level but also the necessity – and even legitimacy – of public support will be increasingly questioned).

4. ADVANCED TECHNOLOGIES

The fourth change has been the development of advanced technologies. On the face of it, this should enhance the role of universities as the source of much of the basic research on which these technologies are based (and increasingly in terms of their role in developing these technologies through applied research and other entrepreneurial activities). However, in the UK advanced technologies may have been experienced as much through consumption (iPhones manufactured in China), and therefore changing social behaviour, as through direct production in the shape of advanced engineering (of which there are far fewer examples in the UK than Germany or Switzerland). One of the features of globalization is that products can be sourced from almost anywhere, even if primary research and design work is – for the moment – concentrated in a small number of developed countries.

While many advanced engineering processes, and their analogues in business and services, have been exported to lower-wage economies, many European countries, including the UK and also the USA, have become heavily dependent on importing scientific and technical talent to service the research and design activities that have been retained (as well as, of course, their higher education and research systems in key subjects) often from the same countries. The result of this 'export' of jobs and 'import' of talent is far from reassuring. As a result, the development of advanced technologies may create challenges of sustainability in a country such as the UK, in terms of both employment and expertise.

5. GLOBALIZATION

A fifth trend has been the impact of globalization, an overused and much abused term. Science and research, and to a lesser degree higher education, have always been global domains. Global divisions of labour and global flows of people are hardly new phenomena, although the current enthusiasm for lightly regulated capitalist markets and the development of new advanced technologies have certainly intensified these divisions of labour and exacerbated these people flows. The novelty of twenty-first-century globalization, of which the hegemonic model (for the moment) remains free-market exchanges characterized by lightly restricted flows of capital, does not derive so much from new patterns of production. Two other aspects of globalization are having potentially more radical effects. The first is a fundamental reconceptualization, and reconfiguration, of both time and space, creating new temporary and spatial possibilities. Virtual, border-free, even imaginary communities are now transforming social relations. The second is the emergence of global cultures (notably of consumption, material and symbolic). While we are now global consumers, we are global producers to a more limited degree, and global citizens hardly at all.

Conclusion

All these changes in the twenty-first-century economy complicate the more stable relationships that had grown up between the mass higher education systems and welfare-state social-market economies that evolved in the third quarter of the twentieth century. A splintered and volatile graduate labour market has led universities to ask searching questions about the purposes of the higher education they offer. General or liberal education has tended to be redefined in terms of employability and transferability of skills. Vocational education has shifted its emphasis from the formation of expert professional skills to the inculcation of entrepreneurial behaviours. In research, curiosity-driven inquiry has struggled to maintain its position within more open knowledge systems – which sadly, for the present, have placed greater emphasis on narrowly conceived 'impact', as defined by market-dominated norms of performativity, than on broader, more socially distributed, and potentially more democratic forms of knowledge production. Universities themselves have redefined their purposes and missions, which has led to important changes not only in their organizational structures, but also management cultures. Although encouraged (and often bullied) to tighten their embrace with a free-market post-industrial economy that is very different from the regulated 'social market' economy with which mass higher education systems were aligned, they have found themselves far from being the ascendant institutions in this new global knowledge economy.

However, these changes in the situation of the university, in terms of their educational goals, research practices, and organizational and management cultures, have not necessarily led to a better 'fit' between their outputs, in terms of either skilled graduates or expert knowledge, and the 'needs' of the economy – despite the policy-driven rhetoric urging them to give such relationships a near-absolute priority. One reason is that in a more fluid hyper-capitalist market economy 'needs' are difficult to define authoritatively, and also the very idea of 'fit' may be too redolent of older ideas of a more ordered and planned economy for current ideological tastes, both of which factors necessarily impose limits on how far such efforts can be pursued. But a more important reason is the fundamental indeterminacy of the contemporary socio-economy. This indeterminacy is not only inherent in the admittedly creative destruction-ism of markets, their ceaseless redeployment of capital from less to more profitable activities. It also arises from chronic and accumulating uncertainties. These include the social and individual effects of destabilizing technologies, the limits that successful efforts to combat climate change might impose on economic growth, the impact of new social movements on established ideas of community and solidarity, and the rise of conflicts fuelled by increasing inequalities that have been produced, but also laid bare, by global integration.

The hope for the future must be that the university has not been sufficiently impoverished by this relentless drive to align it more closely with the needs of the economy, a drive perhaps doomed to failure because of the restless nature of that economy, that it will be unable to address these issues, the 'big questions' facing humankind. Other skills-and-knowledge generating institutions are able to deliver 'relevance' and 'impact' with regard to economic development. But perhaps only the university is still constituted to be able to begin to increase human understanding of these truly epochal challenges.

References

Bell, D. (1973) *The Coming of Post-Industrial Society: A venture in social forecasting*. New York: Basic Books.

Brown, P. (2013) 'Education, opportunity and the prospects for social mobility'. *British Journal of Sociology of Education*, 34 (5–6), 678–700.

Brown P. and Lauder, H. (2012) 'The great transformation in the global labour market'. *Soundings: A Journal of Politics and Culture*, 51, 41–53.

Bush, V. (1945) *Science: The endless frontier: A report to the president.* Washington: US Government Printing Office.

Clark, B. (1998) *Creating Entrepreneurial Universities: Organizational pathways of transformation.* Oxford: IAU Press/Pergamon.

Committee on Higher Education (1963) *Higher Education: Report of the Committee appointed by the Prime Minister under the chairmanship of Lord Robbins, 1961–63.* The Robbins Report. Cmnd 2154. London: Her Majesty's Stationery Office.

Cribb, J., Disney, R., and Sibieta, L. (2014) *The Public Sector Workforce: Past, present and future.* Briefing Note 145. London: Institute for Fiscal Studies.

Douglass, J. (2010) *From Chaos to Order and Back? A revisionist reflection on the California master plan for higher education@50 and thoughts about its future.* Research and Occasional Paper Series 7.10. Berkeley, CA: Center for Studies in Higher Education.

Etzkowitz, H. (2008) *The Triple Helix: University–industry–government innovation in action.* London: Routledge.

— (2014) 'The entrepreneurial university wave: From ivory tower to global economic engine'. *Industry and Higher Education,* 28 (4), 223–32.

Florida, R. (2005) *Cities and the Creative Class.* London: Routledge.

Gibbons, M., Limoges, C., Nowotny, H., Schwartzman, S., Scott, P., and Trow, M. (1994) *The New Production of Knowledge: The dynamics of science and research in contemporary societies.* London: SAGE.

House of Commons Library (2012) *Education: Historical statistics.* Standard Note SG/SN/4256. London: House of Commons.

Jerrim, J. (2013) *Family Background and Access to 'High Status' Universities.* London: The Sutton Trust.

Johnstone, B. (2004) 'The economics and politics of cost sharing in higher education: Comparative perspectives'. *Economics of Education Review,* 23 (4), 403–10.

Nowotny, H., Scott, P., and Gibbons, M. (2003) '"Mode 2" revisited: The new production of knowledge'. *Minerva,* 41, 179–94.

Patterson, M. (1972) 'French university reform: Renaissance or reformation?' *Comparative Education Review,* 16 (2), 281–302.

Piketty, T. (2014) *Capital in the Twenty-First Century.* Cambridge, MA: Harvard University Press.

Stehr, N. (1994) *Knowledge Societies.* London: SAGE.

Response

Gareth Williams

Fifty years of research into higher education

How does one respond to such a generous collection of essays from friends and colleagues? Between them they have covered much of higher education policy, and research into it, during the past half century and have reminded me of many of the topics that have interested me during my academic life. In this response I will offer some personal reflections on my involvement in higher education research during these decades: it really has been a lifelong learning experience. I will conclude with some of my own speculations about the future.

Maureen Woodhall recalls that I first became interested in the economics of education as an undergraduate when I was invited to address the university Political Economy Club, whose members included some of the leading economists of the post-war years. I was not confident that I had anything new to say on trade cycle theory or mathematical theories of economic growth that were fashionable at the time, so my supervisor suggested that I write a paper on the economics of education, a topic that was, in the mid-1950s, beginning to attract some attention in the USA, but was almost completely unknown in this country. Mark Blaug (1970) has dated its arrival on the world stage as 1961, with the inaugural presidential address to the American Economic Association of Theodore Schultz, who was essentially reporting on recent work by graduate students in Chicago (Schultz, 1961). The Robbins Report (Committee on Higher Education, 1963) regretted the absence of research into the economics of higher education in the UK, but it acknowledged the work in the USA and recognized that higher education was important for the economy and needed further work here. However, the Committee considered it premature to try to build economic analysis into its own forecasts and recommendations.

More generally, the early years of policy-oriented economic analysis of education owed much to the work of the newly established OECD which, in 1961, took over from the OEEC (Organization for European Economic Cooperation), which had been set up to ensure effective use of the Marshall aid from the USA to help in Europe's reconstruction after the Second World War. At the time there was much concern in the USA and Western Europe about the early successes of the Soviet Union in launching Sputnik and Yuri

Gagarin's orbit of the Earth, also in 1961. It was widely believed that this success was at least partly due to the priority given to education and research in the Soviet five-year plans. Education and especially higher education were prominent in the programmes of the OECD from the outset. This was an age of economic planning, not only in the Soviet Union, and the input–output model, which interpreted the economy as a series of matrices showing the specified inputs and outputs of each economic activity, provided the basis for detailed economic planning. Wassily Leontieff was awarded the Nobel Prize for economics in 1973 for his positive analysis of this interpretation of an economy (Leontieff, 1951). The OECD extended this idea to the creation and use of qualified 'manpower'. Just as the raw materials and intermediate products required to produce, for example, a thousand motor cars could be specified, so the number of engineers, technicians, accountants, and managers, and the education they needed, could be calculated and thence the education and training courses necessary to produce them could be determined.

This was the intellectual climate in which I was recruited by the OECD in 1962 to work on its Mediterranean Regional Project (MRP), an attempt to forecast the educational needs of the, then relatively underdeveloped, OECD countries of Southern Europe using input–output inspired techniques. This was extremely influential at the time and the methodology of the MRP was exported to several other developing countries. The first book I wrote, under the OECD imprint (OECD, 1967) on statistical needs for educational planning, was an attempt to identify the information needed to link flows of pupils and students through the educational system into the various specified job vacancies that economic planners expected to be available.

Shortly after this was published, I moved to the somewhat different intellectual environment of the LSE, where the Unit for Economic and Statistical Studies in Higher Education (UESSHE) had been established by the Robbins statistician, Claus Moser, to start to answer some of the questions raised by the Robbins Committee on the possible value for policymaking of economic interpretations of education. Although manpower planning was still influential amongst economists and several early studies by the UESSHE used input-output ideas, the LSE economists were much more convinced by the work of other US economists, especially Gary Becker (another Nobel Prize winner, in 1970), in Chicago who were using data on the earnings of people with different amounts of education as a basis for calculating the economic benefits of education (Becker, 1962). Their assumptions about the way the economy operated were very different from those of Leontieff. For them 'human capital' was at least as important as physical capital in increasing economic output, and the earnings of individuals with different levels of qualifications indicated the labour market demand for their services and this reflected their productivity. Relative earnings were thus ever-changing signals in an evolving economy rather than the rigid 'requirements' suggested by the Leontieffian models.

For several decades these two competing models underpinned much of the research into the economics of education. Now, although for at least two decades the human capital, market-based model has been in the ascendant, echoes of manpower planning ideas are still to be found, for example in Ulrich Teichler's contribution to this volume considering the debates about whether there are too many or too few graduates at present. Estimates of manpower needs (now usually called qualified personnel needs) still play a major part in discussions of medical and teacher education and influence much of the debate about STEM (science, technology, engineering, mathematics) subjects.

There was, however, another influence on policy debates that prevented either of these rival economic approaches from having much influence on policy until the 1980s. The Robbins Report regarded higher education as an activity to which all who had the ability and prior attainment should have access if they wanted it. Essentially this treats higher education as an end in itself which does not need a utilitarian economic rationale to justify its public provision. Robbins amply demonstrated that far more than the then 7 per cent of each generation had the ability to benefit from higher education. Expansion, it was believed, would increase social mobility and hence help continue the progress towards greater social and economic equality, which had been one of the main aims of policy in most countries throughout the post-war period (Piketty, 2014). It would also help economic progress, but Robbins was too canny to try to quantify this with the information available at the time. Projections of the number of school leavers with the necessary qualifications dominated higher education policy for nearly two decades after Robbins. By 1981 the 'age participation rate' stood at 12.1 per cent (Farrant, 1981), almost exactly the figure projected by Robbins two decades earlier.

However, the path by which this was achieved had been very different from that foreseen by Robbins, whose forecasts were for a steady expansion between 1964 and 1981. In the event, the Robbins 1981 participation forecast was reached by 1970 and then remained stagnant throughout the 1970s. This stagnation was caused mainly by lack of demand from qualified school leavers: the official policy of both main political parties remained what Robbins had recommended, to provide places for all who sufficiently qualified and wished to undertake higher education. Many sociologists and economists turned to consider why this apparent plateau in higher education participation had been reached. Some suggested that the graduate labour market was saturated (see Teichler *et al.*, 1980). Others, of which I was one, thought that it was the rate of growth of graduate output that was too rapid for employers to absorb in the kind of jobs graduates had traditionally expected. In one paper, still influenced by manpower planning ideas, I compared the output of graduates with specialist skills with the well-known cobweb cycle of economists. Shortages at one point in time led to larger numbers of people seeking these qualifications: these emerged on to the graduate labour market a few years later and resulted in surpluses, which resulted in fewer people seeking the qualification and so on (Williams, 1973). There was indeed evidence that the very rapid expansion in the late 1960s in many OECD countries had had a depressing effect on graduate starting salaries and the kind of jobs they were able to secure (Freeman, 1976).

Another example of the doubts about the value of higher education in the 1970s was the idea of the diploma disease (Dore, 1976). Based mainly on what had been happening in Japan and other Asian countries this postulated that what most students sought was a formal statement of a suitable qualification rather than the education or training itself. This was because many employers seemed more concerned with possession of the diploma rather than any learning acquired in the course of obtaining it. Educated unemployment had been experienced in many Asian countries for some years (see for example Blaug *et al.*, 1969), but was beginning to appear in OECD countries by the mid-1970s and, in a period still strongly influenced by the input–output model of the economy and the associated manpower planning of higher education, the diploma disease based on the idea of higher education qualifications as simply signals of potential achievement acquired some currency.

It was also in the 1970s that one of the most perceptive and widely quoted essays in higher education policy research was published, Martin Trow's paper on the transition from elite to mass higher education (Trow, 1974). Although the terms 'elite', 'mass', and 'universal' higher education are widely quoted, the original essay itself is, I suspect, not so widely read, partly because its source is not easily obtainable. Its title makes clear that it was concerned with *problems in the transition* from elite to mass higher education and argued that the latter should not to be seen simply as an enlargement of the former. Trow's underlying thinking was based on a comparison of the Californian Master Plan (for higher education) enacted in 1960 and the higher education future for the UK foreseen in the Robbins Report. The former recognized that a much expanded system would need to cater for a wide diversity of abilities, interests, and aspirations, while the latter essentially saw an expanded higher education as consisting of an ever-increasing number of Britain's intellectually challenging universities, which, long before league tables were invented, were seen as being very close to the best in the world. The Master Plan created a clear three-tier system catering for different types of students' abilities and aspirations. Robbins explicitly saw the university as the peak of an intellectual pyramid to which all post-secondary educations could aspire after some years of maturation. Although the government rejected this part of the Robbins proposals and went instead in the direction of the Master Plan by creating a system of polytechnics, these institutions were modelled in many ways on the universities, especially through the Council for National Academic Awards (CNAA), which was required to ensure that their degrees were comparable to those of universities and, of course, in 1992, the polytechnics and many other institutions were redesignated as universities.

The immediate impact of Trow's categorization was limited in most European countries by the slow pace of growth during that decade. Mass, much less universal, higher education seemed a rather remote possibility. Instead attention was given to exploring why young people did or did not decide to go to university. My own contribution to this debate claimed that while most school teachers and academics saw higher education as a process of personal development, most young people themselves and their parents considered it primarily as a pathway to better jobs (Williams and Gordon, 1981), a finding I see repeated in a recent report from the Higher Education Policy Institute (HEPI, 2015).

The early 1980s Society for Research into Higher Education (SRHE) Leverhulme studies into the future of higher education were strongly influenced by the events of the 1970s, particularly the stagnation in student demand over much of that decade following the earlier explosive post-Robbins expansion. They were undertaken at a time when the long-term Robbins projections were expiring, and since there was no sign of any government intentions to set up any major inquiry to update Robbins, the SRHE supported by the Leverhulme Trust ambitiously decided to set up an independent series of studies loosely modelled on those of the Carnegie Commission in the USA. By this time higher education research had become an established field of study with its own journals, at least one specialized research centre in most countries, and several thousand students studying the subject at postgraduate level. The SRHE-Leverhulme study set out to apply the findings of research in this specialized field to the major policy issues then confronting higher education in the UK and make policymakers aware of this research. Its reports show the main areas in which researchers at the time felt they had a contribution to make to policy development: the labour market, access and participation, institutional change, role of research in universities, the place of arts in higher education, changes in learning and teaching, governance, and finance (Lindley, 1981; Fulton, 1981; Bligh, 1982a, 1982b; Morris and Sizer, 1982; Oldham, 1982; Robinson, 1982; Wagner, 1982; Shattock, 1983; Williams and Blackstone, 1983). Even though there is little evidence of the reports having a direct influence on policy, the list of topics shows some prescience in identifying many of the areas that began to preoccupy policymakers during the next two decades and several of its predictions and recommendations are now in operation.

In the event, the 1980s was a decade of radical ideological change in many countries. In the UK, cuts in public expenditure resulted in the first peacetime reduction in public expenditure on higher education for over half a century. This was followed in 1988 by the Education Reform Act, the effects of which on education departments in universities was dramatic. Up to 1988, the backdrop of nearly all their research and teaching was the 1944 Education Act. The 1988 Act changed this in almost every detail. As far as higher education was concerned the most important change was the abolition of the University Grants Committee, the transformation of institutional subsidy into a payment for services rendered, and the abolition of guaranteed lifetime tenure for academic staff, so that academic staff could be dismissed if there was no longer sufficient demand for their services. In addition, the polytechnics and other major public sector higher education institutions were taken out of local authority control and given a legal status similar to universities, a process that was completed in the complementary 1992 Higher and Further Education Act which enabled them to become universities. The Robbins ideal of a unitary university-based system had arrived, though not in the way Robbins had envisaged.

It is misleading to view these changes solely as resulting from higher education policymaking. They were part of a much wider shift in social and economic policy aimed at unravelling the collectivist welfare state of the post-war years and replacing it with one in which private market behaviour played a much larger role. These changes were not unique to the UK; throughout the OECD area there were moves in this direction and most radical of all, communist state planning imploded in Eastern Europe.

The effect on higher education was that it quickly became marketized, partly through changes in the arrangements in which universities and colleges received money from governments and partly through the expansion of private, often fully commercial, universities and colleges, some of which were linked to established public universities (Altbach and Levy, 2005).

Higher education policy research was, unsurprisingly, radically affected by these developments. Manpower planning finally disappeared from view. Analysis of graduate labour markets based largely on information about relative earnings and employment patterns took its place. For the most part these studies continued to show that the possession of a higher education qualification brought significantly higher lifetime incomes for most people. They were supplemented by evidence that many other social benefits accrue to individuals and societies with high levels of educational achievement (Schuller *et al.*, 2004).

However, the change which occupied most of my interest in the 1980s and 1990s was the transformation of universities as organizations as they shifted from being institutions receiving regular government subsidies, which usually increased from year to year and almost guaranteed that no university would have insufficient funds to meet its commitments, to being in effect commercial organizations whose income depended on the number of students they were able to recruit and the amount of research and consultancy income they could earn.

It would be presumptuous to claim that I saw these changes coming, but as someone whose early academic years had been as a research officer and subsequently a research director whose staff depended on the next successful grant, I had long had a personal interest in the difference between what was then known as 'hard' money and 'soft' money. Hard money was the guaranteed government grant, and academic staff could be given lifetime contracts after a relatively short period of probation. Research staff, on the other hand, had contracts that were only good until that research grant was finished. Renewal depended on securing a new contract. As a manager of research I had to submit regular reports to show that the money was being well spent and that the outcomes were worthwhile. At the same time, I observed that some colleagues concerned mainly with teaching were able to use the same lecture notes year after year with very little fear of losing their jobs, partly because no one was monitoring what they were doing. I remember one occasion shortly after I was appointed a professor at Lancaster University with virtually no teaching experience: I decided to sit in on a few lectures to help me get an idea of what the department was teaching. Some colleagues thought it scandalous that a professor was checking up on their teaching.

It was becoming clear during the 1980s that the cuts of 1981 were beginning to result in wider recognition of such anomalies. Led by Warwick University it soon became apparent that full-cost fees for students from outside the EU could be an important source of supplementary income. Courses other than those for first degrees and other initial qualifications were also able to charge fees that seemed appropriate. I did a study for the OECD in the late 1980s exploring changes in the mechanisms of higher education finance in its member countries and simultaneously a more detailed study of the changes that were taking place in the UK (Williams, 1992). In the UK these changes were boosted by the 1988 Act, which linked most of the income received from government to the number of students recruited and assessments of the quantity and quality of the research. For several years after that there was a frantic scramble by most universities to increase their enrolments and the total number of students increased extremely rapidly for a few years. By the mid-1990s the Conservative Government was alarmed by the total public expenditure this free-for-all was incurring (even though expenditure per student declined) and imposed a cap on each university's student numbers on a year-by-year basis.

Study of the implications of the shift from publicly subsidized institutions to commercial and quasi-commercial enterprises dominated the last decade of my full-time academic work. The most obvious change was that of the vice chancellor who was transformed from a *primus inter pares*, first among otherwise equal members of the academic staff, to being the chief executive of a business enterprise. University Councils changed from being not much more than debating societies with a loose responsibility to keep an eye on the work of vice chancellors and their senates, into boards of directors with detailed responsibility for the financial activities of the institution and consequently overall control of much of its substantive work. For me, one of the most interesting transformations was that of the finance officer, who shifted from being in the words of one of them to me a 'bean counter' well below the registrar in the university hierarchy to being, after the vice chancellor, the most influential member of the planning and strategy committee, the key decision initiating body that all universities established in the 1990s.

As in all organizations, public and private, the management revolution was expedited by the spectacular developments in information technology. Strategy committees could keep a close eye on teaching and research and the other university processes: key performance indicators facilitated monitoring. IT also gave rise to the possibility of implementing the theoretical ideas of what came to be known as 'new public management' (NPM). This received considerable attention from higher education researchers under various names: 'steering from a distance' (Neave and van Vught, 1991), the 'audit society' (Power, 1997), among others. In practice it meant that universities (as well as many other public service organizations) could have considerable apparent financial and administrative autonomy, while at the same time their strategies were being steered and their implementation monitored by governments. University and college managers as well as politicians stressed the need for 'culture change', which at root meant that staff needed to recognize that all their activities used resources that must come from somewhere. Some sort of cost–benefit analysis should be applied even when something was worth doing for its own sake. The analysis had to take account of the magnitude and probability of risk in any new venture.

By the turn of the millennium, higher education had become a regulated market in many countries and moving in that direction in many others (Brown and Carasso, 2013). Research publications on entrepreneurial universities began to appear (e.g. Clark, 1998; Shattock, 2005), as well as critiques of the commodification of higher education (*THE*, 2014). The concept of the knowledge economy and higher education's key role in it became one of the main drivers of continued expansion (Temple, 2013). Worldwide expansion and improved communication, especially the Internet, but also air travel, resulted in considerable increase in higher education as a global network of linked activities: students and staff crossed national borders, international collaboration in research flourished. These resulted in attempts at harmonizing at least the first degree systems of different countries, of which the Bologna agreements were the best known and most influential, and their arrangements for the finance of research projects. Media-generated international league tables of universities' performance, mainly in research, achieved considerable prominence.

Where does higher education research go from here?

Higher education policy research which, when I first became involved in it half a century ago, was largely a matter of forecasting student numbers and the likely employment opportunities for them when they graduated, has become a major multidimensional, multi-disciplinary research area concerned with a major sector of the economy. In my opinion the three most important changes in the 50 years I have been working on it are expansion in size and scope, the consequential impossibility of understanding higher education policy separately from economic and social policy more generally, and the scientific revolution, especially the explosion of information technology.

During the next 50 years, expansion in purely numerical terms is unlikely to be a major issue in most countries because mass and near universal higher education participation has already been achieved. Instead, patterns of participation in mass systems will be of increasing importance. Already higher education systems must cater for a very wide range of interests and abilities stretching from the relatively few individuals who will become scientific and intellectual leaders, through the leading engineers, physicians, lawyers, and other professionals to those in occupations that do not make the highest intellectual demands but which do require care, integrity, and common sense. How best can higher education meet these wide-ranging demands on its services? Market-type solutions are based ultimately on the assumption that supply and demand will bring about the best, or at least satisfactory, solutions through the operation of prices, wages, and information including self-knowledge. But markets are not perfect, especially in activities where there is a considerable delay between signals being sent out and the effects of individuals' reactions to them. Much further work is needed on post-market solutions to the problems of the economic, social, political, and cultural obstacles to achieving higher education systems that are efficient as far as economic and social progress is concerned, that distribute the benefits as fairly as possible, and that use information technology to improve quality of learning.

Another dimension is the subject of study. Hard evidence is becoming available supporting long-held beliefs about the different learning experiences of students of different subjects (and in different institutions) (Buckley *et al.*, 2015), and the different career patterns that follow. The average income of graduates in different subjects varies considerably and within subjects earning differences between the highest and lowest earners are considerable, often linked to university of graduation (Britton *et al.*, 2016). Much more research is needed into the extent and causes and consequences of these differences.

At present it is implicitly assumed that consumers' (student) choice abetted by media-produced league tables will ensure that some universities cater mainly for those who require very demanding courses through to those that provide worthwhile learning experiences for much larger numbers of people. This competition between students for places in what they consider the university for them, and universities for the most promising entrants, is supplemented by a rapidly growing system of higher degrees and other forms of lifelong learning.

Will this continue to be the shape of the higher education systems of the future? The picture is complicated by concerns about equality.

While half a century ago it was believed that higher education expansion would increase social mobility and hence help to bring about greater social equality, several decades of expansion accompanied by increasing inequality have cast doubt on this hypothesis. Much more research is needed into the relationship between higher education, social mobility, and reduction in economic and social inequality that goes well beyond looking at the postcode and secondary school of university applicants. Higher education researchers need to collaborate with those interested in primary and secondary school research. In my opinion, higher education programmes should persuade students and graduates to respect the interests and abilities of all their contemporaries, but it is futile and ultimately self-defeating for them to take on the task of remedying social inequality other than by ensuring equity in the opportunities to enter courses which any particular individual has the interest and the potential ability to benefit from. Different universities and colleges will concentrate on different aspects of higher and lifelong education, but it is important to aim for all to have parity of esteem and equitable access to the resources needed to perform their particular functions.

Higher education policies in the future will continue to be closely linked to other national policies. While private and corporate markets are at present hegemonic, this may not always be so, especially if inequalities of income and wealth continue to grow. There needs to be some thinking by researchers about post-marketization, perhaps with more power being returned to the providers of academic services and students being given more explicit guidance about which higher education experiences are likely to be most appropriate for them. Part of the reason why young people from advantaged backgrounds do better throughout their time in education is that they tend to receive much more explicit guidance from family and friends, and often from their private school teachers. 'Students as customers' has some merits in reminding their teachers that educational establishments exist primarily for the benefit of their students, but it needs never to be forgotten that most students are at best ill-informed customers and their higher education will bring about irreversible changes in them as human beings.

The role of universities as research establishments will come under increasing scrutiny. The Humboldtian ideal of the unity of teaching and research has been the dominant belief of the past two centuries, but in an age of mass higher education there are doubts about its universal validity and, in practice, research and teaching have become increasingly separated both within and between universities. At the very least higher education researchers need to establish closer contact with the science policy research community and much more needs to be known, other than the opinions of academics, who have their own vested interests, about the ways in which these two activities interact.

Finally, and most importantly for future higher education policy researchers, will be the continuing growth of the influence of information technology (IT) in its various forms. Mention has already been made of its transformation of university management and administration. Performance indicators and league tables based on them will continue to develop in more and more detail. But the most important developments will be on the substance of higher education, its content, and academic processes. Already the Internet and email and their offshoots have brought about huge changes in the experiences of students and the work of academic staff without transforming the basic structure of universities and colleges. However, we are already beginning to see signs of possible university forms of the future: mixed mode courses, massive open online courses (MOOCs), and global university conglomerates. This is where the other main branch of higher education research, the processes of learning and teaching, with which I have not been personally involved to any significant extent, will meet the research into policy and management. Defenders of nineteenth- and twentieth-century university values and practices point out with some justice that there have been several false alarms about computers taking over the university. But this is to ignore the many peripheral changes that IT has already brought about and to be blind to what is happening in many related areas of activity, particularly the mass media.

The essential rationale of the university of the nineteenth and much of the twentieth centuries was that it provided a haven where scholars, from first-year students to professors, could best advance and disseminate knowledge and understanding by interacting with others of similar interests and abilities. For many reasons, of which expansion and IT are the most important, this is no longer the case. Scholars can interact with others of similar interest the other side of the world as easily as with colleagues in the next office. Vast amounts of knowledge no longer need to be stored in university libraries; search engines make much knowledge instantly available. One of the reasons why earlier stages of the computer revolution have had relatively little impact on the core activities of universities is that they have been seen by policymakers primarily as a means of reducing costs. Now it is possible to claim that they not only can reduce costs but they can also improve the quality of many aspects of learning and research. One important task for higher education researchers will be to identify whether there remain essential functions that geographically distinct universities can perform and what sort of universities can best perform them. The role of universities as research institutions in the information-rich world also needs further clarification. At present higher education research and science policy research are two separate areas of study with very little overlap. Higher education researchers need to be much more aware of the work of science policy researchers.

I do not believe that universities as we have known them will disappear as a consequence of the IT revolution. I see analogies with mass entertainment. The invention of photography did not make painting redundant; moving pictures did not destroy the live theatre; the rise of television did not mean the end of cinema; YouTube will not supplant television. But in all cases the new developments brought about radical changes in the earlier art form. So it must be with universities. It is for researchers into higher education to identify the necessary and optimal form of these changes and to monitor and evaluate them when they occur. They will need to take into account the very great differences between academic subjects. What is appropriate for Engineering or Medicine is not necessarily best or most efficient for Social Sciences or Literature.

I have two alternative images of higher education in 50 years' time. One is optimistic: the information revolution will enable universities to recover their role as guardians of scholarship in the best and broadest sense of the word. When almost any information is instantly accessible on mobile phones, and probably by that time able to be fed directly into human brains, the evaluation and interpretation of that information will become of central importance. Universities will become primarily centres of understanding and logical thinking.

The other is that economic and social inequalities will continue to grow and universities as havens of person-to-person learning supported by ever-more powerful information technology will be reserved for the wealthy and a few very able young people, while for the great mass of the population, higher education and lifelong learning will be delivered in various electronic forms with only occasional human contact, although that too will be mostly via electronic media. This is the story of the mass media. Will it also be the story of mass higher education?

In either case there will be much for higher education researchers to observe, analyse, and, hopefully, influence.

References

Altbach, P. and Levy, D. (2005) *Private Higher Education: A global revolution.* Rotterdam: Sense Publishers.

Becker, G. (1962) 'Investment in human capital: A theoretical analysis'. *Journal of Political Economy*, 70 (5), 9–49.

Blaug, M. (1970) *Introduction to the Economics of Education.* London: Allen Lane.

Blaug, M., Layard, R., and Woodhall, M. (1969) *The Causes of Graduate Unemployment in India.* London: Allen Lane.

Bligh, D. (1982a) *Professionalism and Flexibility in Learning.* SRHE/Leverhulme Report 6. Guildford: Society for Research into Higher Education.

— (1982b) *Accountability or Freedom for Teachers.* SRHE/Leverhulme Report 7. Guildford: Society for Research into Higher Education.

Britton, J., Dearden, L., Shephard, N., and Vignoles, A. (2016) *How English Domiciled Graduate Earnings Vary with Gender, Institution Attended, Subject and Socio-Economic Background.* London: Institute for Fiscal Studies.

Brown, R. with Carasso, H. (2013) *Everything for Sale: The marketisation of UK higher education.* Abingdon: Routledge/SRHE.

Buckley, A., Soilemetzidis, I., and Hillman N. (2015) *The 2015 Student Academic Experience Survey.* Oxford: Higher Education Policy Institute. Online. www.heacademy.ac.uk/sites/default/files/resources/StudentAcademicExperienceSurvey2015.pdf (accessed 16 April 2016).

Clark, B. (1998) *Creating Entrepreneurial Universities: Organizational pathways of transformation.* Oxford: IAU Press/Pergamon.

Committee on Higher Education (1963) *Higher Education: Report of the Committee appointed by the Prime Minister under the chairmanship of Lord Robbins, 1961–63.* The Robbins Report. Cmnd 2154. London: Her Majesty's Stationery Office.

Dore, R. (1976) *The Diploma Disease.* London: George Allen and Unwin.

Farrant, J. (1981) 'Trends in admissions'. In Fulton, O. (ed.) *Access to Higher Education.* SRHE/Leverhulme Series 2. Guildford: Society for Research into Higher Education.

Freeman, R. (1976) *The Overeducated American.* Cambridge, MA: Academic Press.

Fulton, O. (ed.) (1981) *Access to Higher Education.* SRHE Leverhulme Report 2. Guildford: Society for Research into Higher Education.

HEPI (2015) *I Worked Hard to Get to Where I Am Today.* HEPI occasional paper, 12. Oxford: Higher Education Policy Institute.

Leontief, W. (1951) 'Input–output economics'. *Scientific American*, 185 (4), 15–21.

Lindley, R. (1981) *Higher Education and the Labour Market.* SRHE/Leverhulme Report 1. Guildford: Society for Research into Higher Education.

Morris, A. and Sizer, J. (1982) (eds) *Resources and Higher Education.* SRHE/Leverhulme Report 8. Guildford: Society for Research into Higher Education.

Neave, G. and van Vught, F. (1991) *Prometheus Bound: The changing relationship between government and higher education in Western Europe.* Oxford: Oxford University Press.

OECD (1967) *Methods and Statistical Needs for Educational Planning.* Paris: OECD.

Oldham, G. (1982) (ed.) *The Future of Research.* SRHE/Leverhulme Report 4. Guildford: Society for Research into Higher Education.

Piketty, T. (2014) *Capital in the Twenty-First Century.* Cambridge, MA: Harvard University Press.

Power, M. (1997) *The Audit Society: Rituals of verification.* Oxford: Oxford University Press.

Robinson, K. (1982) (ed.) *The Arts and Higher Education.* SRHE/Leverhulme Report 5. Guildford: Society for Research into Higher Education.

Schuller, T., Preston, J., Hammond, C., Brassett-Grundy, A., and Bynner, J. (2004) (eds) *The Benefits of Learning: The impact of education on health, family life and social capital.* London: RoutledgeFalmer.

Schultz, T. (1961) 'Investment in human capital'. *The American Economic Review,* 51 (1), 1–17.

Shattock, M. (1983) (ed.) *The Structure and Governance of Higher Education.* SRHE/Leverhulme Report 9. Guildford: Society for Research into Higher Education.

— (2005) 'European universities for entrepreneurship: their role in the Europe of knowledge – the theoretical context'. *Higher Education Management and Policy,* 17 (3), 13–25.

Teichler, U., Hartung, D., and Nuthmann, R. (1980) *Higher Education and the Needs of Society.* Windsor: NFER Publishing Company.

Temple, P. (2013) (ed.) *Universities in the Knowledge Economy: Higher education organisation and global change.* Abingdon: Routledge.

THE (2014) '1,300 universities, one shared fear: The commodification of education'. *Times Higher Education,* 5 April.

Trow, M. (1974) 'Problems in the transition from elite to mass higher education'. In *General Report on Future Structures of Post-Secondary Education.* Paris: OECD.

Wagner, L. (1982) (ed.) *Agenda for Institutional Change in Higher Education.* SRHE/Leverhulme Report 3. Guildford: Society for Research into Higher Education.

Williams, G. (1973) 'The labour market for graduates'. *Three Banks Review,* September.

— (1992) *Changing Patterns of Finance in Higher Education.* Buckingham: SRHE/ Open University Press.

Williams, G. and Blackstone, T. (1983) *Response to Adversity: Higher education in a harsh climate.* London: Society for Research into Higher Education.

Williams, G. and Gordon, A. (1981) 'Perceived earnings functions and ex ante rates of return to post-compulsory education in England'. *Higher Education,* 10 (2), 199–227.

The works of
Gareth Williams

Books and monographs

Brosan, G., Carter, C., Layard, R., Venables, P., and Williams, G. (1971) *Patterns and Policies in Higher Education*. Harmondsworth: Penguin.

Filippakou, O. and Williams, G. (2015) *Higher Education as a Public Good: Critical perspectives on theory, policy and practice*. New York: Peter Lang.

OECD (1965) *Econometric Models of Education: Some applications*. Paris: OECD.

Williams, G. (1967) *Methods and Statistical Needs for Educational Planning*. Paris: OECD.

— (1977) *Towards Lifelong Education: A new role for higher education institutions*. Paris: UNESCO.

— (1987) *New Ways of Paying the Piper: An inaugural lecture*. London: Institute of Education, University of London.

— (1992) *Changing Patterns of Finance in Higher Education*. Buckingham: SRHE/ Open University Press.

Williams, G. and Blackstone, T. (1983) *Response to Adversity: Higher education in a harsh climate*. Guildford: Society for Research into Higher Education.

Williams, G. and Greenaway, H. (1973) *Patterns of Graduate Employment*. London: Society for Research into Higher Education.

Williams, G. and Woodhall, M. (1979) *Independent Further Education*. London: Policy Studies Institute.

Williams, G., Blackstone, T., and Metcalf, D. (1974) *The Academic Labour Market: Economic and social aspects of a profession*. Amsterdam: Elsevier.

Williams, G., Fulton, O., and Gordon, A. (1982) *Higher Education and Manpower Planning: A comparative study of planned and market economies*. Geneva: International Labour Office.

Williams, G., Morley, L., Unterhalter, E., and Gold, A. (eds) (2003) *The Enterprising University: Reform, excellence, and equity*. Buckingham: SRHE/ Open University Press.

Williams, G., Woodhall, M., and O'Brien, U. (1986) *Overseas Students and Their Place of Study*. 3 vols. London: Overseas Students Trust.

Williams, G., Zabalza, A., and Turnbull, P. (1979) *The Economics of Teacher Supply*. Cambridge: Cambridge University Press.

Articles and chapters in books

Williams, G. (1969) 'Towards a national educational planning model'. *Socio-Economic Planning Sciences*, 2.

— (1972) 'What educational planning is about'. *Higher Education*, 1, (4), 381–90.

— (1973) 'The labour market for graduates'. *Three Banks Review*, September.

— (1981) 'Of adversity and innovation in higher education'. *Studies in Higher Education*, 6 (2).

— (1984) 'Research and research policy'. *Higher Education in Europe*, IX (4), October–December.

— (1984) 'The economic approach'. In Clark, B. (ed.) *Perspectives on Higher Education: Eight disciplinary and comparative views*. Los Angeles, CA: University of California Press.

— (1985) 'Graduate employment and vocationalisation in higher education'. *European Journal of Education*, 20 (2–3), 181–92.

— (1987) 'The international market for overseas students in the English speaking world'. *European Journal of Education*, 22 (1), 15–25.

— (1988) 'Current debates on the funding of mass higher education in the United Kingdom'. *European Journal of Education*, 33 (1), 77–87.

— (1988) 'The debate about funding mechanisms'. *Oxford Review of Education*, 14 (1), 59–68.

— (1989) 'Prospects for higher education finance'. In Ball, C. and Eggins, H. (eds) *Higher Education into the 1990s: New dimensions*. Stony Stratford: Open University Press/SRHE.

— (1992a) 'An evaluation of new funding mechanisms in British higher education: Some micro-economic and institutional management issues'. *Higher Education in Europe*, XVII (1), 65–85.

— (1992b) 'British higher education in the world league'. *Oxford Review of Economic Policy*, 8 (2), 146–58.

— (1992c) 'Introduction'. In Williams, G. (ed.) *The Encyclopedia of Higher Education, Vol. 2: Analytical Perspectives*. General editors Clark, B. and Neave, G. Oxford: Pergamon Press.

— (1995) 'The "marketization" of higher education: Reform and potential reforms in higher education finance'. In Dill, D. and Sporn, B. (eds) *Emerging Patterns of Social Demand and University Reform: Through a glass darkly*. Oxford: IAU Press/Pergamon.

— (1996) 'The many faces of privatisation'. *Higher Education Management*, 8 (3), 39–57.

— (1997) 'The market route to mass higher education: British experience 1979–1996'. *Higher Education Policy*, 10 (3/4), 275–89.

— (1998) 'Advantages and disadvantages of diversified funding in universities'. *Tertiary Education and Management*, 4 (2), 85–93.

— (1999) 'State finance of higher education: An overview of theoretical and empirical issues'. In Henkel, M. and Little, B. (eds) *Changing Relationships between Higher Education and the State*. London and Philadelphia: Jessica Kingsley Publishers, 142–61.

— (2004a) 'The higher education market in the United Kingdom'. In Teixeira, P., Jongbloed, B., Dill, D., and Amaral, A. (eds) *Markets in Higher Education: Rhetoric or reality?* Dordrecht: Kluwer Academic Publishers.

— (2004b) 'The changing political economy of higher education'. In Shattock, M. (ed.) *Entrepreneurialism and the Transformation of Russian Universities*. Paris: International Institute for Educational Planning.

— (2009) 'An economic view of higher education theory'. Paper presented at the SHRE Conference, Newport, South Wales, 8–10 December.

— (2010) 'Subject benchmarking in the United Kingdom'. In Dill, D. and Beerkens, M. (eds) *Public Policy for Academic Quality: Analyses of innovative policy instruments*. Dordrecht: Springer.

— (2011) 'Will higher education be the next bubble to burst?' In *The Europa World of Learning 2011*. Online. www.educationarena.com/pdf/sample/sample-essay-williams.pdf (accessed 15 April 2016).

— (2012) 'Some wicked questions from the dismal science'. In Temple, P. (ed.) *Universities in the Knowledge Economy: Higher education organisation and global change*. Abingdon: Routledge.

— (2013) 'A bridge too far: An economic critique of marketization of higher education'. In Callender, C. and Scott, P. (eds) *Browne and Beyond: Modernizing English higher education*. London: IOE Press.

— (2015) 'Reflections on the debate'. In Filippakou, O. and Williams, G. (eds) *Higher Education As a Public Good: Critical perspectives on theory, policy and practice*. New York: Peter Lang.

Williams, G. and Filippakou, O. (2010) 'Higher education and UK elite formation in the twentieth century'. *Higher Education*, 59 (1), 1–20.

Williams, G. and Gordon, A. (1981) 'Perceived earnings functions and ex ante rates of return to post-compulsory education in England'. *Higher Education*, 10 (2), 199–227.

Williams, G. and Kay, G.B. (1961) 'A survey of recent theories of economic growth'. *Economics*, Spring 1961 and Autumn 1961.

Williams, G. and Kitaev, I. (2005) 'Overview of national policy contexts for entrepreneurialism in higher education institutions'. *Higher Education Management and Policy*, 17 (3), 125–41.

Williams, G. and Light, G. (1999) 'Student income and costs of study in the United Kingdom'. *European Journal of Education*, 34 (1), 23–41.

Williams, G. and Psacharopoulos, G. (1973) 'Public sector earnings and educational planning'. *International Labour Review*, July.

Williams, G. and Turnbull, P. (1974) 'Sex differentials in teachers' pay'. *Journal of the Royal Statistical Society*, Series A, 137 (2), 245–58.

— (1975) 'Supply and demand in the labour market for teachers: Qualifications and differentials in teachers' pay'. *The British Journal of Industrial Relations*, 13.

Subject index

Major references are in bold.

Index

Name index

Index